Men'sHealth
Total-Body
Health & Fitness
Guide
2011

RODALE

© 2011 by Rodale Inc.

All rights reserved.
No part of this publication may be reproduced or transmitted in any form or by any means, electronic or mechanical, including photocopying, recording, or any other information storage and retrieval system, without the written permission of the publisher.

Men's Health is a registered trademark of Rodale Inc.

Printed in the United States of America

Rodale Inc. makes every effort to use acid-free ♾, recycled paper ♲.

Book design by George Karabotsos, Davia de Croix, Courtney Eltringham, Laura White, and Elizabeth Neal

ISBN-13 978–1–60529–169–7   hardcover

2   4   6   8   10   9   7   5   3   1   hardcover

Contents

vii   Introduction

Part 1:
Lose Your Gut
2   The New American Diet
13   The Truth about Sugar
18   Ultimate Fat Fighting
25   The New Science of Fat Loss
30   The Fat Burner
36   18 Exercise Upgrades
40   Prove It
42   You Asked

Part 2:
Flat Belly Foods
46   16 New Lessons of Great Guy Food
73   Five MIA Nutrients
79   Six Stealth Health Foods
82   Supermarket Survival Guide
90   What the Food Industry Doesn't Want
     You to Know
96   The No-Carb Noodle
100 The Beauty of the Beast
118 The Scoop on Protein
123 Check Your Oil
126 Change the World (and Your Life)
     One Apple at a Time
136 Prove It
139 You Asked

Part 3:

Muscle Up Fast

146 The 5-Second Muscle Test

149 Strong Shoulders Ahead

152 A Rock-Solid Chest

157 The Best Ab Workout You've
Never Done

162 The Bun Blaster

167 Small Muscles, Big Results

172 The Best New Fitness Gear

178 Prove It

182 You Asked

Part 4:

Look Better Instantly

188 Dress It Up

191 The DNA of Jeans

200 American Classics, Renewed

207 Ultimate Age Erasers

214 Prove It

218 You Asked

Part 5:

Live Longer, Live Better

225 Five Tests That Could Save Your Life
232 Bad Habits to Break
238 The Doctor Will See You Now
243 Your Service Plan
249 The Prostate-Protection Plan
260 Extra-Strength Pain Relief
272 The Alzheimer's Virus
282 The Bad Mood Buster
290 The Fountain of Youth
304 Prove It
307 You Asked

Part 6:

Improve Your Game

312 Your Best Shot
317 Your Body Guards
321 The Champion Within
326 Raising the Stakes
333 The Persistence Factor
337 Prove It
341 You Asked

344 Credits
345 Index

According to the most recent stats from the Bureau of Labor Statistics, on any given day, only 21 percent of men spent any time at all exercising— and that includes playing sports. However, a whopping 82 percent of men find time to watch TV each day!

But what if those numbers were reversed? What if 82 percent of us exercised our bodies instead of our eyes? The benefits to exercise and fitness are huge. It can…

- **Improve your mood**
- **Prevent heart disease, diabetes, and other chronic diseases**
- **Manage your weight**
- **Boost your energy**
- **Sleep better**
- **Ramp up your sex life**

Ponce de Leon was clearly looking in the wrong place for the fountain of youth. He should have tried the gym.

We've gathered together all of the best health and fitness information from Men's Health to create this total-body health and fitness guide. This book will help you boost your fitness, and also your overall health.

In **Part 1**, you'll take the first step and Lose Your Gut. Taste the "New American Diet," discover "The Truth about Sugar," and hit your fighting weight with our "Fat Burner" workout.

Life is short; learn how to fill it with great foods in **Part 2**, Flat Belly Foods. Here you'll read about the "16 New Lessons of Great Guy Food," "Six Stealth Health Foods," and "Five MIA Nutrients." Are you getting enough?

In **Part 3**, you'll save time and get strong in Muscle Up Fast. First take our "5-Second Muscle Test." Then build strong shoulders, chest, abs, buns, and even those small, easily forgotten muscles—for big results.

You'll Look Better Instantly after reading **Part 4**. Find out how to "Dress It Up," wear your jeans well, and turn back time.

In **Part 5**, you'll find out how to Live Longer, Live Better. Discover the "Five Tests That Could Save Your Life." Find out about the "Bad Habits to Break," before they break you. Bust a bad mood, and more.

Last, in **Part 6**, you can Improve Your Game. Take "Your Best Shot" and improve your golf score. See what you need to know to shred the peak and park this winter. And save your body from injury with our "Body Guards."

We hope this book will inspire you to watch less, and move more. To spend less time observing, and more time living. Here's to your health! ■

1

Lose Your Gut

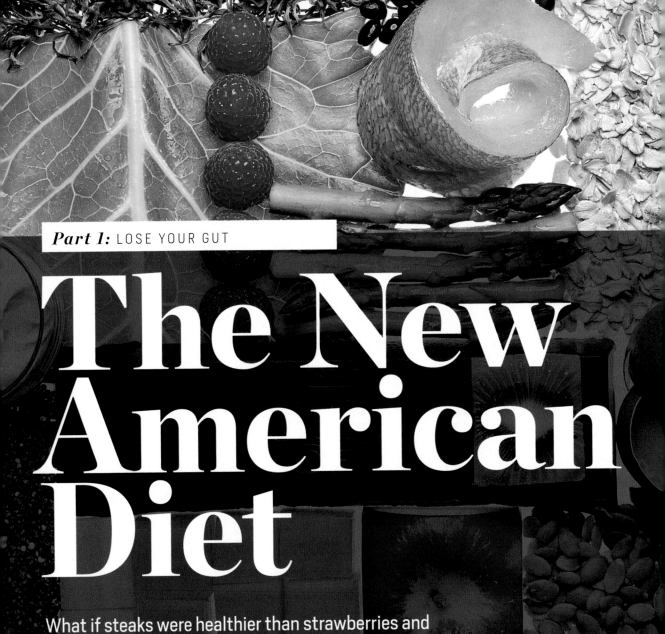

The New American Diet

What if steaks were healthier than strawberries and
ice cream a better weight–loss tool than carrots?
It's time to rethink what you know about the food you eat.

It's not just about calories in versus calories out. If that were all it took to lose weight—eating a little less and exercising a little more—then weight loss would be as simple as grade-school math: Subtract Y from Z and end up with X.

But if you've ever followed a diet program and achieved less than your desired result, you probably came away feeling frustrated, depressed, and maybe a bit guilty. What did I do wrong?

Instead of X, it's XXL.

Why?

Because there's probably more at work here than just calories in/calories out. More and more research is indicating that America's obesity crisis can't be blamed entirely on too much fast food and too little exercise. A third factor might be in play: a class of natural and synthetic chemicals known as endocrine-disrupting chemicals (EDCs), or, as researchers have begun to call them, obesogens.

THE NEW WEIGHT-GAIN THREAT

Obesogens are chemicals that disrupt the function of hormonal systems; many researchers believe they lead to weight gain and, in turn, numerous diseases that curse the American populace. They enter our bodies from a variety of sources—natural hormones found in soy products, hormones administered to animals, plastics in some food and drink packaging, ingredients added to processed foods, and pesticides sprayed on produce. They act in a variety of ways: by mimicking human hormones such as estrogen, by misprogramming stem cells to become fat cells, and, researchers think, by altering the function of genes.

Endocrine disruptors are suspected of playing a role in fertility problems, genital malformation, reduced male birth rates, precocious puberty, miscarriage, behavior problems, brain abnormalities, impaired immune function, various cancers, and cardiovascular disease.

"We have data linking environmental chemicals to practically every major human disease, from cardiovascular disease to attention-deficit disorder," says Jerry Heindel, Ph.D., an expert on EDCs at the National Institute of Environmental Health Sciences (NIEHS).

Now new research is finding that some EDCs, the obesogens, might be helping to make us fat. This field of research is dominated by animal and test-tube studies. And while researchers note that the known effects of many obesogens are more potent in the unborn and newly born, some suspect a similar impact on adults.

This combination of factors, along with our growing tendency to put on weight, is what we call the obesogen effect. Understanding it could be the key to freeing ourselves from weight gain and the other hazards of these chemicals.

WHY TRADITIONAL DIETS DON'T WORK

Decades ago, before big, soft guts were the norm in the United States, we referred to overweight people as having "glandular problems." Their weight was not their fault, doctors explained; their bodies just didn't have the ability to fight off weight gain like most people's bodies did.

We don't use that polite phrase any longer. What changed? Now that about two-thirds of American adults are overweight or obese, did those folks with "glandular problems" disappear? No; it's just that many others have caught the same disease. Thanks to the obesogen effect, we might all be at risk for some glandular problems.

Your endocrine system is a finely tuned instrument that can easily be thrown out of kilter.

Your endocrine system is the contingent of glands producing the hormones that regulate your body. Growth and development, sexual function, reproductive processes, mood, sleep, hunger, stress, metabolism—they're all controlled by hormones. And the pancreas, hypothalamus, adrenal glands, thyroid, pituitary gland, and testes are all part of that system. So whether you're male or female, tall or short, hirsute or hairless, lean or heavy—that's all determined in a big way by your endocrine system.

"Obesogens are thought to act by hijacking the regulatory systems that control body weight," says Frederick vom Saal, Ph.D., curators' professor of biological sciences at the University of Missouri. "And any chemical that interferes with body weight is an endocrine disruptor."

That's why obesogens seem to be good at making us fat—and why researchers are so bent on uncovering the truth about these chemicals. The NIEHS is funding studies that target them. The Endocrine Society, the largest organization for hormone research and clinical endocrinology, has also noted the connection.

"The rise in the incidence in obesity matches the rise in the use and distribution of industrial chemicals that may be playing a role in generation of obesity," it stated in a recent report, "suggesting that EDCs may be linked to this epidemic."

That's one reason why weight-loss advice might not always work. Even strictly following the smartest traditional advice won't lower your obesogen exposure. An apple a day may have kept the doctor away 150 years ago. But if that apple now comes with chemicals believed to promote obesity, then that advice is way out of date. In fact, apples have been named one of the most pesticide-laden produce choices out there.

The obesogen effect may be part of the reason why traditional dieting practices—choosing chicken over beef, eating more fish, loading up on fruits and vegetables—might not work anymore.

But here's some good news: There's no reason why our favorite foods—steak, burgers, pasta, ice cream—can't be part of a reasonable weight-loss program. We just need to move past the old thinking and adopt some new laws of leanness.

LEANNESS LAW 1:
Know When to Go Organic

Every day the average American is exposed to an estimated 10 to 13 different pesticides and/or their metabolites (breakdown products) through food, beverages, and drinking water.

Some of those chemicals can mimic estrogen during development, which can lead to weight gain later in life. Others can spur unnecessary fat-cell formation at any age. At the University of California at Irvine, Bruce Blumberg, Ph.D., recently reported that prenatal exposure to obesogens among mice can predispose them to weight gain later in life. The effect is likely the same in humans. In one study, the adult daughters of women who had the highest levels of DDE (a breakdown

Your New Weight-Loss Checklist

QUESTION THE SOURCE. Find out where your food comes from—whether you're at the market, restaurant, or farm stand.

EAT GRASS-FED BEEF. This healthier choice can have more conjugated linoleic acid than grain-fed beef has, so it's better for you.

SKIP THE SWEET STUFF. Check the label; if the item contains high-fructose corn syrup, put it back on the shelf.

GO (A LITTLE) ORGANIC. Avoid a few notorious pesticide-coated fruits and vegetables to reduce your obesogen exposure.

DRINK SMART. Toss out any water bottle stamped with a 7 on the bottom; it may have BPA. And avoid Styrofoam cups.

MEET THE BUTCHER. Purchase your meat wrapped in paper instead of plastic, which may contain phthalates.

THE NEW AMERICAN BURGER

- 1   organic egg
- ½   cup oats
- ⅓   cup diced onion
- ½   cup chopped organic spinach
- 1   pound grass-fed ground beef
- 2   tablespoons shredded organic Cheddar cheese
-     Salt
-     Ground black pepper
- 4   whole wheat buns
- 2   large organic tomatoes, sliced
- 1   avocado, peeled, pitted, and sliced

1. In a large bowl, whisk the egg. Add the oats, onion, spinach, beef, cheese, and salt and ground black pepper to season. Mix with your hands until well blended.

2. Form four patties. Place them on a grill and cook for 6 minutes on each side or to your desired level of doneness.

3. Place the burgers on the buns and top with the tomato and avocado.

Makes 4 servings

product of the pesticide DDT) in their blood during childbearing years were found to be 20 pounds heavier, on average, than daughters of women who had the least.

And the evidence continues to accumulate.

• Researchers have noted a link between organochlorine pesticides and impaired thyroid function. According to the Endocrine Society's 2009 report on EDCs, changes in thyroid function can result in metabolic effects. Indeed, the authors of a 2009 *Thyroid Research* article cited hypothyroidism, a symptom of which can be weight gain, as a possible effect of organochlorines on the thyroid.

Ninety-three percent of Americans have detectable levels of bisphenol A (BPA) in their bodies.

• The authors of a study in the journal *BioScience* found that tributyltin, a fungicide, activates components in human cells known as retinoid X receptors, which are part of the metabolic pathway necessary for fat-cell formation. They also found that tributyltin causes the growth of fat cells in mice exposed to it. Although tributyltin is no longer used on crops, experts suspect that a similar compound still used on produce, fenbutatin, is at least as potent.

• The authors of a recent study in *Molecular and Cellular Endocrinology* note that organophosphates and carbamates, two common classes of pesticides, cause obesity in animals.

But there is some hopeful research; a study in the journal *Environmental Health Perspectives* found that children who ate fruits and vegetables free of organophosphorous pesticides for just 5 days reduced their urine concentrations of those pesticides to undetectable levels.

According to the Environmental Working Group, you can reduce your pesticide exposure by nearly 80 percent simply by choosing organic versions of the 12 fruits and vegetables shown in its tests to contain the highest pesticide load. The group calls them the Dirty Dozen: In order of pesticide load, they are peaches, apples, bell peppers, celery, nectarines, strawberries, cherries, kale, lettuce, imported grapes, carrots, and pears. There's a Clean Fifteen, too, a group of conventionally grown fruits and vegetables with the least pesticide residue: onions, avocados, sweet corn, pineapples, mangoes, asparagus, sweet peas, kiwis, cabbages, eggplants, papayas, watermelons, broccoli, tomatoes, and sweet potatoes.

LEANNESS LAW 2:
Stop Eating Plastic

You're thinking, *Well, I don't generally eat plastic.*

Ah, but you do.

Chances are you're among the 93 percent of Americans with detectable levels of bisphenol A (BPA) in their bodies, and you're also among the 75-plus percent of Americans with detectable levels of phthalates in their urine. Both of these synthetic chemicals, found in plastics, mimic estrogen. Like some pesticides, these chemicals can predispose your body to gain fat.

How do they end up inside you? Mostly through what you eat and drink: Phthalates can be found in food packaging, plastic wraps, and pesticides, as well as children's toys, PVC pipe, and medical supplies. Each year, about 18 billion pounds of phthalate esters are created worldwide, and they can easily leach into your body.

More than 6 billion pounds of BPA, found in polycarbonate plastics and epoxy resins, is produced every year; it leaches from food and drink packaging, baby bottles, cans, and bottle tops. Pop the top off a jar of tomato sauce and check out the resin on the inside of the cap—that's where the BPA comes from. A recent study published on BPA's effects on humans found that workers exposed to BPA at Chinese factories had more than four times the risk of erection difficulties. (Japan reduced the use of BPA in cans between 1998 and 2003; as a result, measures of BPA in some Japanese populations dropped more than 50 percent.) According to the Environmental Working Group, canned chicken soup, infant formula, and ravioli have BPA levels of the highest concern. And your sturdy reusable water bottle? After people drank out of a polycarbonate bottle (usually stamped with a 7 on the bottom) for just 1 week, their BPA levels jumped by nearly 70 percent, according to a seminal study from Harvard University and the Centers for Disease Control and Prevention.

Here's how you can limit your exposure.

Follow Dr. vom Saal's rule: "No plastic item ever goes into the oven or the microwave." Heat can damage plastic and increase leaching.

THE NEW AMERICAN OMELET

- **5** organic eggs
- **2** tablespoons chopped flat-leaf parsley
  Dash of reduced-sodium soy sauce
- **½** cup organic spinach
- **2** tablespoons chopped broccoli florets
- **5** spears asparagus, chopped
- **¼** cup halved organic green beans
- **1** clove garlic, finely chopped
  Dash of black pepper
- **2** teaspoons olive oil

1. Beat the eggs, parsley, and soy sauce in a bowl.

2. Add the vegetables, garlic, and pepper to a skillet coated with olive oil, and sauté on medium for 5 minutes.

3. Pour the egg mixture over the vegetables. Stir for about 30 seconds, and then let it sit for 1 minute. Stir again until the eggs firm up, and let it sit for another minute. Fold it and remove it from the pan onto a plate.

Makes 2 servings

Foods canned beans and jarred foods, which are in BPA-free packaging.

Use a nonplastic mug whenever you can. And for good measure, avoid drinking coffee or other hot beverages out of Styrofoam, which can leach styrene, a compound linked to cancer.

LEANNESS LAW 3:
Don't Eat the Viking

When was the last time you took a dose of weight-promoting hormones?

Okay, when was the last time you ate a burger?

The answer to both questions might well be the same. Every time you eat conventionally grown beef, there's a chance you're eating weight-gain hormones—a potential cocktail of natural and synthetic obesogens. In fact, a report in the *International Journal of Obesity* by researchers at 10 universities, including Yale, Johns Hopkins, and Cornell, notes that the use of hormones in meat could be a contributing factor to the obesity epidemic.

A 1999 European study concluded that people who ate meat from cattle treated with growth hormones were taking in hormones and their metabolites: estrogens in the range of 1 to 84 nanograms per person per day, progesterone (64 to 467 ng), and testosterone (5 to 189 ng).

A nanogram is a billionth of a gram: That's tiny. But it might be enough to disrupt the way your hormone system operates, research indicates. Some experts believe that certain obesogens exert influence at below 1 part per billion. And

Avoid plastic-wrapped meat. "The plastic wrap used at the supermarket is mostly PVC, whereas the plastic wrap you buy to wrap things at home is increasingly made from polyethylene," Dr. vom Saal says. PVC contains phthalates that, according to animal studies, may lower testosterone levels. In humans, lower testosterone leads to weight gain as well as a decrease in muscle mass and sex drive. Go to a butcher who uses paper instead.

Cut down on canned goods like tuna, and buy frozen vegetables in bags instead of canned produce. Consider buying Eden

small amounts from many sources add up.

Perhaps even more worrisome are the potent synthetic steroids we ingest from beef. Trenbolone acetate is an anabolic steroid estimated to be 8 to 10 times as potent as testosterone, which is an endocrine-disrupting chemical by definition.

"This cocktail of hormones given to beef has huge consequences," Dr. vom Saal says. We know what happens to the body when it receives large doses of steroids over a short period of time, but there is no research on the effects of small doses over years.

To bring this all home, imagine you've been in a terrible plane crash in the Andes, like those poor souls depicted in the movie *Alive*. The only way to survive is to pick one of the dead folks to eat. You're given the choice of an obese, grotesquely muscled, man-boob-toting Minnesota Vikings lineman with shrunken testicles who's been injecting himself with hormones for a dozen years, or someone of normal size and body type and hormonal function. (One of the Kardashian sisters, maybe.) Which would you choose?

Well, every time you eat conventionally raised beef, you're choosing the Viking.

There's a better way. Organic beef has none of the weight-promoting steroid hormones of conventional beef, while grass-fed beef has been found to have more omega-3s and more conjugated linoleic acid (CLA). CLA is a fatty-acid mixture that's been linked to protection against cardiovascular disease and diabetes; it can also help you lose weight, according to the *American Journal of Clinical Nutrition*.

Similarly, conventionally raised dairy cows are often given hormones to produce more milk, which may lead to some nutrient dilution. Grass grazing, however, may increase omega-3 content in milk. By choosing to eat and drink more omega-3s, more CLA, and more nutrients, you're choosing to fill your body with more nutrition—feeding your brain, fueling weight loss, and keeping hunger at bay.

LEANNESS LAW 4:
Beware of the Sneaky Saboteurs

Ingesting pesticides, growth hormones, and plastic-based chemicals obviously isn't a good idea. But other, sneakier obesogens are at work. We're talking about high fructose corn syrup (HFCS) and soy, which are added into your diet and the diet of the animals you eat, and which carry or are converted into natural obesogens.

But wait: Isn't soy good for your heart? Not necessarily. A review in the American Heart Association's journal *Circulation* notes that soy protein can lower LDL cholesterol, but only a measly 3 percent. You'd have to eat the equivalent of 2 pounds of tofu a day to reap that benefit. As a result, the AHA withdrew support for definitive health claims for soy protein and coronary heart disease. Yet soy is in hiding in everything from cookies to french fries.

The result of all that extra soy could be— get ready for it—more fat. This is particularly true for people who were given soy-based formula as infants. Soy contains two naturally occurring chemicals, genistein and daidzein, both of which are estrogenics, which can spur the formation of fat cells.

Guess who else is on a soy diet? The animals we depend on for food. (Many fish, too, are chowing down on soy.) Chickens that once ate natural grasses and forage now feed on a high-energy diet of which soybean meal is a large component.

According to British researchers, this type of diet is partly to blame for the fact that some modern chickens contain two to three times as many calories from fat as from protein. (That's right: The chicken's proportion of muscle is dropping, just like ours! Sounds like the obesogen effect.)

So when you eat modern, supermarket chicken and beef, you're eating more fat, less protein, and more obesogens.

High fructose corn syrup, too, has been fingered by some experts as a possible player in the obesity crisis. HFCS is found in countless items, from bread to ketchup to Life Savers to cough medicine. Recent research indicates that a diet high in HFCS might trick your brain into craving more food even when you don't need it. And preliminary research indicates that HFCS may even play a role in disrupting the endocrine system, says Robert Lustig, M.D., a pediatric endocrinologist at UCSF. In overweight people, it interferes with leptin, a hormone that regulates appetite.

You can reconsider the old weight-loss advice—the "diet wisdom" that told you to stop eating burgers, pasta, and ice cream—and go back to eating what you love. Of course, you should eat reasonably sized portions. But the key is to eat natural, obesogen-free versions. Do this while keeping up your exercise program, and over time you'll see results. Your waistline, taste buds, and even muscles and libido will thank you. ■

The Perfect Day of Weight Loss

You can always use your time better. Boost metabolism, burn calories, and torch your belly for 24 hours with these secrets.

7:00 a.m.
Wake up and do 2 minutes of jumping jacks, high knee skips, pushups, or crunches.

7:15 a.m.
Have two scrambled eggs and a slice of Canadian bacon. A 2009 Purdue University study found that a high-protein breakfast makes people feel fuller throughout the day, so they're less likely to overeat.

7:45 a.m.
Hit the gym, and lower weights slowly. Taking 3 seconds to lower weights during full-body resistance training can rev your metabolism for up to 3 days, according to a Wayne State University study. (Study participants used a challenging weight for 5 sets of 6 reps for each exercise.)

9:00 a.m.
Chug some milk. A diet with plenty of calcium-rich dairy can enhance weight loss, according to a 2007 study of overweight people.

10:00 a.m.
Grab a protein-rich snack, such as half a turkey sandwich on whole grain bread with Swiss cheese. In a Georgia State University study, athletes who ate three 250-calorie snacks a day were more likely to lose body fat and have more energy than those who didn't.

11:00 a.m.
Walk briskly around the office for a while. A recent Mayo Clinic study found that lean people walk an average of 3.5 miles per day more than obese people do.

1:00 p.m.
For lunch, eat a spinach salad with grilled halibut and almond slices. All contain magnesium, a metabolism-friendly mineral.

2:00 p.m.
If your meeting is with just one or two people, do it West Wing–style, walking the halls as you talk.

10

9

8

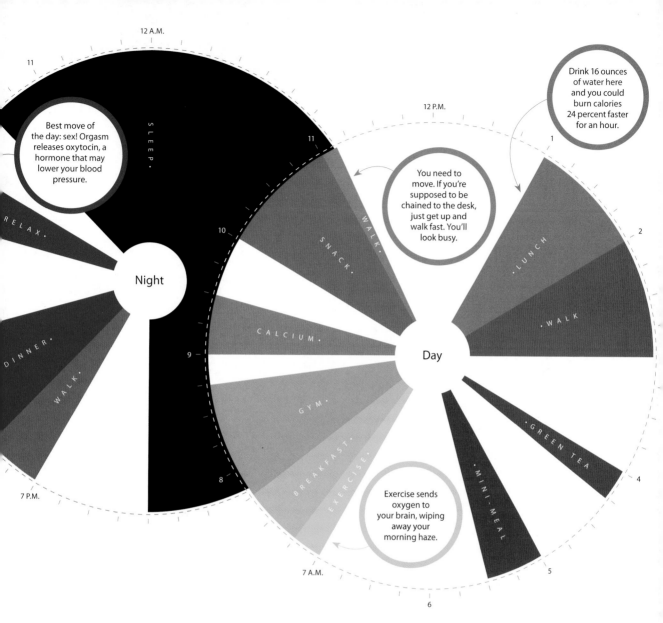

The clock diagram contains the following labels:

- 12 A.M.
- 11
- SLEEP.
- 12 P.M.
- 11
- Best move of the day: sex! Orgasm releases oxytocin, a hormone that may lower your blood pressure.
- Drink 16 ounces of water here and you could burn calories 24 percent faster for an hour.
- You need to move. If you're supposed to be chained to the desk, just get up and walk fast. You'll look busy.
- RELAX.
- WALK.
- SNACK.
- 10
- LUNCH
- 1
- 2
- Night
- CALCIUM.
- Day
- WALK
- 9
- DINNER.
- WALK.
- GYM.
- BREAKFAST.
- EXERCISE.
- GREEN TEA
- MINI-MEAL
- 8
- Exercise sends oxygen to your brain, wiping away your morning haze.
- 7 P.M.
- 7 A.M.
- 6
- 5
- 4

4:00 p.m.
Down a glass of iced green tea. According to a study in the *Journal of Nutrition*, the catechins in green tea decrease body fat.

5:00 p.m.
Have another mini-meal— and make it a fiery one. According to a 2006 study review, spicy foods help burn fat and calories.

7:00 p.m.
Take a short walk before dinner.

7:30 p.m.
Eat dinner. If you ate lightly today, don't worry about a heavier meal now: "It doesn't matter when you fuel up; it's how many gallons you put in the tank," says Gary Foster, Ph.D., director of Temple University's Center for Obesity Research and Education.

9:30 p.m.
Grab a good book (or magazine!), pop in some tunes, and relax. Stress jacks up your levels of cortisol, a chemical that boosts abdominal fat.

10:30 p.m.
Draw your shades so the sun won't rouse you early. According to a 2008 review, losing sleep affects the hormones that turn your appetite on and off, making you feel less satiated by food and hungrier overall.

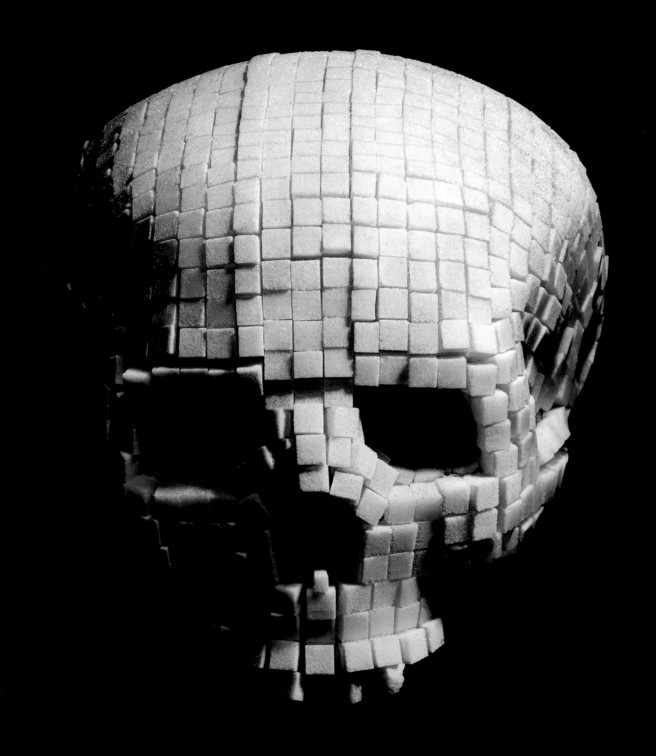

White death or fundamental fuel?
Here are five facts you need to know.

The Truth about Sugar

Say anything nasty about sugar, and folks will swallow it. Sugar caused the recession. Sugar makes your nipples grow. Sugar keyed your car. Sugar's crazy—it knifed my cousin down at the corner bar last Saturday night. Somebody should drop a safe on sugar. Well, maybe.

It's true that sugar is insidious—diabolical, even—and hidden in countless processed foods. It certainly contributes to the obesity crisis. It makes people fat and diabetic. These claims are correct—to a limited and oversimplified extent.

But sugar doesn't point a gun to our heads and force us to eat it. It's only as big a bogeyman as we make it out to be. We need some truth about sugar. It's too important. The sugar in our bodies, glucose, is a fundamental fuel for body and brain, says Dr. David Levitsky, Ph.D., a professor of psychology and nutritional sciences at Cornell University. The health threat to the vast American public arises from a very personal level, Dr. Levitsky says: "It's that sugars taste good. Sweetened foods tend to make us overeat. And that threatens the energy balance in our bodies."

Read this and learn a few facts about the sweet stuff hiding in some of your favorite meals and drinks. Then, the next time some uninformed punk says sugar's out of line, you won't be tempted to drag sugar behind a Dumpster and kick the crap out of it. The fact is, you might be the one who's out of line.

TRUTH #1

Sugar doesn't cause diabetes

Too much sugar does. Diabetes means your body can't clear glucose from your blood. And when glucose isn't processed quickly enough, it destroys tissue, Dr. Levitsky says. People with type 1 diabetes were born that way; sugar didn't cause their diabetes. But weight gain in children and adults can cause metabolic syndrome, which leads to type 2 diabetes.

"That's what diabetes is all about—being unable to eliminate glucose," says Dr. Levitsky. "The negative effect of eating a lot of sugar is a rise in glucose. A normal

> Sugar doesn't point a gun to our heads and force us to eat it. It's only as big a bogeyman as we make it out to be.

pancreas and normal insulin receptors can handle it, clear it out, or store it in some packaged form, like fat."

What matters: That "normal" pancreas. Overeating forces your pancreas to work overtime cranking out insulin to clear glucose. Eric Westman, M.D., an obesity researcher at the Duke University Medical Center, says that in today's world, "it's certainly possible that the unprecedented increase in sugar and starch consumption leads to pancreatic burnout." But researchers can't be sure; everyone's body and diet are different, so generalization is iffy. One thing that is sure, Dr. Westman says, is that the rise in sugar consumption over the past 100 years is unprecedented.

Your job: Drop the pounds if you're overweight, and watch your sugar intake. Research has shown for years that dropping 5 percent to 7 percent of your body weight can reduce your odds of developing diabetes.

SUGAR by the Numbers

88 pounds of sweeteners an American ate in 1909

142 pounds we ate in 2005

9 teaspoons of added sugar men should eat daily, at most

30 teaspoons men actually eat

8 teaspoons in a 12-ounce can of soda

TRUTH #2

Simply avoiding high fructose corn syrup won't save you from obesity

In the 1970s and 1980s, the average American's body weight increased in tandem with the food industry's use of high fructose corn syrup (HFCS), a staple because it's cheap. But it's not a smoking gun, as we talked about in the previous chapter, merely a piece of the puzzle.

Obesity is largely about consuming too many calories, says Lillian Lien, M.D., the medical director of inpatient diabetes management at the Duke University medical center.

"It just so happens that a lot of overweight people have been drinking HFCS in sodas and eating foods that are high on the glycemic index—sweet snacks, white bread, and so forth," says Dr. Lien. "The calorie totals are huge, and the source just happens to be sugar-based."

Dr. Westman notes that the effect of a high-glycemic food can be lessened by adding fat and protein. Spreading peanut butter (protein and fat) on a bagel (starch, which becomes glucose in your body), for example, slows your body's absorption of the sugar.

What matters: We can demonize food manufacturers because they produce crap with enough salt and sugar to make us eat more of it than we should—or even want to. But it comes down to how much we allow down our throats.

"A practical guide for anyone is weight," says Dr. Lien. "If your weight is under control, then your calorie intake across the board is reasonable. If your weight rises, it's not. That's more important than paying attention to any specific macronutrient." Still, skinny isn't always safe. (Keep reading.)

TRUTH #3

Too much sugar fills your blood with fat

Studies dating back decades show that eating too much fructose, which is a sugar found naturally in fruit and also added to processed foods, raises blood lipid levels. And while the relatively modest quantities in fruit shouldn't worry you, a University of Minnesota study shows that the large amounts of fructose we take in from processed foods may prove especially nasty: Men on high-fructose diets had 32 percent higher triglycerides than men on high-glucose diets.

Why? Your body can't metabolize a sweet snack as fast as you can eat it, says Dr. Levitsky. So your liver puts some of the snack's glucose into your bloodstream or stores it for later use. But if your liver's tank is full, it packages the excess as triglycerides. The snack's fructose goes to your liver as well, but instead of being deposited into your bloodstream, it's stored as glycogen. Your liver can store about 90 to 100 grams of glycogen, so it converts the excess to fat (the triglycerides).

What matters: By maintaining a healthy weight, most people can keep their triglycerides at acceptable levels. "If you're overweight or gaining weight, however, they'll accumulate and become

a core predictor of heart disease and stroke," Dr. Levitsky says.

If you're one of those overweight people, your first step is to lay off sugary and starchy foods, beer, and sweet drinks. Your body wasn't built to handle all that sugar. Consider this: You'd have to eat four apples in order to ingest roughly the same amount of fructose in one large McDonald's Coke.

TRUTH #4

Too much sugar stresses your system

Doctors use the oral glucose tolerance test (OGTT) to diagnose prediabetes and diabetes. For an OGTT, you consume 75 grams of glucose to see how your system processes sugar. It's a kind of stress test; downing that kind of sugar load is not something you should normally do.

And yet a 24-ounce soda often contains more than 75 grams of sugar, most of it likely HFCS. Roughly half of that 75 grams is fructose, so that soda shock may be worse than the doctor's test. "The way people eat and drink these days, unintentional stress tests probably happen quite often," says Dr. Lien.

What matters: Maybe you figure your body can process a big sugar load without damage. But that's like pointing to a man who smokes until he's 90 and dodges emphysema or cancer, Dr. Westman says. Why gamble?

Severe hyperglycemia (high blood sugar) can cause blurred vision, extreme thirst, and frequent urges to urinate. Hypoglycemia (low blood sugar) is easier to spot: You feel weak with cold sweats and anxiety, blurred vision, or tiredness a couple of hours after a sugar binge. Sound familiar? Ask about an OGTT, which is more accurate than the simpler fasting glucose blood test.

TRUTH #5

Fewer blood sugar spikes help you live longer

If you live large—big meals, lots of beer, little moderation—you might be shortening your life even if your weight is okay. Repeated blood sugar spikes stress the organs that make up the metabolic engine of your body. That takes a toll.

And you might not notice. "People can live symptom-free for years in a prediabetic state even though they've lost as much as 50 percent of their pancreatic function," says Dr. Lien. "And they don't even know it." People with prediabetes share the same health risks, especially for heart disease, that haunt people with full-blown diabetes.

What matters: Moderation. It's simple, yet difficult. Think about what you put in your mouth. Sugar is diabolical; it tastes great and is less filling. Back off on the high-impact glycemics: beer, sugary soft drinks and sport drinks, potatoes, pasta, baked goods, pancakes.

"The less sugar stress you put on your system, the longer it will function properly," says Dr. Levitsky. And stop blaming sugar for all the world's problems. Even if it is diabolical. ■

Ultimate Fat Fighting

Martin Rooney helps warriors get fighting fit, and he can whip your weight problem with five simple exercises.

The "hurricane workout" is comprised of five challenging exercises performed for 60 seconds each, with no rest in between.

Watching from the sidelines, it's clear: Even this guy's warmup would make most men puke.

"This guy" is 37-year-old Martin Rooney, one of the world's top strength and conditioning coaches. As chief operating officer of the Parisi Speed School franchise in Fair Lawn, New Jersey, he has worked with thousands of elite athletes, including Olympians and pros from the NFL, the NBA, and Major League Baseball.

And the men he's training right now? Well, you might call them warriors. Consider two world champions in Brazilian jujitsu, one national judo champ, and three Ultimate Fighters. They're here because Rooney is best known for his ability to prepare mixed martial artists physically and mentally for the ring. It's easy to see why.

Only after a 45-minute warmup that features agility drills, abdominal training, and wind sprints are the fighters ready for their actual workout. And it's not about to become easier. Next on the docket is one of Rooney's trademark "hurricane" training sessions: Three 5-minute rounds of five different exercises, performed for 1 minute each. Today he's demanding these lung- and muscle-busting moves:

1 A 300-pound tire flip
2 Quick-feet drills through a ladder
3 Pushing a weighted sled
4 Sprinting with added resistance
5 Pounding a tire with a sledgehammer

Go fast, go hard, go for a minute, and move to the next station—for 5 minutes straight. Then catch your breath and do it all over again.

"If a guy we compete against can't do on one day what we do every day," says Rooney, "he's going to be in trouble."

So ask yourself this: Can you handle a hurricane? Or would you be "in trouble"? Find out by trying the routine for yourself, using Rooney's mix-and-match system. Even if you're not quite ready for the ring, you'll burn blubber, build muscle, and take your conditioning to an all-time high.

Simply pick one exercise from the options (A, B, or C) listed in each group. Then do all five exercises in the order shown, without resting. That's one round. Rest for 2 minutes between rounds, and then repeat up to 2 more times. Use this plan twice a week, on the days between your regular workouts.

1

1A
Jump Rope

Skip or jump at the highest intensity you can maintain for a total of 60 seconds.

1B
Treadmill Run

Go at the fastest pace that you can maintain for the entire 60 seconds.

1C
Shadowboxing

Throw punches at an imaginary opponent—alternate hands, and mix jabs and hooks to the body and head—while you dance and duck as if you were in the ring.

2

2A
Stepup

Place your left foot on a bench and push your body up until both feet are on it. Step down with your left foot, and then your right. Repeat, this time starting with your right foot. Continue to alternate.

2B
Bench Jump

With your feet shoulder-width apart, dip down and jump up onto a bench. Step down and repeat.

2C
Scissor Bench Jump

Place your left foot on a bench with your right foot on the floor. In one movement, jump up and switch leg positions in midair. Continue to alternate to the left and right.

1B

Swing your arms forward, not across your body.

2A

Press your heel into the bench as you step onto it.

3

3A
Medicine Ball Crunch

Perform a classic crunch while holding a medicine ball against your chest.

3B
Medicine Ball Russian Twist

Sit holding a medicine ball in front of your chest. Lean your torso back slightly and raise your feet off the floor. Now rotate the ball to your left and then to your right. Move back and forth quickly.

3C
Medicine Ball Pike

Lie on your back with your body straight, holding a medicine ball behind your head. Now simultaneously raise your legs and arms until the ball touches your feet.

4

4A
Pushup

Keeping your body rigid, lower yourself until your chest touches the floor. Repeat as many times as you can in 60 seconds, even if you have to stop. Just rest and start again.

4B
Chinup

Using a shoulder-width, underhand grip, pull your chest to the bar. Repeat as many times as you can in 60 seconds, just as you did on the pushup.

4C
Dip

Lower your body until your elbows are bent 90 degrees. Repeat as many times as you can in 60 seconds, just as you did on the pushup.

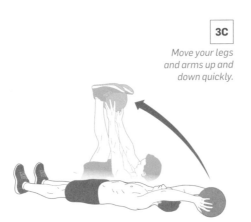

3C

Move your legs and arms up and down quickly.

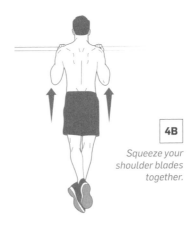

4B

Squeeze your shoulder blades together.

Go fast, go hard, go for a minute, and move to the next station—for 5 minutes straight.

5A
Walking Lunge

Step forward with your left foot, lower your body into a lunge, and then bring your right foot forward. Now push your body back to a standing position.

5B
Squat Thrust

Squat and lean forward so that your hands are on the floor and you're on the balls of your feet. Then kick both legs back into a pushup position, reverse back to a squat, and jump as high as you can.

5C
Jump Squat

Stand with your feet shoulder-width apart, lower your body until your thighs are parallel to the floor, and then jump as high as you can.

5C

Try to land softly on your toes.

Create Your Own Hurricane

You can do hurricane training anytime, anywhere.

Martin Rooney's hurricane training system will melt your midsection, and it'll also help keep you motivated. That's because the variety of exercise combinations you can use is nearly limitless, which is key to keeping your workout fresh and exciting.

"You can do arm curls for only so long before you become bored," says Rooney. "There's nothing better than designing a workout that has people sweating and smiling."

Spartacus: Blood and Sand lead warrior Andy Whitfield stays gladiator-fit with just three workouts a week.

The New Science of Fat Loss

Lift this way to find your abs and stay lean for life.

Ponder this scenario: You've just received a treasured job offer—a dream situation for your career, in fact—but it comes with a few unusual requirements. You have to go shirtless on the job, millions of people will watch you work that way, and oh yeah, you need to achieve and maintain 10 percent body fat or they'll fire your ass.

However, because you're so busy doing this job, you have only 45 minutes, 3 days a week to exercise. Assuming you take the position, what would you do with that time? Go for a run? Hit the elliptical machine? Search the job boards? Hire a body double?

This is precisely the predicament faced by Andy Whitfield, who plays the lead in the new Starz television drama *Spartacus: Blood and Sand* (think *Gladiator* meets *300*).

"I'm filmed virtually naked in my Roman skivvies all day long," says the 37-year-old actor. "So when I look in the mirror, I'm driven by both vanity and fear." You can probably relate.

It's natural to assume that an actor has far more time for exercise than the average guy does. But Whitfield's schedule probably isn't much different from your own. After all, he has a wife and two young children and spends most days on set from 7 a.m. to 7 p.m.

"For Spartacus, we've committed 100 percent of our production time to creating great scenes," says Whitfield. "So all the training I do is on my own time. And that's pretty limited."

Sound familiar?

Now consider that job offer again. If you were Andy Whitfield, what kind of exercises would you do to stay lean on the job? Warning: Most people have the answer all wrong.

THE GREAT AEROBIC HOAX

For decades, we've been told that the best activity for burning calories and fat is aerobic exercise. In fact, you can practically pinpoint the year this idea started to take hold: 1977. That's when Jim Fixx's *The Complete Book of Running* was published. This bestseller popularized the notion of running to improve health and lose weight, and it's widely credited with kicking off the jogging boom of the 1980s. Hundreds of studies since then have reported that aerobic exercise offers many benefits, from improving markers of heart-disease risk to coping with mental stress to enhancing cognitive function. That's all good. But if you're looking to shed fat, the newest weight-loss research will tell you to look elsewhere for your exercise routine.

"It's sort of like a self-fulfilling prophecy," says Jeff Volek, Ph.D., R.D., an exercise and nutrition scientist at the University of Connecticut. "Any type of exercise burns calories. So if you're told that running is ideal and you start dropping pounds once you take it up, then you have no reason to believe otherwise."

But Dr. Volek's research gives him good reason to doubt the conventional wisdom about the superiority of aerobic exercise for fat loss. In one study, Volek and his team put overweight people on a reduced-calorie diet and divided them into three groups. One group didn't exercise, another per-

Gym rats everywhere have wondered why an intense, energy-boosting workout supposedly burned fewer calories than a run.

T-PUSHUP
The T-pushup starts with a dumbbell push-up and then extends to a T, working your abs extra hard.

formed aerobic exercise 3 days a week, and a third did both aerobic exercise and weight training 3 days a week.

The results: Each group lost nearly the same amount of weight—about 21 pounds per person in 12 weeks. But the lifters shed 5 more pounds of fat than those who didn't pump iron. The weight they lost was almost pure fat, while the other two groups shed 15 pounds of lard but also gave up 5-plus pounds of muscle.

This isn't a one-time finding, either. Research on low-calorie dieters who don't lift shows that, on average, 75 percent of their weight loss is from fat and 25 percent of it is muscle. That 25 percent may reduce your scale weight, but it doesn't do a lot for your reflection in the mirror. (Can you say "skinny-fat"?) However, if you weight train as you diet, you protect your hard-earned muscle and burn extra fat instead.

THE NEW SCIENCE OF CALORIE BURNING

There's one argument for aerobic exercise that's always been rock solid. It's well documented that an activity like moderate jogging burns more calories than weight training, an activity that's highly anaerobic. In fact, if you go by the numbers, you find that even golfing beats out a light circuit workout. But recent research shows a new perspective.

When Christopher Scott, Ph.D., an

exercise physiologist at the University of Southern Maine, began using an advanced method to estimate energy expenditure during exercise, his data indicated that weight training burns more calories than originally thought—up to 71 percent more. Based on these findings, it's estimated that performing just one circuit of eight exercises—which takes about 8 minutes—can expend 159 to 231 calories. That's about the same as running at a 6-minute-mile pace for the same duration.

"Exercise physiologists often use the techniques for estimating the energy expenditure of walking and jogging and apply them to weightlifting," says Dr. Scott. "But clearly, aerobic and anaerobic activities differ, and so too should the way we estimate their energy expenditures."

That's a relief to gym rats everywhere, who no doubt wondered why an intense, energy-sapping weight workout supposedly burned so few calories.

REAL-WORLD RESULTS

The unfortunate reality is that science is slow.

"If we waited around for studies to tell us what works best for fat loss, we'd go out of business," says Rachel Cosgrove, C.S.C.S., who co-owns Results Fitness in Santa Clarita, California, with her husband, Alwyn. Over the past 10 years, the Cosgroves have risen to the top of the fitness industry because of their clients' successes. From the beginning, their programs were scientifically based.

"Starting out, we knew that weight training was necessary to avoid muscle loss, and that it appears to boost your metabolism for hours after you work out," Cosgrove says. "We also knew that according to studies, higher-intensity exercises such as interval training and weight

DUMBBELL ROW
Dumbbell rows can harden your core, back, and arms.

SWING
For this "swing" exercise, you can use either a dumbbell or a kettlebell, and either one or both arms. Your glutes, hamstrings, and core benefit.

MOUNTAIN CLIMBER
The mountain climber is
another weight-loss wonder.

training resulted in greater fat loss than lower-intensity exercise did."

But from there, the Cosgroves started their own experiments.

"As time went by, we began to drop aerobic exercise from our fat-loss programs altogether. And guess what? Our clients achieved even faster results," says Cosgrove. Keep in mind that the Cosgroves' clients aren't like *Biggest Loser* contestants. In other words, they don't have 4 to 6 hours a day to work out.

That's why the Cosgroves rely on what they call "metabolic circuits." These are fast-paced weight-training routines in which you alternate between upper- and lower-body exercises. You might compare this type of activity to running repeated bouts of 30- to 60-second sprints. While sprinting has been shown to burn calories at a high rate, it can't be sustained for long

because the muscles in your lower body become fatigued—and that's even if you're resting between sprints.

"But with metabolic circuits, you're emphasizing different muscles in each exercise," says Cosgrove. "So you can maintain a high-intensity effort for a much longer duration and with almost no rest." The result: the muscle-saving, calorie-burning benefits of intense resistance training and sprints, combined with the nonstop movement of long, steady-state aerobic exercise.

Of course, if you try to find evidence of this workout's effectiveness in the scientific journals, you'll be disappointed: No one has studied it yet. But researchers like Drs. Volek and Scott are beginning to put the pieces together. Just as important, trainers like the Cosgroves are already using this kind of routine to help their real-world clients achieve faster results than ever. ∎

The Fat Burner

Hit your fighting weight with this high-intensity workout.

If you're like most men, you have a time in your past when you remember looking and feeling your best. But now when you look in the mirror, maybe that body seems like it belonged to someone else. Fitness expert Todd Durkin, C.S.C.S., hears stories like this from many of the guys at his gym, Fitness Quest 10, in San Diego. Whether they weighed 10 or 20 pounds less or were significantly stronger and could bench 50 to 100 pounds more, they look back fondly at their former selves.

But here's some good news: You don't need to reminisce about your glory days. Durkin uses the past as a baseline for improvement and not necessarily an ultimate goal. That's because your body just needs a new stimulus that can shock your muscles into dramatic changes and help you reach a new physical peak.

This program is based on the same cutting-edge concepts that Durkin uses with his NFL players, including athletes such as LaDainian Tomlinson, Drew Brees, and Kellen Winslow, who need to be in prime condition when the season starts.

The routine incorporates everything you need to transform your body: compound exercises that work all your muscles, fast-paced supersets that shred fat, and new variations of old favorites that make the routine both challenging and fun. And after only 4 weeks, you'll be amazed by the changes you see and confident that you're on your way to achieving the best shape of your life.

Your Strong and Lean Plan

Reach your physical prime using this blend of unique exercises.

DIRECTIONS

Perform each workout (A, B, and C) once a week, resting at least a day between sessions. Alternate between exercises of the same number (1A and 1B, for example) until you complete all the sets in that pairing. In other words, do 1 set of the first exercise and follow it up with 1 set of the second exercise. Rest 30 to 60 seconds between and after each exercise pair, and then repeat the cycle until you've completed all prescribed sets before moving on to the next exercise. To speed fat loss, do the conditioning work listed with each workout.

Workout A
Complete exercises 1, 2, and 3 (2 to 3 sets of each).
Conditioning: Plate pushes. Put a weight plate flat on the floor. Place your hands on the plate; keeping your back flat and your butt low, drive with your legs to push the plate 10 yards, and return. That's 1 set; do 5.

Workout B
Complete exercises 1, 2, 3, and 4 (2 to 3 sets of each).
Conditioning: Set a treadmill for the fastest pace you can consistently maintain for 30 seconds. Run for 30 seconds and then step off the treadmill for 30 seconds. That's 1 set. Complete a total of 6.

Workout C
Complete all the exercises, 1 through 5 (2 to 3 sets of each).
Conditioning: Set a treadmill at the fastest pace you can maintain for 60 seconds. Run for 60 seconds, stop, and then— with as little rest as possible — complete as many pushups as you can. Do this 3 times.

1A
Barbell Overhead Lunge
Stand holding a barbell overhead with your arms straight. Maintain that position as you take a large step forward until your front knee is bent 90 degrees and your back knee is an inch or two off the floor. Return to the starting position, and repeat with the other leg. (20 reps)

A

B

TIP:
Squeeze your shoulder blades together during the entire move.

1B
Hyperextension with Dumbbell Scarecrow and Twist

Hold a pair of light dumbbells as you bend over a back-extension machine with your hips fully supported and arms extended. Without rounding your back, bend your elbows to 90 degrees, raise your upper body, and twist to the right. Your elbows should remain at 90 degrees with your shoulder blades flexed. Return to the starting position and repeat the twist in the opposite direction. (12 to 20 reps)

2A
Barbell Bus Driver Rotation

Wrap a towel around the end of a barbell and wedge that end firmly into a bench. Grab the other end with both hands and hold it in front of your right hip. Your left (back) foot should rotate inward. In a sweeping arc (while keeping your arms straight), twist your torso to bring the barbell in front of your body. Finish with the barbell on your opposite hip. (Twist your left foot a bit as the bar moves across your body.) Repeat on the other side. That's 1 rep. (12 to 20 reps)

TIP: Wedge a barbell into a bench for exercises 2A–2C.

2B
Barbell Squat and One-Arm Press

Wedge one end of a barbell into a bench as in 2A. Squat and hold the other end in your right hand. Stand and push the barbell until your arm is extended. Return to the starting position. That's 1 rep. Do all your reps on the right, and repeat on the left. (10 reps each side)

2C
Barbell Drop Squat and Row

Wedge one end of a barbell into a bench as in 2A. Squat and grab the other end with your right hand; your arm should be fully extended. Now step back with your right foot and pull the barbell up to your rib cage. As you do this, stand and rotate your body so you face the barbell, finishing with the bar at shoulder height. That's 1 rep. Complete all your right-arm reps, switch sides, and repeat with your left arm. (10 reps each side)

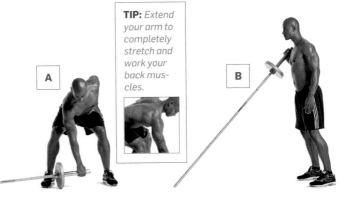

TIP: *Extend your arm to completely stretch and work your back muscles.*

3A
Pushup and Row Combination

Assume a pushup position with your arms straight and your hands resting on light dumbbells. Keep your feet about hip-width apart. Lower your body to just above the floor, pause, and then push yourself back up. Now bring one dumbbell toward your rib cage and return it to the floor. Do another pushup, and repeat with your other arm. That's 1 rep. (10 to 20 pushups)

3B
Inverted Row

Lie under a barbell that's been secured slightly higher than arm's length above the floor. Grab the bar with an overhand grip and hang from it with your body in a straight line from ankles to shoulders. Pull your chest to the bar, pause, and lower yourself until your arms are straight. (To count as a rep, your chest must touch the bar.) (as many reps as you can)

4A
Dumbbell Curl with Static Hold

Hold a dumbbell in each hand with your arms extended and palms facing forward. While keeping your left arm bent 90 degrees, curl the right dumbbell as close to your chest as you can without moving your upper arms. Pause and lower the weight to the starting position. Do 10 reps. Then keep your right arm bent and do 10 curls with your left arm. Finally, do 10 curls with both arms. That's 1 set. (30 reps total: 10 left, 10 right, 10 both)

TIP: *Keep your non-working arm flexed to add more size to your biceps.*

4B
Pushup

Assume a pushup position: Your hands should be slightly wider than and in line with your shoulders, your feet slightly wider than hip-width apart, and your arms straight. Keeping your back flat, lower your body until your chest nearly touches the floor. Pause, and push yourself back up to the starting position. (15 reps)

5
Single-Leg Balance Touch

Remove your shoes and stand on your left leg. Now bend at the waist (while keeping your back flat and hips pushed back), and extend your right leg behind you. Reach down, moving your right hand across your body and toward your left foot. Then raise your upper body to the starting position, but without touching your right foot to the floor. That's 1 rep. Complete all your reps on one leg, and then switch sides and repeat. (15 reps each leg)

TIP: *Try to mimic a pitcher's throwing motion but without losing your balance.*

18 Exercise Upgrades

Use these training secrets to build more muscle and lose fat faster.

What if you could instantly make any exercise 10 times more effective? Chances are, you can. That's because most men make tiny but key technique errors on even the most basic movements. As it turns out, these seemingly minor mistakes may be preventing you from achieving the body you want. You see, an exercise may feel right, but smart lifting isn't just about moving a weight from point A to point B. For big-time gains, you need to master the small details.

The good news: Use these 18 tips from the top trainers in the industry to help you perfect your form, engage the right muscles, burn more calories, and lower your risk of injury. Think about it this way: It takes the same amount of time to do an exercise right as it does to do it wrong. So start squeezing more from every second of your workout.

PUSHUP

What you're doing wrong: You're letting your hips sag as you raise and lower your body.

Perfect Your Form

1

"When you're in a pushup position, your posture should look the same as it would if you were standing up straight and tall," says Vern Gambetta, the owner of Gambetta Sports Training Systems in Sarasota, Florida. "So your hips shouldn't sag or be hiked, and your upper back shouldn't be rounded."

2

"Before you start, contract and stiffen your core the way you would if you had to zip up a really tight jacket," says Kaitlyn Weiss, an NASM-certified trainer based in Southern California. Hold it that way for the duration of your set. "This helps your body remain rigid—with perfect posture—as you perform the exercise."

3

"Don't just push your body up; push your hands through the floor," Gambetta says. You'll generate more power with every repetition.

The only movement during a pushup should occur in your arms.

BENCH PRESS

What you're doing wrong: You're thinking only about pushing the bar up from your chest.

Perfect Your Form

4

"Every time you lower the weight, squeeze your shoulder blades together and pull the bar to your chest," says Craig Rasmussen, C.S.C.S., a fitness coach at Results Fitness in Santa Clarita, California. This will help you build up energy in your upper body so that you can press the bar up with more force.

5

"As you pull the weight down, lift your chest to meet the barbell," Rasmussen says. "This will aid your efforts to create a springlike effect when you start to push the bar back up."

6

"When you press the weight, try to bend the bar with your hands," says Pavel Tsatsouline, a fitness expert and the author of *Enter the Kettlebell!* The benefit: You'll activate more muscle fibers in your lats and move the bar in a stronger and safer path for your shoulders.

Focus on lowering the bar to maximize how much weight you can bench.

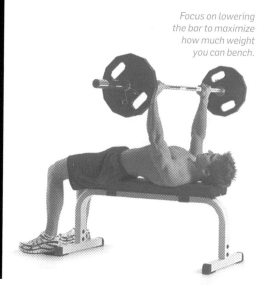

SQUAT

What you're doing wrong: You're starting the movement by bending your knees.

Perfect Your Form
7

"Sit back between your legs, not on top of your knees," says Dan John, a strength coach based in Draper, Utah. Start your squats by pushing your hips back. "Most men tend to bend their knees first, which puts more stress on their joints."

8

"When you squat, imagine you're standing on a paper towel," says Charlie Weingroff, director of sports performance and physical therapy for CentraState Sports Performance in Monroe, New Jersey. "Then try to rip the towel apart by pressing your feet hard into the floor and outward." This activates your glutes, which helps you use heavier weights.

9

"Instead of raising your body, think about pushing the floor away from your body," says Alwyn Cosgrove, C.S.C.S., co-owner of Results Fitness. "This helps you better engage the muscles in your legs."

Press through your heels as you stand and avoid shifting your weight to your toes.

STRAIGHT-LEG DEADLIFT

What you're doing wrong: You're rounding your lower back as you bend over.

Perfect Your Form
10

"To lower the weight, pretend you're holding a tray of drinks and need to close the door behind you with your butt," says Cosgrove. This cues you to bend over by pushing your hips back instead of rounding your lower back—a form blunder that puts you at risk for back problems.

11

"Try to 'shave your legs' with the bar," says Weiss. The reason: Every degree the bar is away from your body places more strain on your back, which increases your chance of injury and limits the emphasis on your hamstrings and glutes.

12

"As you lift the bar, squeeze your glutes like two fists," says Nick Grantham, a top strength and conditioning coach in the U.K. and the owner of Smart Fitness. You'll ensure that you're engaging your butt muscles. This helps you generate more power, lift more weight, and produce better results.

Remember to push your hips back to help activate your hamstrings and glutes.

ROWS AND PULLUPS

What you're doing wrong: You're ignoring the muscles that retract your shoulder blades.

Perfect Your Form
13

"When doing bent-over and seated rows, and any pullup variation, create as much space between your ears and shoulders as you can," says Rasmussen. Pull your shoulders down and back and hold them that way as you do the exercise. This ensures you're working the intended middle- and upper-back muscles.

14

"As you row the weight, stick your chest out," says Mike Boyle, M.A., A.T.C., owner of Mike Boyle Strength and Conditioning in Winchester and North Andover, Massachusetts. This allows you to better retract your shoulder blades, which will lead to better results.

15

"Imagine there's an orange between your shoulder blades," says Grantham. "Then try to squeeze the juice out of it with your shoulder blades as you pull the weight or your body up."

Pull your shoulder blades down and back before rows and pullups.

LUNGE

What you're doing wrong: You're leaning forward, causing your front heel to rise.

Perfect Your Form
16

"When you lunge, keep your torso upright, and focus on moving it up and down, not backward and forward," says Rasmussen. This will keep your weight balanced evenly through your front foot, allowing you to press hard into the floor with your heel—and target more muscle.

17

"Drop your back knee straight down to the floor," says Boyle. Consider this a second strategy to help you remember that you should drop your torso down, not push it forward, as you do the exercise.

18

"To work your core harder, narrow your starting stance," says Gray Cook, M.S.P.T., the author of *Athletic Body in Balance*. The smaller the gap between your feet, the more your core has to work to stabilize your body. Your goal: Lunge so that it's almost like you're walking on a tightrope as you perform the exercise.

Think of the lunge as an up-and-down movement for the best results.

PROVE IT.

KNOW THE TRUTH

Are you being fooled by what you see in the mirror? In a University of Kansas study, a group of flabby guys were asked to choose an image that best represented their bodies. The finding: **Obese men almost always believe they're thinner than their doctors think they are.**

People deny the severity of a weight problem in order to buffer their self-esteem, says the lead study author, Kim Pulvers, Ph.D. Ask your physician to assess the state of your weight problem—and trust him. After all, the truth can hurt, but it may provide the kick in the pants you need.

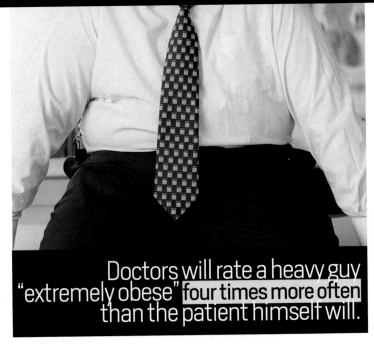

Doctors will rate a heavy guy "extremely obese" four times more often than the patient himself will.

DON'T WORRY YOURSELF FAT

A stressful job might make you fat, suggest Harvard researchers who followed 1,355 Americans for 9 years. They found that overweight men with little authority gained more weight than men with more authority did. **Not being able to make decisions is linked to stress.** Eating can be calming because it releases mood-improving endorphins, says study author Jason Block, M.D. Best stress-busting fat burner? Exercise.

WRITE OFF THE POUNDS

Hold yourself accountable: In a 13-week study, dieters who kept a food record for 3 weeks or longer lost 3.5 pounds more than those who didn't, say researchers at the University of Arkansas. And over the long term, this strategy may be even more important for enhancing your results. "Keeping a detailed account of what you eat, even for a short period of time, helps you learn how to accurately estimate portion sizes," says the *Men's Health* weight-loss coach, Alan Aragon, M.S. To eyeball calories like an expert, log and analyze your daily meals for at least 2 weeks on a free Web site such as SparkPeople.com.

QUENCH YOUR APPETITE

Pepper your diet with fat-fighting vegetables.
Here's a weight-loss trick: Fill your belly to shrink it. Penn State researchers found that when people swapped half the roast beef and rice on their plates with lightly buttered broccoli, they ate 86 fewer calories—and felt just as full.

"Vegetables are satiating because they contain water, which bulks food up," says study coauthor Jennifer Meengs, R.D. The top picks? Cabbage, zucchini, cucumbers, cauliflower, and peppers.

REV UP YOUR METABOLISM

If you're overweight, eating protein instead of carbohydrates can speed up your metabolism. Australian scientists recently discovered that **heavy people burn fat more quickly after they eat high-protein meals than after they eat high-carb ones.**

To experience the benefit, the study participants simply tweaked two meals of their daily menu. Instead of a large bowl of cereal for breakfast, they substituted a cheese-and-tomato omelet; for lunch, they opted for an open-faced meat sandwich.

GET AN EXERCISE RX

A piece of paper could solve the obesity epidemic. Researchers in Spain found that people were more likely to exercise if their doctors gave them written workout "prescriptions," along with delivering the advice verbally. And while doctors will need more training to properly prescribe exercises, the scientists believe it'll be worth the effort: **Research shows that a sedentary life can make people sitting ducks for disease.**

YOU ASKED.

Should I measure my body fat?

A: Tracking your progress can be helpful, but every testing method, from calipers to dual-energy X-ray absorptiometry, is flawed. Your two best indicators are the mirror and your clothes. Use a pair of jeans that you want to fit into as a measure of progress. How tight are they? Is the button in any danger of popping off? As they loosen up, you'll know you're nearing your goal.

Q: I'm losing pounds but not inches. What's wrong?

A: "My guess is you're not weight training and eating enough protein," says Alan Aragon, M.S., a nutritionist in Westlake Village, California. Doing both is key to eliminating fat and building muscle. Resistance training burns calories during your sessions and stimulates your metabolism afterward.

To achieve the second goal, fortify your diet with either 6 additional ounces of meat or 2 scoops of protein powder; each option yields about 40 grams of protein.

Q: Can a "cheat meal" ever be helpful?

A: A high-calorie meal can temporarily raise metabolism, but not by enough to override the extra calorie intake. Still, there's a psychological benefit: It's healthy to momentarily ease up and realize that you can make progress without being boxed into diet foods.

Q: If pairing protein with carbs helps build muscle, will it help weight loss?

A: Yes. Although you might think that the carbs will slow weight loss, the opposite can be true. Carbs plus protein helps build muscle (especially if you eat the combo just before and after exercise), and that can indirectly enhance fat loss, because muscle is metabolically active tissue that helps burn more calories around the clock.

Q: What's a great way to keep my diet on track?

A: Users of an online weight-loss program dropped more pounds when they were sent e-mail encouragements, says a study in the *Archives of Internal Medicine*. E-mail recipients shed between 11 and 16 pounds, compared with just a 6-pound drop among the unprodded. Sign up for weekly reminders and tips at bellyoff.com.

Q: I'm a vegetarian. Besides eggs and beans, how can I eat more protein?

A: Cheese, milk, yogurt, and cottage cheese are all good, as is 40 grams (or about 2 scoops) of whey-protein powder. Unless you're vegan, we'd advise against a soy-protein isolate. You probably eat a lot of soy already, and too much might increase estrogen levels.

Q: I lost 5 pounds my first week on a new diet and exercise program but only 2 pounds the next. What gives?

A: This is common at the start of a diet. You're probably dropping water weight because of the carbs and salt you've stopped eating. That weight goes fast but slows after a week or two.

Q: I've been told not to eat late, but usually I'm starving after my shift. What should I do?

A: Your body isn't on a 24-hour clock. What counts is whether you burn more calories than you ingest by the end of the day (or better yet, the week). If the munchies surface at night, any combination of fruit, nuts, nut butter, or dairy (such as milk, yogurt, or cheese) makes a perfect prebed snack.

Q: I watch my calories, but I've been known to binge during the holidays. Should I eat less the next day?

A: You don't have to eat less, just eat smarter.

"Depriving yourself after a binge can actually lead to more bingeing," says Louis Aronne, M.D., a clinical professor of medicine at Cornell University. Your stomach capacity can increase about 25 percent during a pig-out. And it won't shrink back to its pregorge size for another 2 weeks. That means you could feel unsatisfied—despite yesterday's feeding frenzy—if you restrict calories.

To stay full, opt for high-protein, high-fiber foods. "For breakfast, have an omelet with vegetables and light cheese, or some peanut butter on a slice of whole wheat toast," Dr. Aronne says. Choose lean meats and colorful vegetables for lunch and dinner.

Just stay away from the sweets. "Desserts can actually stimulate your appetite and make you lose your sense of fullness, potentially prompting another binge," he says. Munch on some fruit instead.

2

Flat Belly Foods

16 New Lessons of Great Guy Food

Life is short. Fill it with amazing food.

You eat three times a day, so you should do it really well. Plus, it's one of those pleasures that you can appreciate even more in a bum economy, because your own kitchen is the place where you can spend less, eat more, and eat better.

That's what the following pages are all about: pleasing yourself, pleasing her, pleasing friends, and improving your life, bite by bite.

From incredible cheap eats to cutting-edge kitchen science, there's never been a better time to be a man with an appetite. Here's why.

NEW FLAVORS ARE STILL BEING DISCOVERED

Remember the diagram from school? The tongue is divided like a map, with four basic tastes claiming territory on that slimy surface: sweet, sour, bitter, salty. For centuries, Western culture's understanding of taste relied on those four categories.

Made sense. Except the diagram was missing something. It couldn't account for the savory deliciousness in, say, a bite of aged Parmesan.

Back in 1908, Japanese chemist Kikunae Ikeda sought to identify the mysterious flavor in his seaweed soup. He concluded that it was an amino acid called glutamate. Ikeda named the flavor "umami," meaning "yummy," and wrote of "a singular taste which cannot be called sweet, or sour, or salty, or bitter." Nearly 100 years later, the scientific community vindicated Ikeda with the discovery of separate taste receptors on the tongue for umami.

"Umami has a mushroomy, earthy quality," says *Top Chef*'s Tom Colicchio. "But it's elusive. It doesn't hit your tongue the way the other stuff does." The Umami Information Center ranks kelp, Parmesan cheese, cured ham, and ripe tomatoes particularly high in rich umami flavor.

There is an evolutionary imperative behind our recognition of the taste. Protein-rich foods are thick with glutamate; the taste of umami signaled to our tree-swinging ancestors that they were eating the good stuff. Plus, umami blends well with other flavors, upping what food geeks call the "amplitude" (flavor balance) of many dishes. If you've ever shaken Worcestershire sauce onto a burger, you understand the concept.

Ikeda was hip to this. He patented MSG—pure, crystallized umami—and we've been mainlining it in our Doritos ever since. But when you're ready to evolve past Frito-Lay for your umami fix, Colicchio offers a strategy for packing more of the fifth flavor into your meals: Soak a pack of dried mushrooms in warm water for 20 minutes and use the resulting stock to spike soups, sauces, and stir-fries. Or taste umami in all its earthy splendor with a few thick tomato slices topped with shaved Parmesan.

CHOOSING WINES JUST BECAME EASIER

Gone are the days when champagne was reserved for weddings and women. Wine snobs and bargain hounds alike are embracing bubbly for its ability to pair well with anything, even red meat.

"When people want to drink one wine for eight different courses, I tell them sparkling is the way to go," says Jim Rollston, the wine director at Cyrus restaurant in Healdsburg, California. "It has a little sweetness balanced with great acidity." Even better is that you don't need to call it champagne anymore, because the pricey French stuff is now competing with delicious, affordable proseccos from Italy and cavas from Spain. Bonus: She'll love it.

Around $20: Chandon Brut Classic

This California bubbly is made using the same techniques as the French stuff.

Pair with: Sushi. "Bubbles usually work well in place of sake or beer, and this one is especially great with any white fish," Rollston says. Also, few pairings make more sense than bubbly and a plate of raw oysters. Douse the mollusks with lemon and Tabasco.

Around $15: Mionetto Prosecco Brut

This bubbly is from the north of Italy, made with the prosecco grape.

Pair with: Anything salty or fatty, from potato chips to cured meats. Rollston says prosecco's sweetness and softness help it balance those foods.

Around $10: Segura Viudas Brut Reserva

This Spanish sparkling wine known as cava is made from a blend of three local grapes and aged in the bottle for 3 years.

Pair with: Snacks. "I love this with popcorn, chips and salsa, or a soft pretzel," says Rollston. "And it's affordable enough to pop while just watching the game."

IT'S NEVER BEEN SIMPLER TO LEARN TO COOK

As men flock to the kitchen, an army of bloggers and their savvy food sites are on hand to guide your every move. You now have at your fingertips a deep reservoir of healthy cooking tips, strategies for saving money, and food pics worthy of centerfold treatment. Whether it's reliable recipes or hunger stimulation you seek, these three sites deliver the delicious goods.

tastespotting.com: Click on any one of a huge collection of *Bon Appétit* cover-worthy photos at this gastronomic community potluck, and you'll be sent to the user

blog, where the "Damn, that looks awesome" recipe resides. Try not to lick the computer screen.

imcooked.com: At this watch-and-salivate video recipe site, users create and upload instructional films of themselves cooking family faves in their kitchens. Watch Christopher Walken take a shot at roasted chicken with pears. There's a channel (try Soups, Pastas, or Cocktails) for everything.

behindtheburner.com: If imcooked.com is the YouTube of home cooking, this is the Paramount Pictures. Pros contribute educational articles, Q&As, topnotch videos, and ambrosial recipes plump with insider tips. Chefs, mixologists, sommeliers, and nutritionists also offer ingredients and tools at discount prices.

SCIENCE CAN MAKE OUR BEEF BETTER

Harold McGee comes up with world-changing ideas, sort of like Einstein, except McGee's universe is the kitchen. Lots of traditionalists reject new concepts, such as cooking pasta in just a little water or making ice cream in a plastic bag. But McGee has science on his side.

"Food and eating are really complex processes that benefit from study," says McGee, whose tireless research is documented in the seminal book *On Food and Cooking: The Science and Lore of the Kitchen.*

Our favorite McGee discovery starts with a hunk of beef. Everyone knows that high heat and two turns of a steak will seal in juices and flavor. Yeah, so why is the result often overcooked and dry? McGee found that searing creates flavor but doesn't seal in juices. Then a friend showed him computer software that simulates heat conduction.

After tweaking the variables, McGee came up with this conclusion: Starting a steak at room temperature and flipping it every 10 to 15 seconds over very high heat allows it to acquire a brown and flavorful exterior while the interior cooks much faster and more evenly to 140°F, the perfect medium rare. Every 10 to 15 seconds sound like too much work? Flipping your strip steak once a minute still yields amazing flavor, similar to the results you'd get from rotisserie cooking, where the meat is repeatedly heated and cooled. You don't need to understand this; just know that unconventional wisdom never tasted so great.

HEAVY METAL ROCKS THE STOVE

Every man needs one pan he can count on, whether he's searing a steak or churning out piles of hash browns. Griswold—a now-defunct manufacturer—made cast-iron behemoths with surfaces that shone like black ice. It's worth your trouble to track one down.

What makes a Griswold skillet better? To start with, even heat distribution makes it capable of charring a burger or delicately frying an egg. Add relentless durability and you have a cooking vessel for a lifetime.

Modern cast iron is fine, but it's nothing like the old classics. Doris Mosier, spokeswoman for the Griswold & Cast Iron Cookware Association, suggests looking for a vintage skillet with a smooth surface. Clean it down to bare metal, rub a thin coating of vegetable oil all over it—top and bottom—and place it upside down in a

300°F oven. After 30 minutes, turn the oven off and let the pan cool, creating an oxidized, nonstick surface.

"Seasoned properly, the pan should be good for another 50 years," says Mosier.

YOUR BIRD IS NOW JUICIER

For decades, the chicken breast has been the go-to lean protein for smart eaters. But let's change that: Its flavor is weak, and the cooking margin of error is thin. You've choked down enough dry white meat to know this. Besides, you've always been a thigh man. Thighs are succulent, tasty, and cheap, like so many good things in life. They cost a buck less per pound than breasts do, but here's the stunner: All that juicy flavor adds just 1 measly gram of saturated fat per 4-ounce serving compared with the white stuff. Plus, you get more zinc and a tad more iron to fuel and build your muscles. Chef Hinnerk Von Bargen, an associate professor at the Culinary Institute of America's San Antonio campus, suggests these easy dishes. It's time to go moist.

Skillet: Slowly simmer thighs over medium-low heat for an hour in a mixture of chicken broth, soy sauce, rice wine, fresh ginger, dried shiitake mushrooms, and star anise. Serve with Chinese noodles that you've cooked in the sauce.

Grill: Puree sliced lemongrass, garlic, and ginger in a blender, adding water as necessary to ease blending. Mix in sugar, turmeric, ground peanuts, and kosher salt. Pour the mixture over boneless thighs and let them marinate overnight. Cut the chicken into long strips, thread them onto soaked bamboo skewers, and grill over medium heat for 8 to 10 minutes.

Oven: Bake the thighs at 375°F for 20 minutes or until they reach an internal temperature of 165°F. Make a mango salsa by dicing and combining mango, red pepper, jalapeño, red onion, and fresh cilantro. Add fresh lime or lemon juice and scoop the salsa on top of the cooked thighs.

NOT ALL CARBS ARE CREATED EVIL

Long before U.S. politicians legislated corn as the nation's Manifest Destiny, the Aztecs were building an empire fueled by the grain. So it's no wonder Mexicans still know how to cook the King of Crops into such a delicious state. It may be your birthright as a North American to stuff yourself silly with corn on the cob in summer, but when it comes to cooking it, take a cue from the street vendors of Mexico. They grill corn over charcoal, paint it with a light sheen of mayo and lime juice, and finish it with a spicy-salty flourish of chili powder and cheese. Viva Mexico!

SUMMER CORN

4 ears fresh corn
2 tablespoons mayonnaise, thinned with the juice of 1 lime
1 teaspoon chili powder
2 tablespoons finely grated Parmesan cheese

Fire up a charcoal or gas grill. Peel back the husks and remove the silk, and then re-cover the ears with the husks and soak them in cold water for 10 minutes. Place the ears on the grill and cook for 15 minutes, turning so the husks don't burn. Now pull back the husks and grill the ears for another 5 to 10 minutes, until the corn is lightly charred. Paint the ears with a sheen of the lime mayo and dust them with the chili powder and cheese.

IMPRESSING HER HAS NEVER BEEN SO CHEAP

Sure, you could spend 4 years at the Culinary Institute of America—or you could spend $70 and pick up the CliffsNotes. The 1,232-page *The Professional Chef* contains 600-plus recipes that can help you soak up the secrets of top chefs. Invite a guest and try these tips from your new kitchen bible.

Page 463: Ratchet up the flavor quotient in sauces, rubs, and stir-frys by roasting spices, nuts, seeds, and chilies at 350°F for 5 minutes before using.

Page 813: Cook grains in chicken or vegetable stock. As they simmer, add a bay leaf or a few sprigs of fresh thyme or rosemary. Remove the herbs before serving.

Page 1,061: To sweeten (or close) the deal with a dinner date, boil 1 cup of sugar in 1 cup of water. Let the syrup cool, and then drizzle it over sliced peaches or strawberries. Top with whipped cream. Dessert is served.

YOU CAN CATCH A COOL BUZZ THIS SUMMER

Coffee, in all its brain-preserving, diabetes-defending, cancer-fighting glory, may be one of the world's most enjoyable superfoods. But as the mercury climbs, the quality of your caffeine fix plummets. That's because most coffee shops charge extra for iced coffee, only to melt a feeble cup of cubes with piping-hot java. Skip the diluted version and cold-brew a batch at home.

Of course, the effort is wasted if you don't start with good beans. Luckily, the artisan coffee movement is fully percolating in the United States. Among our

ICED COFFEE

⅔ cup coffee grounds
3 cups cold water

Combine the coffee grounds and water in a glass jar or French press, stir, and let the brew sit overnight. In the morning, pour it through a sieve (or lower the French press plunger) to strain out the grounds. Combine this concentrate with an equal amount of cold water. As for the cubes? Make them with the concentrate: As they melt, your joe gets better.

favorite coffees right now are the Panama Esmeralda Especial from Stumptown Coffee Roasters (stumptowncoffee.com) and the Finca Santuario from Intelligentsia Coffee & Tea (intelligentsiacoffee.com).

SUBSTITUTE FOR SALMON

Wild salmon costs $20 a pound, and the farmed stuff gives farming a bad name. Want an alternative? Try mackerel: For around $5 a pound, you'll eat a fish with more life-extending omega-3s than tilapia, cod, catfish, tuna, and snapper combined. One problem: Mackerel's oily texture can overpower your palate. The fix? "Grill it on the bone. You'll tame the flavor and create a moist,

tender texture," says Pano Karatassos, executive chef at Kyma, in Atlanta.

PERFECT GRILLED MACKEREL

½   cup olive oil
3   tablespoons Dijon mustard
    Juice of 2 lemons
    Handful chopped parsley
1   whole mackerel
    Salt
    Ground black pepper

Whisk together the oil, mustard, lemon juice, and parsley. Season the fish with salt and pepper and a spoonful of the vinaigrette, and cook it over medium heat on a clean, oiled grill for 3 to 4 minutes a side, until it's lightly charred and firm to the touch. Drizzle on plenty of extra vinaigrette before serving.

GO WEST

You never forget your first. That's true for, okay, that. And if you're from Southern California, you never forget your first Double-Double animal-style from In-N-Out Burger. The toasty bun; the beef patties covered in melted cheese and grilled onions, all buffered by crisp produce; the "spread" drippings that collect in the wrapping, ready for mopping with a fistful of freshly made fries. And none of it is touched by microwave, heat lamp, or freezer. It's an almost spiritual awakening, your first In-N-Out—a burger baptism.

In-N-Out has been ministering to a growing flock since 1948, when Harry and Esther Snyder opened California's first drive-thru hamburger stand, in Baldwin Park. The company expanded methodically, never franchised, and remains a privately owned, family-run affair. This has allowed In-N-Out to turn out first-rate fare. That means burgers made to order. Potatoes cut and fried on the line. Shakes made from ice cream, not "shake mix." The simple menu is highly customizable, with secret orders awaiting discovery. In-N-Out's success stands as a rebuke to the idea that fast-food companies grow like fungus, exploit staff, and serve gut-churning crap.

East Coast and Midwestern burger lovers, take heart. In-N-Out added Utah to its roster last year. At this rate, New Yorkers could be enjoying Double-Doubles sometime later this century. Meantime, try these tips from In-N-Out VP Carl Van Fleet: Slather ¼-inch patties in mustard before cooking, top with onions fried next to the burger in a cast-iron skillet, and crown each with a slice of good old American cheese.

A GREAT CONDIMENT JUST GOT BETTER

The condiment aisle is the minefield of the grocery store, its jars exploding with fat (mayo), sugar (ketchup), and sodium (bottled dressing). Your safest route to big flavor: mustard. With virtually zero calories, there's no need to exercise caution with this yellow beauty, which derives its color from antioxidant-rich turmeric. Plus, few foods are so versatile. (Just check out the three hot dog–free uses that follow.) So what could possibly make mustard better? How about a can of dark beer? That's what Anthony Fusco of Manhattan's Harbour

HARBOUR GUINNESS MUSTARD

2 small shallots
½ teaspoon vegetable oil
1 cup mustard seeds
1 can Guinness Draught

Slice the shallots and sauté them in the oil. Add the mustard seeds and stir over low heat for 30 seconds. Add enough beer to barely cover the seeds, and simmer until the seeds become tender. Let the mixture cool, and then puree it in a blender. Add more beer as necessary to adjust the consistency. Keeps in the fridge for up to 6 months.

Reef restaurant uses in his 5-minute homemade mustard.

Stir it into a homemade vinaigrette. Mustard acts as an emulsifier, binding the vinegar to the fat molecules in the oil.

Spread it on one side of your pork chops, chicken, or fish, and then sprinkle bread crumbs and herbs on top before roasting.

Mix it (instead of mayo blobs) into your next potato, tuna, or chicken salad. Keep a bit of mayo, but make your favorite mustard the star.

WE'RE MAKING GAINS WITH GRAINS

Farro—a staple for ancient Egyptians and modern-day Italians alike—has everything you need: nearly twice the protein and fiber of brown rice, along with calcium and iron.

"The health benefits are great, but it's really the soulful flavor and chewy texture that make it so special," says Scott Conant, chef at New York City's Scarpetta restaurant. Conant (pictured above, with his wife, Meltem) stirs cooked farro into soups and stews, tosses it with roasted vegeta-

bles to make salads, and replaces rice with farro in pilafs and risottos.

His most inspired creation, though, comes at breakfast time: Sauté onions and garlic and chili flakes in lots of olive oil, and then stir in some tomato sauce and precooked farro. Crack a few eggs directly into the sauce and let them poach.

"I eat it straight out of the pan with grilled bread. It's amazing hangover food." Pick up a bag at igourmet.com.

THERE'S PLENTY TO SHARE

Here are four organizations feeding the hungry.

Feeding America: If you have a food pantry, soup kitchen, emergency shelter, or after-school program in your neighborhood, chances are this nonprofit helps keep it well stocked. feedingamerica.org

Free Rice: Play an Internet game guilt-free. This site, funded by the UN World Food Program, tests your knowledge in six subjects (you can answer as many questions as you'd like) and donates 10 grains of rice to hunger programs for every correct answer. freerice.com

Heifer International: This Arkansas-based charity funds the delivery of live-stock to more than 50 countries. The best part? You pick the type of animal or other agricultural service you want donated. That's right, you can sponsor your own water buffalo. heifer.org

Doctors Without Borders: DWB treats more than 100,000 malnourished children in dozens of countries with ready-to-eat foods like Plumpynut, a peanut butter/milk paste that delivers essential nutri-ents. doctorswithoutborders.org

GOOD THINGS DO COME FROM CANS

Over the past 5 years, craft brewers have given new kick to the beer can, taking advantage of the ecofriendly, skunkproof enclosures to bring better beer to the masses. If there's one man to thank for the can-do attitude, it's Dale Katechis, founder of Oskar Blues in Lyons, Colorado. Dale's eponymous pale ale destroyed all comers in back-to-back taste tests by the *New York Times* and *New York* magazine in 2005 and 2006. Dale now makes a few brews: There's the malt-driven, hearty Scotch ale called Old Chub; a golden pilsner called Mama's Little Yella Pils (tailor-made for a hot summer day); and our favorite, Gordon, a hoppy, assertive mix of imperial red ale and double IPA that's the best "extreme" beer we've ever sipped. What are you waiting for? Grab an ice bucket and crack a cold one. oskarblues.com

THERE ARE SMARTER WAYS TO CATCH FISH

Do we really need to explain our love for juicy, charred fish topped with smoky chipotle-spiked cream and wrapped in a toasty tortilla? Didn't think so. Purists will remind you that fish tacos are meant to be battered and deep-fried; that's how they're made up and down the Baja California coast. We'll remind purists that burgers were originally served without ketchup, and pizza without cheese, and then continue to enjoy our lean, mean fish tacos with a side of smoke and fire. Feel free to do the same.

GRILLED FISH TACOS WITH CHIPOTLE CREMA

½   cup Mexican crema or sour cream
3   limes
1   tablespoon finely chopped chipotle pepper in adobo sauce
    Fresh cilantro
1   pound mahi-mahi, halibut, or fresh tuna
½   tablespoon chili powder (preferably ancho chili powder)
    Salt
    Freshly ground black pepper
8   soft corn tortillas
1   cup finely shredded cabbage
1   avocado, peeled, pitted, and thinly sliced
    Hot sauce

1. Clean and oil a grill or grill pan thoroughly and preheat it on medium high. Mix together the crema with the juice of 1 lime, the chipotle pepper, and a handful of chopped fresh cilantro. Set aside.

2. Drizzle a light coating of oil over the fish, and rub on the chili powder and a pinch of salt and pepper.

3. Place the fish on the grill and cook, undisturbed, for 4 minutes. Carefully flip it with a spatula and cook for another 4 minutes. Remove. Before turning off the grill, warm the tortillas directly on the surface for 1 to 2 minutes.

4. Divide the fish evenly among the warm tortillas, add a bit of cabbage, spoon on the crema, and top with avocado slices and fresh cilantro. Serve each taco with a wedge of lime and some hot sauce.

Makes 8 tacos

THE 125 BEST FOODS FOR MEN

Simplify your shopping list with our top picks from every section in the supermarket.

We created this list by first comparing the nutrition labels of competing brands in each of our 125 categories. We gave bonus points to products with more protein and fiber and less added sugar and sodium. We also took calories per serving into consideration, but we didn't penalize for fat content, because fat adds flavor and helps keep hunger at bay.

Once we pared down our choices, we matched them in head-to-head taste tests to determine the victors. As for draws, the nod went to the product with the fewest ingredients—which happens to be a good rule of thumb, period.

To find all our top picks, complete with customizable grocery list, go to MensHealth.com/bestfoods.

Breads and Grains

1. Best health cereal: Post Spoon-Size Shredded Wheat
This cereal contains just one ingredient: whole grain wheat.
Per cup: 170 calories, 6 grams (g) protein, 40 g carbs (6 g fiber), 1 g fat

3. Best instant oatmeal: Quaker Weight Control Cinnamon
This fast breakfast is packed with fiber.
Per packet: 160 calories, 7 g protein, 29 g carbs (6 g fiber), 3 g fat

5. Best breakfast bar: Fiber One Chewy Bars Oats & Peanut Butter
Grab and go when you're short on time.
Per bar: 150 calories, 3 g protein, 28 g carbs (9 g fiber), 4.5 g fat

7. Best English muffin: Thomas' Hearty Grains 100% Whole Wheat
For a first-class breakfast, top with eggs (#31), ham (#32), sliced avocado, and a healthy scoop of salsa (#104).
Per muffin: 120 calories, 5 g protein, 23 g carbs (3 g fiber), 1 g fat

2. Best sweet cereal: Kashi Autumn Wheat
It tastes deliciously sweet, but has only a touch of sugar.
Per cup: 190 calories, 5 g protein, 45 g carbs (6 g fiber), 1 g fat

4. Best steel-cut oats: McCann's Steel-Cut Irish Oatmeal
Add berries (#49) and almonds for extra sweetness and crunch.
Per ¼ cup: 150 calories, 4 g protein, 26 g carbs (4 g fiber), 2 g fat

6. Best bagel: Thomas' Hearty Grains 100% Whole Wheat
Always choose products that are made with 100 percent whole wheat flour.
Per bagel: 240 calories, 10 g protein, 49 g carbs (7 g fiber), 2 g fat

8. Best bread: Pepperidge Farm 100% Whole Wheat
Stuff two toasted slices with turkey (#32), tomato, jalapeño, guacamole (#106), and a slice of Swiss (#20).
Per slice: 100 calories, 4 g protein, 20 g carbs (3 g fiber), 2 g fat

9. Best burger bun:
Arnold's Select 100% Whole
Wheat Sandwich Thins
These have 3 times the fiber
of wheat buns.
Per roll: 100 calories, 5 g protein, 21 g carbs (6 g fiber),
1 g fat

12. Best pizza crust: Rustic
Crust Organic Pizza Originale
Build your own pizza and save
calories.
Per shell: 120 calories, 5 g protein, 25 g carbs (1 g fiber),
1.5 g fat

15. Best grain: Bob's Red Mill
Organic Quinoa
For protein-packed quinoa recipes and more, go to
MensHealth.com/quinoa.
Per ¼ cup: 170 calories,
7 g protein, 30 g carbs
(3 g fiber), 2.5 g fat

18. Best chocolate milk:
Organic Valley Reduced Fat 2%
Chug this after an intense
workout: Its combo of sugar
and protein helps refuel and
rebuild your muscles.
Per cup: 170 calories, 8 g protein, 24 g carbs, 5 g fat

10. Best tortilla:
La Tortilla Factory Smart &
Delicious EVOO Multi Grain
To warm, microwave for
20 seconds.
Per wrap: 100 calories,
9 g protein, 18 g carbs
(12 g fiber), 3.5 g fat

13. Best pasta: Ronzoni
Healthy Harvest Whole Wheat
Thin Spaghetti
It doesn't taste gritty like
some of its whole grain competitors.
Per 2 oz: 180 calories,
7 g protein, 41 g carbs
(6 g fiber), 2 g fat

16. Best flour: King Arthur
Traditional 100% Whole Wheat
Why not cook with 100% whole
wheat, too?
Per ¼ cup: 110 calories,
4 g protein, 21 g carbs
(4 g fiber), 0.5 g fat

19. Best all-purpose cheese:
Cypress Grove Fresh Chevre
Add it to pasta for dinner, or
combine it with sliced pears
for an afternoon snack.
Per oz: 70 calories, 4 g protein,
0 g carbs, 6 g fat

Dairy and Deli

11. Best pita: Weight
Watchers 100% Whole Wheat
A great vehicle for meats
and greens.
Per pita: 100 calories,
7 g protein, 24 g carbs
(9 g fiber), 1 g fat

14. Best quick-cooking rice:
Uncle Ben's Ready Rice Whole
Grain Brown
Ready in 90 seconds.
Per cup: 240 calories,
5 g protein, 39 g carbs
(2 g fiber), 3 g fat

17. Best milk: Organic Valley
Reduced Fat 2%
A good compromise between
lower-calorie skim and
richer-tasting whole milk.
Per cup: 130 calories, 8 g protein, 12 g carbs, 5 g fat

20. Best sliced cheese:
Sargento Reduced Fat Swiss
Adds flavor to any sandwich.
Per slice: 60 calories, 7 g protein, 1 g carbs, 4 g fat

21. Best shredded cheese:
Kraft Natural 2% Milk
Mozzarella
Top your nachos with a
handful and bake at 400°F
until it's melted.
Per oz: 70 calories, 8 g protein,
1 g carbs, 4 g fat

24. Best cottage cheese:
Friendship 4% California Style
More protein but half the carbs
of the competition.
Per ½ cup: 110 calories,
15 g protein, 3 g carbs, 5 g fat

27. Best plain yogurt:
Stonyfield Farm Oikos Organic
Greek Yogurt (Plain)
Makes a great hot-wing
dipping sauce.
Per container: 90 calories,
15 g protein, 6 g carbs, 0 g fat

30. Best new dairy product:
Siggi's Icelandic Style
Skyr Plain
This is a strained version
of nonfat yogurt, but with
more protein.
Per container: 100 calories,
17 g protein, 6 g carbs, 0 g fat

22. Best snacking cheese:
Laughing Cow
Mini Babybel Original
Two pieces provide a healthy
dose of protein.
Per piece: 70 calories, 5 g pro-
tein, 0 g carbs, 6 g fat

25. Best sour cream:
Breakstone's All Natural
Opt for the full-fat variety. It
has a few more calories, but
offers loads more flavor.
Per 2 Tbsp: 60 calories,
1 g protein, 1 g carbs, 5 g fat

28. Best flavored yogurt:
Stonyfield Farm Oikos Organic
Greek Yogurt with Honey
Honey adds antioxidants.
Per container: 120 calories,
13 g protein, 18 g carbs, 0 g fat

31. Best eggs: Eggland's Best
Each egg contains 100 milligrams of heart-healthy
omega-3 fatty acids.
Per egg: 70 calories, 6 g protein, 4 g fat

23. Best cream cheese:
Philadelphia Whipped
Add a dash of honey to
softened cream cheese for
extra flavor.
Per 2 Tbsp: 60 calories,
1 g protein, 1 g carbs, 6 g fat

26. Best butter:
Organic Valley Sweet Cream
Cultured Unsalted Butter
Don't be afraid of real butter.
Research shows that the fat in
a pat of butter helps you better
absorb vitamins A, E, and K.
Per Tbsp: 100 calories, 11 g fat

29. Best kefir:
Lifeway Lowfat Blueberry
Think of this product as drink-
able yogurt or an extra-thick,
protein-packed smoothie.
Per cup: 174 calories, 14 g protein, 25 g carbs (3 g fiber),
2 g fat

32. Best cold cuts:
Hormel Natural Choice
Pre-Sliced Turkey and Ham
Made without preservatives.
Per 4 slices turkey: 60 calories,
10 g protein, 3 g carbs, 1 g fat

33. Best bacon: Oscar Mayer Center Cut Naturally Smoked
Wrap a slice around a firm, white fish fillet and roast at 400°F for 15 to 20 minutes.
Per 3 slices: 60 calories, 6 g protein, 4 g fat

36. Best salami:
Columbus Salame Company Salame Toscano
Add thin slices to a pizza, along with marinated artichokes (#60).
Per oz: 80 calories, 7 g protein, 1 g carbs, 5 g fat

39. Best turkey entrée: Marie Callender's Honey Roasted Turkey
A hearty meal that'll fill you up without filling you out.
Per serving: 320 calories, 25 g protein, 31 g carbs (8 g fiber), 10 g fat

42. Best single-serving pizza: South Beach Living Deluxe Pizza
Packed with protein and fiber.
Per pizza: 340 calories, 30 g protein, 37 g carbs (10 g fiber), 11 g fat

Frozen Foods

34. Best sausage:
Al Fresco Sundried Tomato & Basil Chicken Sausage
Low in calories.
Per link: 140 calories, 15 g protein, 2 g carbs, 7 g fat

37. Best beef entrée:
Stouffer's Homestyle Classics Beef Pot Roast
This beef actually tastes like real food.
Per 9 oz serving: 240 calories, 16 g protein, 27 g carbs (3 g fiber), 8 g fat

40. Best fish entrée:
SeaPak Sun-Dried Tomato Wild Salmon
Place it on a baking tray, add onions and carrots tossed in olive oil, and bake for 22 minutes at 425°F.
Per meal: 220 calories, 22 g protein, 14 g carbs (1 g fiber), 7 g fat

43. Best family-sized pizza: Kashi Thin Crust Margherita
The thin crust slashes calories, not flavor.
Per ⅓ pizza: 260 calories, 14 g protein, 29 g carbs (4 g fiber), 9 g fat

35. Best hot dog: Applegate Farms Uncured Beef Hot Dogs
These dogs are uncured, and they're all beef, with no chemical preservatives.
Per dog: 80 calories, 5 g protein, 6 g fat

38. Best chicken entrée:
Marie Callender's Grilled Chicken Breast
Plenty of protein; enough fat and calories to satisfy.
Per serving: 450 calories, 33 g protein, 39 g carbs (4 g fiber), 17 g fat

41. Best pasta entrée:
Kashi Pesto Pasta Primavera
Multigrain penne with Parmesan cheese, peas, carrots, and red peppers.
Per meal: 290 calories, 11 g protein, 37 g carbs (7 g fiber), 11 g fat

44. Best burrito:
Amy's Burrito Especial
Top with a generous scoop of guacamole (#106) and chopped fresh cilantro.
Per burrito: 270 calories, 9 g protein, 45 g carbs (4 g fiber), 6 g fat

45. Best breakfast sandwich: Van's Huevos Rancheros Breakfast Panini
This fiber-filled sandwich heats up in under 3 minutes.
Per sandwich: 270 calories, 11 g protein, 33 g carbs (5 g fiber), 11 g fat

48. Best frozen vegetable: Birds Eye Garden Peas
This perennial winner is nutritious, tasty, and easy to add as a side dish to any lunch or dinner.
Per ⅔ cup: 70 calories, 5 g protein, 12 g carbs (4 g fiber)

51. Best frozen treat: Klondike Slim a Bear No Sugar Added Bars
Individual packaging acts as a built-in portion monitor—as long as you eat just one.
Per bar: 170 calories, 4 g protein, 21 g carbs (4 g fiber), 9 g fat

54. Best canned beans: Goya Black Beans
No matter how you serve these beans, doctor them with a pinch of cumin and cayenne pepper, and a squeeze of fresh lime juice.
Per ½ cup: 100 calories, 7 g protein, 18 g carbs (8 g fiber)

Packaged Foods and Snacks

46. Best frozen waffle: Van's Multigrain Waffles
Make a handheld breakfast: Slather a toasted waffle with peanut butter (#107).
Per 2 waffles: 180 calories, 4 g protein, 25 g carbs (3 g fiber), 7 g fat

49. Best frozen fruit: Whole Foods 365 Everyday Value Organic Berry Blend
Health food in a bag.
Per ¾ cup: 70 calories, 1 g protein, 15 g carbs (3 g fiber)

52. Best soup: Lucini Italia Rustic Italian Minestrone Soup
Made with 10 different vegetables.
Per cup: 210 calories, 6 g protein, 28 g carbs (9 g fiber), 9 g fat

55. Best refried beans: Casa Fiesta Spicy Refried Beans
Because a serving has 8 grams of fiber, a side of these beans makes any meal more filling.
Per ½ cup: 130 calories, 8 g protein, 24 g carbs (8 g fiber), 1 g fat

47. Best frozen snack: Cedarlane Garden Vegetable Enchiladas
Low in calories, with a healthy balance of protein, carbs, and fat.
Per enchilada: 140 calories, 9 g protein, 20 g carbs (3 g fiber), 3 g fat

50. Best ice cream: Breyers Natural Vanilla
With only five ingredients, it's as unadulterated as you'll get without churning it yourself.
Per ½ cup: 130 calories, 3 g protein, 14 g carbs, 7 g fat

53. Best chili: Hormel Chili with Beans
Sprinkle on some raw onion and shredded cheese (#21).
Per cup: 260 calories, 16 g protein, 33 g carbs (7 g fiber), 7 g fat

56. Best lentils: Goya Lentils
Simmer lentils with chunks of onion, carrot, and minced garlic. Splash them with red-wine vinegar before serving them with your favorite grilled protein.
Per ¼ cup: 70 calories, 8 g protein, 19 g carbs (9 g fiber), 0 g fat

57. Best canned tomatoes:
Muir Glen Organic Whole
Peeled Tomatoes
They're minimally
processed, which keeps
them tasting fresh.
Per ½ cup: 25 calories,
1 g protein, 5 g carbs (1 g fiber)

60. Best jarred vegetable:
Flora Marinated Artichokes
Brings a briny bite to salads,
sandwiches, and pasta dishes.
Per oz: 25 calories, 0.5 g protein, 2 g carbs (0.5 g fiber),
1.5 g fat

63. Best ready-to-eat tuna:
Ortiz Bonito del Norte in
Olive Oil
Sure, it's more expensive than
the classic canned kind.
But it tastes so good you can
skip the mayo.
Per ¼ cup: 160 calories,
14 g protein, 11 g fat

66. Best potato chip:
Popchips All Natural Barbecue
Not fried or baked! Fewer
calories than most other chips.
Per oz: 120 calories,
1 g protein, 20 g carbs
(1 g fiber), 4 g fat

58. Best salad topping:
Melissa's Fire Roasted
Sweet Red Bell Peppers
These can transform a plain
salad into the highlight of
your meal.
Per oz: 10 calories, 1 g carbs

61. Best pickle: Vlasic
Stackers Kosher Dill
With just 5 calories in an
ounce, pickles make a great
crunchy, tangy, light snack.
Per oz: 5 calories, 1 g carbs

**64. Best ready-to-eat
salmon:** Bumble Bee
Premium Wild Pink Salmon
A top source of heart-healthy
omega-3 fat.
Per 2 oz: 60 calories,
14 g protein

67. Best tortilla chip:
FoodShouldTasteGood
Sweet Potato Tortilla Chips
Salty and sweet.
Per oz: 140 calories,
2 g protein, 18 g carbs
(3 g fiber), 6 g fat

59. Best sandwich topping:
Cento Red & Yellow Roasted
Peppers
This versatile vegetable
works well as a topping on any
salad, sandwich, or pizza.
Per oz: 5 calories, 1 g carbs

62. Best canned fruit:
Del Monte 100% Juice
Tropical Fruit Salad
Canned fruit should be
packed in juice, not syrup.
Per ½ cup: 60 calories,
16 g carbs (1 g fiber)

65. Best pretzel:
Utz Select Honey Wheat
Braided Twists
Pair these with hummus
(#112).
Per 7 sticks: 110 calories,
3 g protein, 23 g carbs
(1 g fiber), 1.5 g fat

68. Best cracker:
Doctor Kracker Klassic
3 Seed Flatbreads
Just 8 grams of digestible
carbs per flatbread.
Per flatbread: 100 calories,
5 g protein, 11 g carbs
(3 g fiber), 4 g fat

THE 125 BEST FOODS FOR MEN

69. Best popcorn: Orville
Redenbacher's Light Butter
A satisfying popcorn crunch
with just the right amount
of flavor.
Per cup: 15 calories, 3 g carbs,
0.5 g fat

72. Best almonds:
Blue Diamond Roasted Salted
A great salty taste without the
sodium overload (just 85 milligrams per serving).
Per 28 nuts: 170 calories,
6 g protein, 5 g carbs (3 g fiber),
16 g fat

75. Best dried fruit:
Mariani Premium Mixed Fruit
Limit yourself to one
handful per snack.
Per ¼ cup: 110 calories,
1 g protein, 25 g carbs
(4 g fiber)

78. Best chocolate bar:
Chocolove Strong Dark
Chocolate 70% Cocoa
Enjoy all the health benefits
of dark chocolate, but without
the bitter taste.
Per ⅓ bar: 160 calories,
3 g protein, 15 g carbs
(4 g fiber), 12 g fat

70. Best beef jerky:
Jack Link's Premium Cuts
Original Beef Jerky
A take-anywhere snack that's
almost pure protein.
Per oz: 80 calories, 15 g pro-
tein, 3 g carbs, 1 g fat

73. Best flavored nuts:
Emerald Cocoa Roast
Almonds, Dark Chocolate
This snack tastes like candy,
but it has almost no sugar.
Per ¼ cup: 150 calories,
6 g protein, 6 g carbs
(3 g fiber), 13 g fat

76. Best trail mix: Sahale
Snacks Soledad Almonds
The mix also includes apples,
flaxseeds, dates, and red-
pepper flakes.
Per ¼ cup: 130 calories,
4 g protein, 10 g carbs
(3 g fiber), 9 g fat

79. Best cookie:
Newman-O's Mint Creme
Filled Chocolate Cookies
Eat in moderation.
(We have to say it!)
Per 2 cookies: 130 calories,
2 g protein, 20 g carbs
(1 g fiber), 4.5 g fat

Drinks

71. Best mixed nuts:
Planters Mixed Nuts, Unsalted
Enjoy the health benefits
of peanuts, cashews, almonds,
brazil nuts, hazelnuts,
and pecans.
Per 30 nuts: 170 calories,
6 g protein, 6 g carbs (2 g fiber),
15 g fat

74. Best nut alternative:
Hapi Hot Wasabi Peas
They have an addictive kick.
Per oz: 130 calories, 4 g pro-
tein, 18 g carbs (1 g fiber),
4 g fat

77. Best snack bar:
Larabar Pecan Pie
The only ingredients in this
delicious snack bar are dates,
pecans, and almonds.
Per bar: 200 calories, 3 g protein, 22 g carbs (4 g fiber),
14 g fat

80. Best flavored water:
Hint Mango Grapefruit
This refreshing beverage
contains no calories, sugar, or
artificial sweeteners.
0 calories

81. Best sports drink:
Gatorade Tiger Focus
Cold Fusion
A great fuel for long
endurance runs.
Per 8 fl oz: 25 calories,
7 g carbs, 0 g fat

84. Best vegetable juice:
R.W. Knudsen Very Veggie
Low Sodium
Six ounces is equivalent to
one serving of vegetables.
Per 8 fl oz: 50 calories, 2 g protein, 11 g carbs (2 g fiber)

87. Best decaf bag tea:
Stash Peppermint
Peppermint tea is packed with
disease-fighting antioxidants,
and may help calm an upset
stomach.
0 calories

90. Best hot chocolate:
Bellagio Sipping Chocolate
It's made with 100% cocoa
powder, so a cup delivers
2 grams of fiber.
Per oz: 110 calories, 2 g protein, 23 g carbs (2 g fiber),
1 g fat

82. Best orange juice:
Tropicana Pure Premium
No Pulp
OJ is nutritious, but don't
overdo it: It packs as much
sugar as empty-calorie soda.
Per 8 fl oz: 110 calories,
2 g protein, 26 g carbs

85. Best bottled tea: Honest
Tea Organic Honey Green Tea
This one has the highest
antioxidant content of any
tea we checked out. Plus, it's
not overloaded with sugar.
Per 8 fl oz: 35 calories,
9 g carbs

88. Best coffee:
Illy Espresso Coffee
Medium Grind
As deep and rich as store-
bought coffee gets.
0 calories

91. Best beer:
Guinness Draught
You really can't find a more
robustly flavored beer for
126 calories.
Per bottle: 126 calories,
1 g protein, 10 g carbs, 0 g fat

83. Best fruit juice:
Lakewood Organic
Pure Cranberry
It's loaded with antioxidants
and antibacterial properties.
Per 8 fl oz: 70 calories, 1 g protein, 18 g carbs (1 g fiber)

86. Best caffeinated bag tea:
Mighty Leaf Organic Earl Grey
A healthy drink by any
standard.
0 calories

89. Best canned coffee:
Starbucks Doubleshot Light
A quick pick-me-up that's
low in sugar.
Per 6½ fl oz: 70 calories,
3 g protein, 6 g carbs, 4 g fat

92. Best light beer:
Amstel Light
Smooth, but not watery.
Per 12 fl oz: 95 calories

THE 125 BEST FOODS FOR MEN

93. Best white wine under $20: St.-Urbans-Hof Riesling Mosel-Saar-Ruwer, Germany, 2007 $15
With great acidity and peach/citrus flavors, this versatile white goes with just about any meal.
Per 4 fl oz: about 95 calories

94. Best red wine under $20: Salentein Malbec Reserve, Argentina, 2006 $20
This succulent South American red pairs well with a nice slab of red meat.
Per 4 fl oz: about 97 calories

95. Best wine for a special occasion: Argyle Brut, Oregon, 2005 $30
A great-tasting sparkling wine that's also relatively inexpensive.
Per 4 fl oz: about 90 calories

Condiments

96. Best mustard: Inglehoffer Original Stone Ground Mustard
Spice up tuna salad with a 2-to-1 ratio of mayo to mustard.
Per tsp: 10 calories, 1 g carbs (1 g fiber)

97. Best ketchup: Heinz Organic
Perfectly balanced. And researchers found that organic ketchup has close to double the lycopene of regular ketchups.
Per Tbsp: 20 calories, 5 g carbs

98. Best mayonnaise: Kraft with Olive Oil Reduced Fat
Made with heart-healthy olive oil.
Per Tbsp: 45 calories, 2 g carbs, 4 g fat

99. Best BBQ sauce: Dinosaur Bar-B-Que Roasted Garlic Honey BBQ Sauce
Tangy and sweet, but not overloaded with sugar.
Per 2 Tbsp: 27 calories, 6 g carbs

100. Best steak sauce: Peter Luger Steak House Old Fashioned Sauce
This famed Brooklyn restaurant's special blend is still our favorite.
Per Tbsp: 30 calories, 7 g carbs

101. Best marinade: Drew's All-Natural Rosemary Balsamic 10 Minute Marinade
A versatile marinade that can also double as a salad dressing.
Per Tbsp: 80 calories, 1 g carbs, 9 g fat

102. Best pasta sauce: Muir Glen Organic Tomato Basil
This hearty sauce has a minimum of sugar.
Per ½ cup: 60 calories, 2 g protein, 12 g carbs (2 g fiber), 1 g fat

103. Best Alfredo sauce: Classico Roasted Red Pepper Alfredo
Most other Alfredo sauces are laden with nearly twice the calories. This is the only one worth eating.
Per ¼ cup: 60 calories, 1 g protein, 3 g carbs, 5 g fat

104. Best salsa: Desert Pepper Roasted Tomato Chipotle Corn
Add black beans (#54) for extra flavor.
Per 2 Tbsp: 10 calories, 2 g carbs

105. Best hot sauce:
Tuong Ot Sriracha
Mix four parts yogurt (#27) with one part of Sriracha and a handful of chopped scallions for a spicy-cool sauce to drizzle over grilled lamb or chicken.
Per tsp: 5 calories, 1 g carbs

108. Best jelly/fruit spread:
Sarabeth's Mixed Berry
The only item to receive a perfect score from our tasters.
Per Tbsp: 40 calories, 9 g carbs (1 g fiber)

111. Best dip: Guiltless
Gourmet Mild Black Bean Dip
Great with chips, burritos, or vegetables.
Per 2 Tbsp: 40 calories, 2 g protein, 7 g carbs (2 g fiber)

114. Best vinaigrette:
Annie's Naturals Shiitake & Sesame Vinaigrette
No added sugars.
Per 2 Tbsp: 130 calories, 1 g carbs, 14 g fat

106. Best premade guacamole: Wholly Guacamole
It's made with real avocados, unlike many competitors.
Per 2 oz: 50 calories, 1 g protein, 2 g carbs (2 g fiber), 4 g fat

109. Best all-purpose condiment: Flora Sundried Tomato Spread
Fold this sauce into pasta, or use it as a sandwich spread.
Per 2 Tbsp: 150 calories, 7 g protein, 1 g carbs, 13 g fat

112. Best hummus: Sabra
Roasted Red Pepper Hummus
Ultrasmooth texture, not chalky.
Per 2 Tbsp: 70 calories, 1 g protein, 3 g carbs, 6 g fat

115. Best everyday cooking oil: Newman's Own Organic Extra Virgin Olive Oil
A nicely balanced oil that's perfect for cooking or making homemade vinaigrettes.
Per Tbsp: 130 calories, 14 g fat

107. Best peanut butter:
Peanut Butter & Co. Crunch Time
This natural spread has just two ingredients: peanuts and salt.
Per 2 Tbsp: 190 calories, 8 g protein, 6 g carbs (2 g fiber), 16 g fat

110. Best sandwich spread:
Flora Italian Foods Pesto Genovese
This garlicky spread elevates any chicken sandwich.
Per 2 Tbsp: 140 calories, 2 g protein, 2 g carbs, 13 g fat

113. Best creamy salad dressing: Drew's All Natural Smoked Tomato
Creamy dressings are usually caloric disasters. But not this one, which provides calories similar to even light dressings.
Per Tbsp: 50 calories, 2 g carbs, 5 g fat

116. Best high-end cooking oil:
Olio Santo California Extra Virgin Olive Oil
The peppery start and mellow finish make it ideal for drizzling on grilled fish or thick slices of tomato and fresh mozzarella.
Per Tbsp: 120 calories, 14 g fat

THE 125 BEST FOODS FOR MEN

117. Best vinegar:
Colavita Aged Balsamic Vinegar Sweet Vinegar of Modena
For a vinaigrette base, mix three parts olive oil with one part vinegar.
Per Tbsp: 5 calories, 3 g carbs

120. Best cooking salt:
Diamond Crystal Kosher Salt
Trade in your shaker of iodized salt for this kosher brand. The larger crystals give you more control over your seasoning.
0 calories

123. Best chocolate sauce:
Hershey's Syrup
It has less sugar and sodium (15 milligrams) than Nestle's.
Per 2 Tbsp: 100 calories, 1 g protein, 24 g carbs (1 g fiber)

118. Best cooking broth:
Swanson Certified Organic Free Range Chicken Broth
Best chicken flavor of all the broths we tasted.
Per cup: 15 calories

121. Best flavor enhancer:
Roland Chipotle Peppers
Puree the whole can, and then add a spoonful to marinades, barbecue sauces, and even mayo.
Per 2 Tbsp: 30 calories, 1 g protein, 5 g carbs, 1 g fat

124. Best syrup: Madhava Agave Nectar, Raw, Organic
A tasty alternative to maple syrup or honey. It works as a sweetener for your tea (#86) or a topping for your pancakes.
Per Tbsp: 60 calories, 16 g carbs

119. Best secret spice:
Star Anise
This spice can be crushed and added to French toast or pancake batter, or used whole to flavor rice, soups, or marinades for meat and vegetables.
0 calories

122. Best soy sauce:
Kikkoman Less Sodium
Combine it with brown sugar, chopped scallions, minced ginger, and minced garlic for a good all-purpose marinade.
Per Tbsp: 10 calories

125. Best protein powder:
Nitrean Vanilla
This whey-casein blend mixes well in a shaker cup.
Per 30 g scoop: 110 calories, 24 g protein, 2 g carbs, 1 g fat

Five MIA Nutrients

Are you getting enough? These nutrients could help you lose weight, build muscle, and beat heart disease.

Five years after telling a bunch of angry apes to keep their filthy paws off him, Charlton Heston starred in *Soylent Green.* In the film, a megacorporation solves a starving world's need for nutritious food by turning the dead into dinner. This is complete science fiction, of course: Most of us are so short on key nutrients we couldn't possibly be someone's square meal.

In fact, studies show that 77 percent of men don't take in enough magnesium, that many of us are deficient in vitamin D, and that the vitamin B_{12} in our diets may be undermined by a common heartburn medication. And we haven't even mentioned our problems with potassium and iodine.

It's time to play catch-up. Follow our advice, and a cannibal will never call you junk food.

VITAMIN D

This vitamin's biggest claim to fame is its role in strengthening your skeleton. But vitamin D isn't a one-trick nutrient: A study in *Circulation* found that people deficient in D were up to 80 percent more likely to suffer a heart attack or stroke. The reason? Vitamin D may reduce inflammation in your arteries.

The shortfall: Vitamin D is created in your body when the sun's ultraviolet B rays penetrate your skin. Problem is, the vitamin D you stockpile during sunnier months is often depleted by winter, especially if you live in the northern half of the United States, where UVB rays are less intense from November through February. Case in point: When Boston University

Cashews
These nuts have 74 milligrams of magnesium per ounce.

researchers measured the vitamin D status of young adults at the end of winter, 36 percent of them were found to be deficient.

Hit the mark: First, ask your doctor to test your blood levels of 25-hydroxyvitamin D.

"You need to be above 30 nanograms per milliliter," says Michael Holick, M.D., Ph.D., a professor of medicine at Boston University. Come up short? Take 1,400 IU of vitamin D daily from a supplement and a multivitamin. That's about seven times the recommended daily intake for men, but it takes that much to boost blood levels of D, says Dr. Holick.

MAGNESIUM

This lightweight mineral is a tireless multitasker: It's involved in more than 300 bodily processes. Plus, a study in the *Journal of the American College of Nutrition* found that low levels of magnesium may increase your blood levels of C-reactive protein, which is a key marker of heart disease.

The shortfall: Nutrition surveys reveal that men consume only about 80 percent of the recommended 400 milligrams of magnesium a day.

"We're just barely getting by," says Dana King, M.D., a professor of family medicine at the Medical University of South Carolina. "Without enough magnesium, every cell in your body has to struggle to generate energy."

Hit the mark: Fortify your diet with more magnesium-rich foods, such as halibut and navy beans. Then hit the supplement aisle: Few men can reach 400 milligrams through diet alone, so Dr. King recommends ingesting some insurance in the form of a 250-milligram supplement. One caveat: Scrutinize the ingredients list. You want a product that uses magnesium citrate, the form best absorbed by your body.

Without potassium, your heart couldn't beat, your muscles wouldn't contract, and your brain couldn't comprehend this sentence.

VITAMIN B$_{12}$

Consider B$_{12}$ the guardian of your gray matter: In a British study, older people with the lowest levels of B$_{12}$ lost brain volume at a faster rate over a span of 5 years than those with the highest levels.

The shortfall: Even though most men do consume the daily quota of 2.4 micrograms, the stats don't tell the whole story.

"We're seeing an increase in B$_{12}$ deficiencies due to interactions with medications," says Katherine Tucker, Ph.D., director of a USDA program at Tufts University. The culprits: acid-blocking drugs, such as Prilosec, and the diabetes medication metformin.

Hit the mark: You'll find B$_{12}$ in lamb and salmon, but the most accessible source may be fortified cereals. That's because the B$_{12}$ in meat is bound to proteins, and your stomach must produce acid to release and absorb it.

Eat a bowl of 100 percent B$_{12}$-boosted cereal and milk every morning and you'll be covered, even if you take the occasional acid-blocking med. However, if you pop Prilosec on a regular basis or are on metformin, talk to your doctor about tracking your B$_{12}$ levels and possibly taking an additional supplement.

POTASSIUM

Without this essential mineral, your heart couldn't beat, your muscles wouldn't contract, and your brain couldn't comprehend this sentence. Why? Potassium helps your cells use glucose for energy.

The shortfall: Despite potassium's can't-live-without-it importance, nutrition surveys indicate that young men consume just 60 percent to 70 percent of the recommended 4,700 milligrams a day. To make matters worse, most guys load up on sodium: High sodium can boost blood pressure, while normal potassium levels work to lower it, says Lydia A. L. Bazzano, M.D., Ph.D., an assistant professor of epidemiology at Tulane University.

Hit the mark: Half an avocado contains nearly 500 milligrams of potassium, while one banana boasts roughly 400 milligrams. Not a fan of either fruit? Pick up some potatoes. A single large spud is packed with 1,600 milligrams.

IODINE

Your thyroid gland requires iodine to produce the hormones T3 and T4, both of which help control how efficiently you burn calories. That means insufficient iodine might cause you to gain weight and feel fatigued.

The shortfall: Because iodized salt is an important source of the element, you might assume you're swimming in the stuff. But when University of Texas at Arlington researchers tested 88 samples of table salt, they found that half contained less than the FDA-recommended amount of iodine. And you're not making up the difference with all the salt hiding in processed foods because U.S. manufacturers aren't required to use iodized salt. The result is that we've been sliding toward iodine deficiency since the 1970s.

Hit the mark: Sprinkling more salt on top of an already sodium-packed diet isn't a great idea, but iodine can also be found in a nearly sodium-free source: milk. Animal feed is fortified with the element, meaning it travels from cows to your cereal bowl. Not a milk man? Eat at least one serving of eggs or yogurt a day; both are good sources of iodine. ∎

These foods fight heart disease and belly fat. (Really.)

Six Stealth Health Foods

Power up your diet by expanding your menu.

Some foods just aren't taken seriously.

Consider celery, for example—forever the garnish, never the main meal. You might even downgrade it to bar fare, because the only stalks most guys eat are served alongside hot wings or immersed in Bloody Marys.

All of which is a shame, really. Besides being a perfect vehicle for peanut butter, this vegetable contains bone-beneficial silicon and cancer-fighting phenolic acids. And those aren't even what makes celery so good for you.

You see, celery is just one of six underappreciated and undereaten foods that can instantly improve your diet. Make a place for them on your plate, and you'll gain a new respect for the health benefits they bestow—from lowering blood pressure to fighting belly fat. And the best part? You'll discover just how delicious health food can be.

CELERY

This water-loaded vegetable has a rep for being all crunch and no nutrition. But ditch that mind-set: Celery contains stealth nutrients that heal.

Why it's healthy: "My patients who eat four sticks of celery a day have seen modest reductions in their blood pressure—about 6 points systolic and 3 points diastolic," says Mark Houston, M.D., director of the Hypertension Institute at St. Thomas Hospital in Nashville.

It's possible that phytochemicals in celery, called phthalides, are responsible for this health boon. These compounds relax muscle tissue in artery walls and increase bloodflow, according to nutritionist Jonny Bowden, Ph.D., author of *The 150 Healthiest Foods on Earth*. And beyond the benefits to your BP, celery also fills you up—with hardly any calories.

How to eat it: Try this low-carbohydrate, protein-packed recipe for a perfect snack any time of day.

In a bowl, mix a 4.5-ounce can of low-sodium tuna (rinsed and drained), 1 tablespoon of balsamic vinegar, ¼ cup of finely chopped onion, ¼ cup of finely chopped apple, 2 tablespoons of fat-free mayonnaise, and some fresh ground pepper. Then spoon the mixture into celery stalks. (Think tuna salad on a log.)

Makes 2 servings
Per serving: 114 calories, 15 g protein, 12 g carbohydrates (3 g fiber), 1 g fat

SEAWEED

While this algae is a popular health food in Japan, it rarely makes it into U.S. homes.

Why it's healthy: There are four classes of seaweeds—green, brown, red, and blue-green—and they're all packed with healthful nutrients.

"Seaweeds are a great plant source of calcium," says nutritionist Alan Aragon, M.S. They're also loaded with potassium, which is essential for maintaining healthy blood-pressure levels.

"Low potassium and high sodium intake can cause high blood pressure," Bowden says. "Most people know to limit sodium, but another way to combat the problem is to take in more potassium."

How to eat it: In sushi, of course. You can also buy sheets of dried seaweed at Asian groceries, specialty health stores, or online at edenfoods.com. Use a coffee grinder to grind the sheets into a powder. Then use the powder as a healthy salt substitute that's great for seasoning salads and soups.

HEMP SEEDS

Despite the *Cannabis* classification, these seeds aren't for smoking. But they may provide medicinal benefits.

Why they're healthy: "Hemp seeds are rich in omega-3 fatty acids, which reduce your risk of heart disease and stroke," says Cassandra Forsythe, Ph.D., a nutrition researcher at the University of Connecticut. What's more, a 1-ounce serving of the seeds provides 11 grams of protein—but not the kind of incomplete protein found in most plant sources. Hemp seeds provide all the essential amino acids, meaning the protein they contain is comparable to that found in meat, eggs, and dairy.

How to eat them: Toss 2 tablespoons of the seeds into your oatmeal or stir-fry. Or add them to your postworkout shake for an extra dose of muscle-building protein.

SCALLOPS

Perhaps these mollusks are considered guilty by association, because they often appear in decadent restaurant meals that are overloaded with calories. (But then again, so does asparagus.)

Why they're healthy: Scallops are more than 80 percent protein. "One 3-ounce serving provides 20 grams of protein and just 95 calories," says Bowden. They're also a good source of both magnesium and potassium. (Clams and oysters provide similar benefits.)

How to eat them: Sear the scallops: It's a fast and easy way to prepare this seafood.

Purchase fresh, dry-packed scallops (not the "wet-packed" kind) and place them on a large plate or cookie sheet. While you preheat a skillet on medium high, pat the scallops dry with a paper towel and season the exposed sides with sea salt and fresh cracked pepper. When the skillet is hot, add a tablespoon of olive oil to it. Being careful not to overcrowd, lay the scallops in the skillet, seasoned-side down, and then season the top sides.

Sear the scallops until the bottoms are caramelized (about 2 minutes), and then flip them to sear for another 1 to 2 minutes, depending on size and thickness. Now they're ready to eat. Pair the scallops with sautéed vegetables, or place them on a bed of brown rice.

DARK MEAT

Sure, dark meat has more fat than white meat does, but have you ever considered what the actual difference is? Once you do, Thanksgiving won't be the only time you "call the drumstick."

Why it's healthy: "The extra fat in dark turkey or chicken meat raises your levels of cholecystokinin (CCK), a hormone that makes you feel fuller longer," says Aragon.

What about your cholesterol? Only a third of the fat in a turkey drumstick is the saturated kind, according to the USDA food database. (The other two-thirds are heart-healthy unsaturated fats.) What's more, 86 percent of that saturated fat either has no impact on cholesterol or raises HDL (good) cholesterol more than LDL (bad) cholesterol—a result that actually lowers your heart-disease risk.

An ounce of dark turkey meat contains just 8 more calories than an ounce of white meat.

How to eat it: Just enjoy, but be conscious of your total portion sizes. A good rule of thumb: Limit yourself to 8 ounces or less at any one sitting, which provides up to 423 calories. Eat that with a big serving of vegetables, and you'll have a flavorful fat-loss meal.

LENTILS

It's no surprise that these hearty legumes are good for you.

Why they're healthy: Boiled lentils have about 16 grams of belly-filling fiber in every cup. Cooked lentils also contain 27 percent more folate per cup than cooked spinach does. And if you eat colored lentils—black, orange, red—there are compounds in the seed hulls that contain disease-fighting antioxidants, says Raymond Glahn, Ph.D., a research physiologist with Cornell University.

How to eat them: Use lentils as a bed for chicken, fish, or beef. They make a great substitute for rice or pasta.

Pour 4 cups of chicken stock into a large pot. Add 1 cup of red or brown lentils and a half cup each of onion and carrot chunks, along with 3 teaspoons of minced garlic. Bring everything to a boil and then reduce the heat to a simmer. Cook the lentils until they're tender, about 20 minutes. Remove the lentils from the heat, add a splash of red wine vinegar, and serve. ∎

Supermarket Survival Guide

The average grocery megastore is bursting with 45,000 products. Some of these foods will compromise your health and happiness. Others can shrink your belly and extend your life. How can you tell one from the other? This section will help you decide what to choose.

When Roald Dahl wrote *Charlie and the Chocolate Factory* nearly half a century ago, he demonstrated how a crafty food marketer could wow us with treats at the same time he was recklessly compromising our health. And while there isn't anything on supermarket shelves that will turn you into an enormous blueberry à la Violet Beauregarde (at least not yet), there are plenty of foods for sale— plenty—that will blow up your waistline and mess with your internal organs.

Many of these boxed offenders are obvious— you already know that the double-cheese- and-pepperoni calzones are a health hazard—but a lot of the worst products are double agents. They pose as healthy choices, labeled with such comforting words as "fortified," "lite," "all-natural," and even "multigrain." But you'd be surprised to discover how meaningless these words are in reality. Indeed, the language on food packaging can be so deceptive that you often have no way of telling the fakers from the real things. And once those frauds make it

past your lips, you're stuck with the results—for a (shortened) lifetime.

And history isn't on your side, either. Since the days when Fonzie ruled the drive-ins, the average salty-snack portion has increased by 93 calories, and soft-drink portions have increased by 49 calories. This information comes from the Nationwide Food Consumption Survey and the Continuing Survey of Food Intakes by Individuals, which together represent a sample of more than 63,000 people. So if you were to indulge in a bag of chips and a soda once a day, you'd be eating 142 more calories every day than Fonzie did. And that's just in one snack! It takes 3,500 calories to create a pound of fat on your body. By eating the same snack every day that Grandpa did, you could take in enough calories to add a pound of flab to your frame every 25 days— or almost 15 pounds of fat a year!

Who Blew Up the Food?

The food industry spends billions of dollars a year on advertising—much of it pitching convenience foods, candy, soda, and desserts. And all the dancing leprechauns and talking teddy bears are obscuring the real story: The food we consume today is simply different from the food that Americans ate 20 or 30 years ago. Here's how.

We've sabotaged our food with time bombs.

A generation ago, it was hard for food manufacturers to create baked goods that would last on store shelves. Most baked goods require oils, and oil leaks at room temperature. But since World War II,

manufacturers have been baking with—and restaurateurs have been frying with—trans fat. Trans fat is cheap and effective: It makes potato chips crispier, cookies tastier, and biscuits flakier. And it lets fry cooks make pound after pound of fries without smoking up their kitchens. The downside: Trans fat increases your bad cholesterol, lowers your good choles-terol, and greatly increases your risk of heart disease.

Our fruits and vegetables aren't as healthy as they once were.

Researchers in a study in the *Journal of the American College of Nutrition* tested 43 different garden crops for nutritional

The average piece of chicken has 165 percent more fat than it did in 1970.

content and discovered that 6 out of 13 nutrients showed major declines between 1950 and 1999: protein, calcium, phosphorus, iron, riboflavin, and ascorbic acid (vitamin C). Researchers say the declines are probably due in part to newer crop varieties that grow faster and can be picked earlier. As a result, the plants aren't able to take in or make nutrients at the same rate.

Even the animals we eat are different today.

The average piece of chicken has 165 percent more fat than it did in 1970, while its protein content has dropped by a third, according to researchers at London Metropolitan University. Because we no longer eat chickens that roam the farm eating bugs and grasses—today they're kept in cages and fed antibiotic-laced soy and corn and other unnatural foods—today's chicken has more fat calories than protein calories. (Even with this food mismanagement, lean chicken—the boneless, skinless chicken breast—is still a good choice for dinner.)

We're drinking more calories than ever.

The University of North Carolina at Chapel Hill found that we consume 450 calories a day from beverages alone, nearly twice as many as 40 years ago. This increase amounts to an extra 29 pounds a year that we're forced to work off—or carry around with us. Many of the calories come

from high fructose corn syrup (HFCS) in our drinks—especially in kids' drinks that are hardly more than sweetened water. In fact, anything you have to drink in your fridge right now—unless it's water, milk, 100 percent juice, or diet soda—probably has HFCS in it. Read the label and weep.

We don't even know what's in our food.

More and more, marketers are adding new types of preservatives, fats, sugars, and other food substances to your daily meals. Just looking at the labels on the shelves might give you uncomfortable flashbacks to high school chemistry. There are now more than 3,000 ingredients on the FDA's list of "safe" food additives, and any one of them could end up on your plate. But often, they go unexplained or, in the case of restaurant food, unmentioned. Unless you're eating it right off the tree, it's hard to know what exactly is in that fruity dish.

These disturbing food-supply trends are a lot to chew on—but chew on them we do, often because we feel we have no choice. But there's a better way. By learning to spot perfect produce, pick lean cuts of meat, and discern truly nutritious packaged foods from the health-touting impostors, you can learn how to maximize nutrition with every bite. While you're satisfying your appetite and saving time and cash, you'll be carving away flab and cutting your risk of heart disease, diabetes, stroke, and cancer. And who doesn't want that?

Packaged Pretenders

Food companies are masters of the nutritional head-fake, using misleading claims to trick us into buying dubious products. Learn the lessons from these two case studies.

1 THE UNNATURAL FRUIT: NUTRI-GRAIN STRAWBERRY CEREAL BARS

The claim: "Naturally and artificially flavored"

The truth: While the FDA requires manufacturers to disclose on the box the use of artificial flavoring, the requirements for what is considered "natural" are not strict. Even a trace amount of the essence or extract of fruit counts as natural. So yes, there is fruit in this bar, but it's third on the ingredients list, behind HFCS and corn syrup.

What you really want: An honest snack with nothing to hide. Larabars, one of our favorite snacks in the aisle, are made with nothing more than dried fruit, nuts, and spices.

INGREDIENTS: FILLING (HIGH FRUCTOSE CORN SYRUP, CORN SYRUP, STRAWBERRY PUREE CONCENTRATE, GLYCERIN, SUGAR, WATER, SODIUM ALGINATE, MODIFIED CORN STARCH, CITRIC ACID, NATURAL AND ARTIFICIAL FLAVOR, SODIUM CITRATE, DICALCIUM PHOSPHATE, METHYLCELLULOSE, CARAMEL COLOR, MALIC ACID, RED #40), WHOLE GRAIN ROLLED OATS, ENRICHED FLOUR (WHEAT FLOUR, NIACIN, REDUCED IRON, THIAMIN MONONITRATE [VITAMIN B1], RIBO-FLAVIN [VITAMIN B2], FOLIC ACID), WHOLE WHEAT FLOUR, SUNFLOWER AND/OR SOYBEAN OIL WITH TBHQ FOR FRESHNESS, HIGH FRUCTOSE CORN SYRUP, SUGAR, CONTAINS TWO PERCENT OR LESS OF HONEY, DEXTROSE, CALCIUM CARBONATE, SOLUBLE CORN FIBER, NONFAT DRY MILK, WHEAT BRAN, SALT, CEL-LULOSE, POTASSIUM BICARBONATE (LEAVENING), NATURAL AND ARTIFICIAL FLAVOR, MONO- AND DIGLYCERIDES, PROPYLENE GLYCOL ESTERS OF FATTY ACIDS, SOY LECITHIN, WHEAT GLUTEN, NIACINAMIDE, SODIUM STEAROYL LACTYLATE, VITAMIN A PALMI-TATE, CARRAGEENAN, ZINC OXIDE, REDUCED IRON, GUAR GUM, PYRIDOXINE HYDROCHLORIDE (VITAMIN

2 THE ABSENT AVOCADO: DEAN'S GUACAMOLE FLAVORED DIP

The claim: "Guacamole"

The truth: This "guacamole" dip is made from less than 2 percent avocado; the rest of the green goo is a cluster of fillers and chemicals, including soybean oil, locust bean gum, and food coloring. Dean's isn't alone in this guacamole caper; most guacs with the word "dip" attached suffer from a lack of avocado. This was brought to light when a California woman filed a lawsuit against Kraft after she noticed that their dip "just didn't taste avocadoey." Similarly, a British judge ruled that Pringles are not technically potato chips because they have only 42 percent potato in them.

What you really want: If you want its heart-healthy fat, you need avocado. Wholly Guacamole makes a great guac, or mash the avocado yourself.

trition cts	Amount/Serving	
ing Size 2 tbsp (30g)	Total Fat 9g	
vings about 11		Saturated Fat 2.5g
ories 90		Trans Fat 0g
Fat Cal 80	Cholesterol less than 5mg	
rcent Daily Values (DV) are ased on a 2,000 calorie diet.	Sodium 170mg	
	Vitamin A 0% • Vitam	

ENTS: SKIM MILK, SOYBEAN OIL, TOMATOES, WATER, COCONUT OIL, CONTAINS LE ... PLUS, SUGAR, NONFAT DRY MILK, WHEY (MILK), LACTIC ACID, SODIUM CASEIN... ...YCERIDES, SPICES, SODIUM BENZOATE AND POTASSIUM SORBATE (TO PRESERVE FRE ...N, LEMON JUICE CONCENTRATE, LOCUST BEAN GUM, DISODIUM PHOSPHATE, GUM ...RRHA, CITRIC ACID, ASCORBIC ACID, BLUE 1, RED 40, YELLOW 5, YELLOW 6. *DEHYDR ...Ventura Foods, LLC, Brea, CA 92821 Dean's® is a registered mark of Dean ...Question or comments, call 1-800-339-1957 Visit our website at www.deansdip.

Food packaging can be **so deceptive that you have no way of telling** the fakers from the real thing.

FOOD ADDITIVE GLOSSARY

One glance at the back of a package, and you'll see that the food industry has kidnapped real ingredients and replaced them with science experiments—and lots of them. Milkshakes with 78 ingredients? Bread with 27? This glossary describes and analyzes the most common food additives in the aisles, from the nutritious (guar gum) to the downright frightening (interesterified fat). Consider it your Ph.D. in food chemistry.

Aspartame

A near-zero-calorie artificial sweetener made by combining two amino acids. Aspartame is 180 times sweeter than sugar.

Found in: More than 6,000 products, including diet sodas, yogurts, and the sugar substitutes NutraSweet and Equal.

What you need to know: Over the past 30 years, the FDA has received thousands of complaints as consumers correlate aspartame consumption with headaches, dizziness, nausea, and mood changes. Human studies have shown aspartame to be completely harmless; a few rodent trials implicate the additive as a carcinogen.

BHA (butylated hydroxyanisole) and BHT (butylated hydroxytoluene)

Antioxidants used to preserve fats and oils.

Found in: Beer, crackers, cereals, butter, and foods with added fats.

What you need to know: Of the two, BHA is considered the more dangerous. Studies have shown it to cause cancer in the forestomachs of rats and hamsters. The Department of Health and Human Services classifies the preservative as "reasonably anticipated to be a human carcinogen."

Blue #1 (brilliant blue) and Blue #2 (indigotine)

These are synthetic dyes that can be used alone or combined with other dyes to make different colors.

Found in: Blue, purple, and green foods, such as beverages, cereals, candy, and icing.

What you need to know: Neither dye has been linked to cancer in humans or animals.

Carrageenan

A thickener, stabilizer, and emulsifier extracted from red seaweed.

Found in: Jellies and jams, ice cream, yogurt, and whipped toppings.

What you need to know: In animal studies, carrageenan has been shown to cause ulcers, colon inflammation, and digestive cancers. While these results are mostly limited to degraded carrageenan—a class that has been treated with heat and acid—a University of Iowa study review concluded that even undegraded carrageenan could become degraded in the human digestive system.

Guar Gum

A thickening, emulsifying, and stabilizing agent made from ground guar seeds.

Found in: Pastry fillings, ice cream, and sauces.

What you need to know: Guar gum is a good source of soluble fiber and might even help decrease blood-glucose levels. One study review found partially hydrolyzed guar gum might be useful in treating irritable bowel syndrome.

High Fructose Corn Syrup (HFCS)

A corn-derived sweetener that makes up more than 40 percent of all caloric sweeteners found in food products. In 2007, Americans consumed 40 pounds of HFCS for each man, woman, and child in the United States. The liquid sweetener is created by breaking down corn-starch with enzymes, and the result is roughly half fructose and half glucose.

Found in: Beverages carry more than half the HFCS consumed in the United States, but it's also an ingredient in ice cream, chips, cookies, cereal, bread, ketchup, jam, canned fruits, yogurt, barbecue sauce, and other products.

What you need to know: Since around 1980, the U.S. obesity rate and HFCS consumption have both risen sharply, and Americans are now consuming an average of 190 calories of the sweetener each day. Some researchers argue that the body metabolizes HFCS differently from table sugar, making it easier to store as fat. However, this theory is not proved.

Interesterified Fats

Semisoft fats that are created by chemically rearranging the structure of natural fats and oils. They're being used more now in response to the public demand for an alternative to trans fat.

Found in: Pastries, pies, margarine, and shortening.

What you need to know: Testing on these fats has not been extensive, but the early evidence doesn't look promising. A study by Malaysian researchers showed a 4-week diet of 22 percent interesterified fats increased the ratio of LDL to HDL cholesterol. Furthermore, this study showed an increase in blood glucose levels and a decrease in insulin response.

Mannitol

A sugar alcohol that's half as sweet as sugar. It provides fewer calories and has a less drastic effect on blood sugar than sugar does.

Found in: Sugar-free candy, reduced-calorie and diet foods, and even in chewing gum.

What you need to know: Because sugar alcohols are not fully digestible in the stomach, they can cause intestinal discomfort: gas, bloating, flatulence, and diarrhea.

Olestra

A synthetic nonfat cooking oil created by Procter & Gamble and sold under the name Olean. It has zero-calorie impact and is not absorbed as it passes through the digestive system.

Found in: Light potato chips and crackers.

What you need to know: Olestra can cause diarrhea and abdominal cramps. Studies show that it impairs the body's ability to absorb fat-soluble vitamins and carotenoids, such as beta-carotene, lycopene, lutein, and zea-xanthin.

Partially Hydrogenated Vegetable Oil

A fat created by adding hydrogen to vegetable fats, an unintended effect of which is the creation of trans fatty acids. Food manufacturers use this fat because of its low cost and long shelf life.

Found in: Margarine, pastries, cakes, cookies, crackers, and non-dairy creamers.

What you need to know: Dozens of studies have linked trans fat to heart disease, which is why Boston and New York, and the state of California, have approved legislation to phase out trans fat in restaurant kitchens. Most health organizations recommend keeping trans fat consumption as low as possible, but a loophole in the FDA's labeling requirements allows processors to add as much as 0.49 gram per serving and still claim zero in their nutrition facts.

Red #3 (erythrosine) and Red #40 (allura red)

Food dyes that are cherry-red and orange-red. Red #40 is the most widely used food dye in the United States.

Found in: Candy, chocolate cake, cereal, beverages, pastries, maraschino cherries, and fruit snacks.

What you need to know: The FDA once considered imposing a ban on the use of Red #3 in food, but thus far has not. However, after the dye was linked to thyroid tumors in rats, the FDA had the liquid form of the dye removed from external-use drugs and cosmetics.

Saccharin

An artificial sweetener that's 300 times sweeter than sugar. Invented in 1879, saccharin is the oldest of the five artificial sweeteners that are used in the United States.

Found in: Diet and reduced-calorie foods, candy, and beverages; chewing gum; toothpaste; and Sweet 'N Low.

What you need to know: Rat studies in the 1970s linked high doses of saccharin with bladder cancer, and the FDA moved to ban it. Congress, however, reacting to public pressure, intervened and mandated that a warning be printed on the label of every product containing saccharin. The warning was removed after 23 years, in the wake of findings that the cancer process saccharin triggers in rats does not apply to humans, and that no human studies found any cancer risk. More recent research found that rats on saccharin-sweetened diets gain more weight than those on sugar-sweetened diets.

Sucralose

A zero-calorie artificial sweetener made by joining chlorine particles and sugar molecules. It's 600 times sweeter than sugar, and its safety has been highly touted.

Found in: Sugar-free foods, beverages, and Splenda.

What you need to know: Before approving sucralose, the FDA reviewed more than 110 human and animal studies for evidence that it might cause cancer, nerve damage, or fertility problems; the agency found no toxic effects.

Yellow #5 (tartrazine) and Yellow #6 (sunset yellow)

The second and third most common food colorings, respectively.

Found in: Cereal, pudding, bread mix, beverages, chips, cookies, and condiments.

What you need to know: Researchers in the United Kingdom found that 3-year-olds given a drink containing both dyes (and other additives) showed more symptoms of hyperactivity than those who didn't ingest the chemicals. One study found that mice fed high doses of sunset yellow had trouble swimming straight and righting themselves in water.

What the Food Industry Doesn't Want You to Know

We found 13 secrets, hidden in plain sight, on the shelves of your local supermarket. Before you fill your cart, make sure you read this.

If you want some insight into the food industry, take a stroll down your supermarket's candy aisle. There, on the labels of such products as Swedish Fish, Mike and Ike, and Good & Plenty, you'll see what is perhaps a surprising claim: "Fat-Free." It's completely true, however. These empty-calorie junk foods are made almost entirely of sugar and processed carbs.

Our point is that food manufacturers think you're stupid. And their marketing strategies rely on it. For instance, the makers of the aforementioned candies may be hoping you'll equate "fat-free" with "healthy" or "nonfattening," so you'll forget about all the sugar their products contain. It's a distraction device: Food companies advertise what they want you to notice, and the candy aisle is just the start.

We scoured grocery-store shelves to expose the secrets that food-industry insiders don't want you to know. The ones they use to prey on your expectations, your wallet, and, most important, your well-being. Use our crib sheet, though, and you can beat Big Food at its own game.

We found that Entenmann's Frosted Mini Donuts had 7 percent more calories than the label said they did.

KEEBLER DOESN'T WANT YOU TO KNOW THAT . . .

. . . Numbers can be deceiving. On the front of a box of reduced-fat Club Crackers—in large, yellow letters—you'll find the claim, "33% Less Fat Than Original Club Crackers." The math is accurate: The original product contains 3 grams of fat per serving, while the reduced-fat version has 2 grams. So statistically, it really is a 33 percent difference.

But is it meaningful? And why doesn't Keebler tout that its reduced-fat cracker has 33 percent more carbs than the original? Maybe the company simply doesn't want you to know that when it removes 1 gram of fat, it replaces it with 3 grams of refined flour and sugar—hardly a healthy trade-off.

BEVERAGE MAKERS DON'T WANT YOU TO KNOW THAT . . .

. . . The bottled green tea you're drinking might not be as healthy as you think it is. Last year, we commissioned ChromaDex Laboratories to analyze 14 different bottled green teas for their levels of catechins, which are the healthful antioxidants in tea that are thought to fight disease.

The finding: The scientists discovered that the catechin content varied widely among brands. While Honest Tea Organic Honey Green Tea topped the charts with an impressive 215 milligrams of total catechins, some products hardly even registered on the antioxidant scale. For instance, Republic of Tea Pomegranate Green Tea had just 9 milligrams, and Ito En Tea's Tea Lemongrass Green had just 28 milligrams.

FOOD COMPANIES DON'T WANT YOU TO KNOW THAT . . .

. . . Your food can legally contain maggots. Sure, the FDA limits the amount of these and other appetite killers in your food, but that limit isn't zero. The allowances aren't harmful to your health, but we can't promise that the thought won't make you sick.

KELLOGG'S DOESN'T WANT YOU TO KNOW THAT . . .

. . . Its Corn Flakes aren't as diabetes friendly as the "Diabetes Friendly" logo on the box's side panel suggests. Australian researchers have shown that carb-loaded cornflakes raise blood glucose faster and to a greater extent than straight table sugar does. (High blood glucose is the primary indicator of diabetes.)

Beneath the logo, the cereal maker does provide a link to its Web site where general nutrition recommendations are provided for people with diabetes. But those recommendations are authored by Kellogg's nutritionists—and are simply "based on" the guidelines of the American Dietetic Association and the American Diabetes Association, not endorsed by those organizations.

QUAKER DOESN'T WANT YOU TO KNOW THAT . . .

. . . Some of its "heart healthy" hot cereals have more sugar than a bowl of Froot Loops, as mentioned in the previous chapter. Even so, the company proudly displays the American Heart Association logo on the Quaker Instant Oatmeal Maple & Brown Sugar box. However, the fine print below the logo reads that the product simply meets the AHA's "food criteria for saturated fat and cholesterol." So it could contain a pound of sugar and still qualify.

But guess what? Froot Loops meets the AHA's criteria, too, only no logo is displayed. That's because . . .

FOOD COMPANIES DON'T WANT YOU TO KNOW THAT . . .

. . . **Companies must pay for a product to be an American Heart Association–certified food.** That's why the AHA check mark might appear on one product but not on another, even when both meet the guidelines.

Artificial food colorings and preservatives might be linked to hyperactivity in kids.

SUPERMARKETS DON'T WANT YOU TO KNOW THAT . . .

. . . **Long checkout lines can make you buy more.** If you're stuck in a line, you'll be up to 25 percent more likely to buy the candy and sodas around you, according to research from the University of Arizona. The authors found that the more exposure people have to temptation, the more likely they are to succumb to it.

This might also help explain why supermarkets place common staples such as milk, bread, and eggs at the rear of the store, forcing you to run the gauntlet of culinary temptation.

THE FOOD INDUSTRY DOESN'T WANT YOU TO KNOW THAT . . .

. . . **Food additives may make your kids misbehave.** U.K. researchers found that some artificial food colorings and preservatives are linked to hyperactivity in children. The additives included Yellow #5, Yellow #6, Red #40, and sodium benzoate,

Popcorn can contain up to 20 gnawed grains or 2 rodent hairs per pound.

tablespoon of traditional half-and-half contains 20 calories; the fat-free version has 10. And after all, how much are you really going to consume?

THE MEAT INDUSTRY DOESN'T WANT YOU TO KNOW THAT . . .

. . . The leanest cuts may have the highest sodium levels. The reason: When you remove fat, you lose juiciness. To counteract this dried-out effect, some manufacturers "enhance" poultry, pork, and beef products by pumping them full of a solution that contains water, salt, and other nutrients that help give them flavor. This practice can dramatically boost the meat's sodium level.

For example, a 4-ounce serving of Shady Brook Farms Fresh Boneless Turkey Tenderloin that hasn't been enhanced contains 55 milligrams of sodium. But the same size serving of Jennie-O Turkey Breast Tenderloin Roast Turkey, which is enhanced by up to 30 percent, packs 840 milligrams.

FOOD COMPANIES DON'T WANT YOU TO KNOW WHAT . . .

. . . The phrase "good source" actually means. No doubt you've seen the claim on labels in every section of your supermarket that a product is a "good source" of one or more vitamins or minerals. But here's what you need to know: To be considered a good source of a specific vitamin or mineral, a serving must contain only 10 percent of the recommended daily value for that nutrient. For perspective, take Nabisco Honey Teddy Grahams, which, the label says, are a "Good Source of Calcium." You'd have to eat 10 servings—the entire box and then some—to hit the amount you

all of which are commonly found in packaged foods in the United States. While the researchers don't know whether a combination of the chemicals is to blame or there's a single primary culprit, you can find Red #40, Yellow #5, and Yellow #6 in Skittles, and sodium benzoate in some soft drinks.

LAND O'LAKES DOESN'T WANT YOU TO KNOW THAT . . .

. . . There's no such thing as fat-free half-and-half. That's because, by definition, half-and-half contains between 10.5 percent and 18 percent butterfat. So what exactly is the product that Land O'Lakes calls "Fat Free Half & Half"? Skim milk— to which a thickening agent and an artificial cream flavor have been added. You may be disappointed in the payoff: One

need for the day. Now think about it: Is that really a good source?

CHEX DOESN'T WANT YOU TO KNOW THAT . . .

. . . Its 100-calorie pack might be a rip-off. In a 2007 study, Brown University researchers found that people ate the same amount of cookies and chips regardless of whether they ate from a large, multiserving bag or single-serving packs. The key factor: The actual amount of cookies or chips people kept in their homes.

Sure, self-control is still your responsibility, but here's the bigger secret: Companies often charge you double for snack-size portions. Take Chex Mix Cheddar, for example, which costs 2.13 times more per gram when packaged in 100-calorie packs than when sold in a normal 8.75-ounce bag.

FOOD COMPANIES DON'T WANT YOU TO KNOW THAT . . .

. . . Their calorie counts might be wrong. That's because in order to make sure you're getting at least as much as you pay for, the FDA is more likely to penalize a food manufacturer for overstating the net weight of a product than for understating it. As a result, it seems that manufacturers often either "generously" package more food than the stated net weight or make servings heavier than the stated serving-size weight. That means you may be eating more calories than you think. Case in point: Using an ordinary food scale, we found that based on the actual weight of a serving, Back to Nature classic granola contained 244 calories—64 more calories than the number listed. Yet another reason to eat with caution. ■

The No-Carb Noodle

No kidding: High in fiber and low in everything else, this mystery food deserves a spot on your menu.

Gone for good are the days when spaghetti was considered a guilt-free food. After all, pasta may be low in fat, but here in the 21st century we know it's loaded with the type of fast-digesting carbs that send your blood sugar soaring. And even more important, men tend to eat pasta in mounds, not moderation.

But what if a noodle existed that was not only Atkins-approved but had virtually no calories? Turns out one does, and it's called shirataki. This translucent noodle, which is made from the powdered root of the Asian konjac yam, consists mostly of a no-calorie, highly soluble fiber called glucomannan. And that fiber is why shirataki is more than just a pasta imposter. According to a study review by University of Connecticut researchers, glucomannan helps lower bad LDL cholesterol, triglycerides, fasting blood sugar, and even body weight. What's more, scientists in Thailand found that just

Almost ready to eat!
Simply rinse the noodles for
2 minutes before preparing.

The User's Guide to Shirataki

After rinsing these noodles with water, you could eat them right out of the bag. And at less than a dollar a serving, shirataki noodles are as cheap as ramen noodles. Find them at miraclenoodle.com, in multiple forms—linguini, orzo, and more.

1 gram has the power to significantly slow the absorption of sugar into your bloodstream after you eat a carb-loaded meal.

So what's the catch? Well, shirataki noodles have almost no flavor, which may explain why you've never seen them on a takeout menu. But the upside is that they soak up the flavors of sauces and spices in any dish—if you know what you're doing. These meals will make you forget all about spaghetti.

SHIRATAKI NOODLE CAKE WITH SHRIMP AND CHORIZO

Try this Spanish-style shirataki dish from Boston chef Ken Oringer, owner of Clio, Uni, Toro, KO Prime, and La Verdad.

1 package (8 oz) shirataki noodles, rinsed and drained
3 eggs
2 cups shredded zucchini
½ cup shredded carrots
½ cup chopped scallions
8 ounces chopped raw shrimp
8 ounces ground chorizo
1 cup flour
Salt
Freshly ground black pepper
1 clove garlic, chopped
1 cup olive oil

1. Chop the noodle strands into thirds. Combine with the other ingredients (except the olive oil) in a mixing bowl.

2. Heat a skillet on medium high and add enough olive oil to coat the bottom of the pan. Scoop one-fourth of the mixture into the pan, cooking until golden brown. Flip and cook again till golden brown.

3. Serve with mayonnaise mixed with minced garlic and lemon juice.

Makes 4 servings (two cakes each)

Per serving: 632 calories, 34 g protein, 30 g carbohydrates, 41 g fat, 5 g fiber

SOY PORK SHIRATAKI STIR-FRY

The shirataki noodles create a high-fiber base in this flavor-packed stir-fry, courtesy of Ming Tsai, chef and owner of Blue Ginger in Wellesley, Massachusetts, and host of American Public Television's *Simply Ming*.

Canola oil
2 tablespoons minced garlic
1 tablespoon minced ginger
Kosher salt
Freshly ground black pepper
¼ cup naturally brewed soy sauce (sub in low-sodium soy, if you prefer)
¼ cup fresh lime juice
¼ cup brown sugar
1 head bok choy, rinsed, spun dry, and cut into pieces
½ bunch scallions, thinly sliced, whites and greens separated
2 red bell peppers, cut into 1-by-1-inch pieces
1 pound ground pork, browned
2 cups fettuccine-type shirataki noodles, packed, rinsed well (three times), and drained

1. Coat the bottom of a saucepan lightly with canola oil and place it on medium heat. Add the garlic and ginger, along with a pinch of salt and pepper. Cook until softened, about 3 minutes.

2. Add the soy sauce, lime juice, and sugar. Bring to a simmer and let the mixture reduce by a third to a syrup consistency, 8 to 10 minutes. To check consistency, pour a line of syrup on a cool dish and hold it vertically. If the line holds with a few drips, it's ready.

3. Use some oil to lightly coat the bottom of a large, hot wok over high heat. (If you don't have a wok, you can use a skillet over high heat.) When the oil is shimmering, add the bok choy, scallion whites, and red bell peppers, and stir-fry until they're slightly softened, about 1 minute. Add the pork, noodles, and garlic-ginger-soy syrup, and stir to coat the noodles with sauce.

4. Check for flavor, and season with salt and pepper if necessary. Serve family-style on a platter, garnished with the scallion greens.

Makes 4 servings

Per serving: 461 calories, 35 g protein, 27 g carbohydrates, 25 g fat, 7 g fiber

**Caprese
Pasta Salad**

Shirataki noodles **soak up the flavor** of fresh herbs.

**Shirataki
Noodle
Cake
with Shrimp
and Chorizo**

CAPRESE PASTA SALAD

Here's a take on an Italian classic from Michael White, the executive chef and a partner at Convivio in New York City.

1   pound asparagus, thinly sliced lengthwise (use a vegetable peeler)
8   ounces shirataki noodles, rinsed and drained
3   large heirloom tomatoes, chopped
½   cup green peas, cooked
1   cup diced fresh mozzarella
¼   cup chopped fresh basil
    Juice of one lemon
⅓   cup extra-virgin olive oil
    Salt
    Freshly ground black pepper

1. Cook the asparagus in boiling salted water for 3 to 5 minutes. Remove the slices with a slotted spoon, drop them into ice water, and then drain them.

2. Place the noodles in the pot of boiling water for 30 seconds to warm them. Then drain the noodles and put them in a large bowl. Add the asparagus and the remaining ingredients—the tomatoes, green peas, mozzarella, basil, lemon juice, oil, and salt and pepper—and toss everything together.

3. Serve with mayonnaise mixed with minced garlic and lemon juice.

Makes 4 servings

Per serving: 386 calories, 15 g protein, 12 g carbohydrates, 31 g fat, 7 g fiber

SHIRATAKI NOODLES AL PESTO

Pesto without pasta? You won't miss it with this shirataki version from Chef White.

2   cups fresh basil leaves
½   cup fresh parsley leaves, packed
¼   cup grated Parmigiano Reggiano cheese
½   cup chilled olive oil
1   clove garlic
¼   cup pine nuts
    Salt
    Freshly ground black pepper
1   cup string beans
1   package (8 ounces) shirataki noodles, rinsed and drained

1. Combine the basil and parsley in a food processor and pulse until a paste begins to form.

2. Add the cheese, oil, garlic, and pine nuts. Pulse again until the mixture is a creamy paste, and then add salt and pepper.

3. Cook the string beans in boiling salted water for 2 to 3 minutes. Spoon them out, drop them briefly into ice water, and drain them. Now drop the noodles into the boiling water for 30 seconds. Drain and transfer them to a bowl, add the pesto and string beans, and toss well. Grate extra cheese on top and serve immediately.

Makes 4 servings

Per serving: 379 calories, 8 g protein, 12 g carbohydrates, 35 g fat, 7 g fiber

The Beauty of the Beast

Writer Matt Goulding shows how a pig from Pennsylvania (plus some really great chefs) can teach you how to savor every last detail of dinner, from tail to snout, from grunt to squeal.

The sound of the blade biting through the neck is almost unbearable—like a band saw hacking through a manhole cover. But after a few thrusts and grunts from the butcher, there's a clean snap, and the hog's head hits the cutting board with a thud.

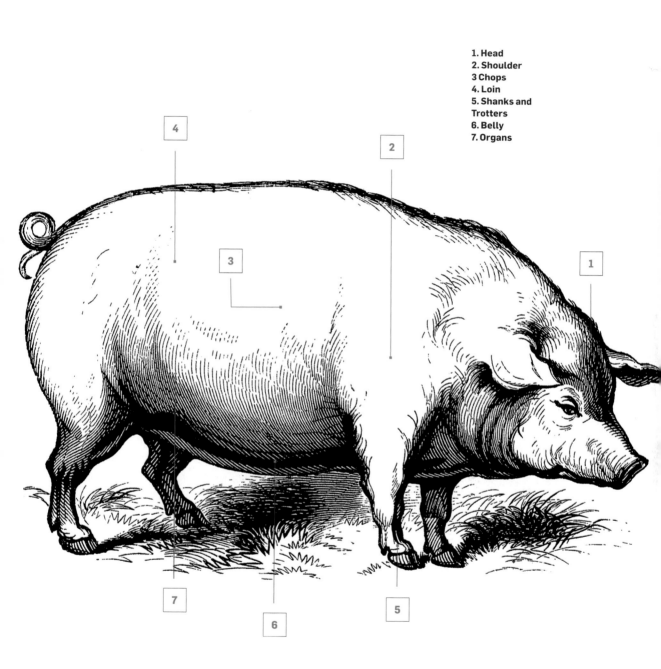

1. Head
2. Shoulder
3 Chops
4. Loin
5. Shanks and
Trotters
6. Belly
7. Organs

The head in question belonged to a 230-pound Berkshire pig that had been delivered that morning from central Pennsylvania. The butcher is Nate Appleman, chef and owner of A16 and SPQR restaurants in San Francisco. As luck would have it, he's in New York City for the week to teach classes on butchering. Appleman looks like he was born to cut meat: short and muscular, shaved head, perma-stubble, thick sleeves of tattoos running up both arms. He goes through about three hogs a week, combined, at his restaurants.

"We waste nothing. Even the skin is stuffed with herbs and bread crumbs and braised."

The pig before us will meet the same fate, and exaltation.

It all started one recent night, when I'd made a wine-lubricated proclamation at dinner: Someday I'd like to eat a whole pig—from snout to curly tail. My companions at the table—men who know pigs—grabbed their phones and began dialing pork farms. Forty-eight hours later, I was with Appleman in the basement of chef Michael Anthony's Gramercy Tavern, severing limbs like some mafioso who needed to scatter evidence.

We'd scatter it, all right. But not to hide anything. My goal was to discover the full potential of the animal, so I sought out a range of chefs with a diverse collection of culinary skills to cook the entire beast, part by delicious part, and along the way we'd taste all the ways the world prepares pig for dinner.

There's a porcine revolution under way across the United States. From specialty pig farmers to menus dedicated entirely to swine dining, the hog has never been so hot in this country. Why pork, you ask? Here's the consensus among the chefs I surveyed: First, few meats are so versatile. Pork holds up to a variety of preparations, from quick grilling to slow braising. You can blast it with bold flavors or accent it with careful, subtle notes. But more than anything else, professional cooks love pork for one simple reason: fat.

Now, you may think of pork as "the other white meat," prized for its decidedly nonpiggy profile. That's how the National Pork Board decided to sell it in 1987, after health-conscious consumers had been

There's a porcine revolution under way across the United States.

turning away from pork and going to poultry in response to a still-unproved link between saturated fat and heart disease. In response, industrial pig operations began breeding the fat out of their hogs. As a result, the average pig has 75 percent less fat today than it did 60 years ago. Which is why the number one complaint you hear about Mom's Wednesday night pork chop is "It's dry. It's bland. It's boring." Applesauce to the rescue.

The truth is, much of the fat those pork producers worked so diligently to eliminate is the heart-healthy monounsaturated variety. Let's take a closer look at the fatty profile of bacon: According to the USDA, 33 percent of bacon fat is saturated. But

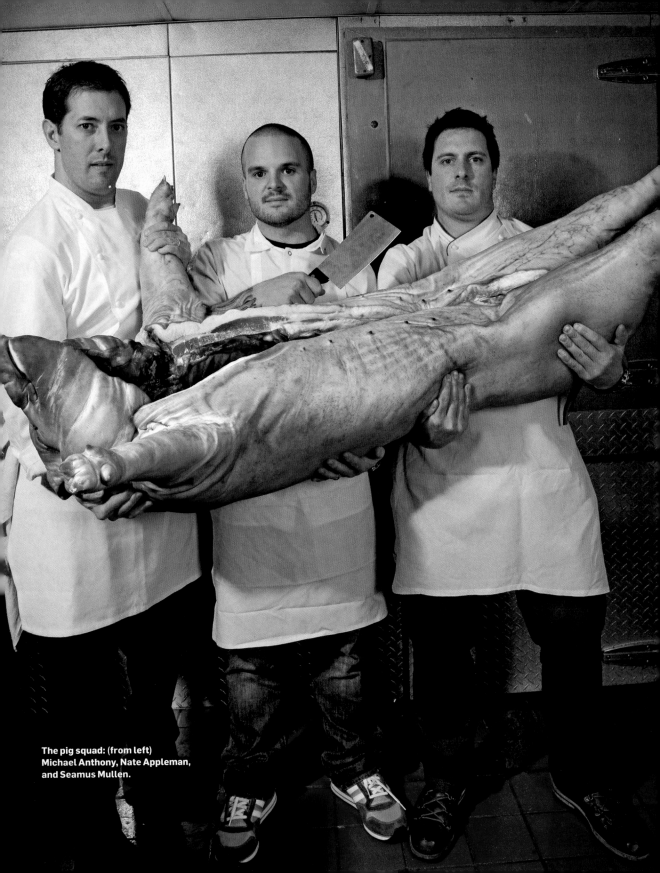

The pig squad: (from left)
Michael Anthony, Nate Appleman,
and Seamus Mullen.

that breaks down like this: 31 percent is stearic acid, and 64 percent is palmitic acid, neither of which has much effect on cholesterol. Plus, 41 percent of the total fat content of bacon is oleic acid, the healthy fat in olive oil.

"When you take a look at the whole picture," says Jeff Volek, Ph.D., R.D., a nutrition researcher at the University of Connecticut, "87 percent of pork fat is predicted to have no effect or a positive effect on cholesterol."

Now they tell me. All the times I turned down bacon over the years! Well, okay, not that many times. But I did feel bad about eating it, occasionally.

To breed out much of this healthy fat, farmers pump their pigs full of antibiotics and other drugs, which stimulate muscle growth and inhibit fat storage, in essence replacing the potbelly with a skinnier, faster-growing frame.

While industrial meat marketers put the nation's hogs on a dubious diet, small farmers have been working hard to introduce (or reintroduce) top-quality heritage hog breeds such as the Ossabaw and the Berkshire. Few are doing it better than Sylvia and Stephen Pryzant, the owners of Four Story Hill Farm in Honesdale, Pennsylvania, where my hog had been roaming freely just 48 hours before its appointment with Mr. Appleman.

But what a life it led. Out in Pennsylvania, things are about as plush as they can be for an animal with a penchant for mud baths. "Fresh air, fresh food, clean surroundings," says Sylvia. "We provide the most comfortable environment possible so that the animal is able to grow stress free."

Your Pig, Roasted to Perfection

Chances are you don't have access to a barbecue pit like the one Pete Daversa uses to slow cook 6,000 pounds of meat every week at New York's *Hill Country*. But you can still cook delicious pork.

"Slow, consistent heat from your oven can produce amazing results," says Daversa. **HERE'S HOW HE DOES IT AT HOME:** Rub a 6- to 12-pound pork shoulder (often sold as Boston butt) generously with kosher salt and fresh cracked pepper (or, alternatively, brine it overnight using the recipe on page 107). Then place it in a roasting oven and cook it at 200°F for 6 to 8 hours, until the meat falls apart with the gentlest pressure from your fingertip. You don't need to watch the pork (or even be awake) while it cooks, but occasional basting with the pan drippings helps. Serve the pulled pork Carolina-style on a warm bun with slaw and spicy vinegar, fold it into warm tortillas with a scoop of guac, or wrap it in lettuce leaves with rice, pickle slices, and chili paste.

Farmers like the Pryzants aspire to do more than simply add more squeal to their stock; they want to reconnect each of us with our food supply. A series of factors—from our industrial food complex to our insistence on convenience cuts of meat—has separated the idea of animals from the meat that comes from them. We think of pork chops and bacon and ignore the wretched creatures

wallowing in their own filth. We focus on the hot dog and bypass the meaty trotters, the hefty shoulders, the marbled jowls. The Pryzants are helping Americans develop pig pride—like the Italians, Spanish, and Mexicans did before them. Pork as pork, not pork as kinda-chicken or beef-lite.

As I watch Appleman cleave pieces from the whole hog, I know that this Berkshire will be like no pork I've eaten before. The chops, for instance, are as thick as a Tokyo phone book, with a rim of creamy white fat.

Wilbur, stand aside. I realize that this, truly, is some pig.

When Appleman's handiwork is complete, I'm left with a head, four shanks, four trotters, two tenderloins, two loins (one on the bone, the other perfectly trimmed with a quarter-inch cap of fat), two huge slabs of belly, two shoulders, two hind legs, kidneys and liver, a rack of baby back ribs, a dozen chops, and a long, squiggly tail.

The smartest guys (plus one woman) I know are going to cook it all, and I'm going to eat it. But here's the best part: The benefits will wind up on your plate. You can do it all yourself, too. What's more, you'll want to.

THE LOIN

FINDING FLAVOR IN THE PRICIEST PIG PART

When I hand over the loin to Wylie Dufresne, he gives me a look.

"It wouldn't be our first choice, but we'll make it work," he says. Make it work? Aren't the loins the most prized parts of any animal? And isn't Dufresne the culinary wizard foodies gasp over? It's like offering Dwight Howard a pass slightly above the rim. It damn well better go through the net.

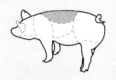

THE LOIN
WYLIE DUFRESNE, WD-50
Cost per pound: $6.47
Best for: Quick cooking, grilling, pan roasting
Recipe relatives: Beef tenderloin, chicken breast

1. Because pork loin is so lean, it dries out easily. Dufresne keeps it moist and flavorful with three steps: (1) Buying loin with a thin cap of fat on top, (2) brining it overnight in 2½ quarts of water mixed with ½ cup salt and ¼ cup sugar, and (3) cooking it to an internal temperature of 150°F.
2. Because loin is "pretty mushy," Dufresne uses a mix of bread crumbs, orange zest, and parsley to add crunch and flavor to the finished dish.
3. Pork and smoke are perfect partners, but most guys don't have smokers. Solution: a few pinches of smoked sea salt to top slices of loin instead.

Dufresne's Manhattan restaurant, wd-50, is a shrine to molecular gastronomy, an avant-garde cooking style that blurs the line between kitchen and laboratory, chef and mad scientist. Over the years, Dufresne has invented noodles made from peanut butter and crafted pepperoni-and-mushroom pizza pebbles. His most infamous creation: cubes of mayonnaise—spiked with stabilizers—breaded and fried to crispy, wobbly perfection. If he can do that to a jar of Hellmann's, he can surely make something of a simple pork loin.

I ask him to create two dishes: one of his patented inventions, and one that you or I could replicate at home—molecular gastronomy for Joe Sixpack.

When I return to the restaurant later that week, I see that Dufresne has been busy. First, he dropped the whole loin in a brine of sugar, salt, and water, and let it rest for 24 hours.

"People love the loin because it's tender, but it doesn't have the flavor you find in the more-used muscles, like the ones around the trotters," says Dufresne. That's where the brine comes into play, imparting both moisture and flavor in a cut that some cooks turn into seasoned rope. After brining, the loin is vacuum packed in a plastic bag and cooked *sous vide*—over a low, carefully controlled heat.

Dufresne calls the rest of the dish "a marriage of pig and barbecue." In Wylie's World of Hypermodern Cooking, that means freezing a homemade barbecue sauce with gelatin; as the sauce defrosts, the solids adhere to the gelatin and you have a clear barbecue broth to stew lentils in. He makes yucca fries by grating the

The author, Matt Goulding, would like to thank his main collaborator on this story and acknowledge its many sacrifices in the line of duty.

should steal immediately. Another chef trick worth trying: basting, which Dufresne does obsessively. Most of the fat stays in the pan, but the pork emerges golden brown and obscenely moist.

Dufresne insists that pork is best cooked medium, with a bit of pink still in the middle. Because loins and chops are already so lean, overcooking them means you'll be left with pig jerky. And given improvements in hog feeding and the handling of pig meat, the trichinosis threat is a thing of the queasy past. As long as the meat hits an internal temperature of 150°F, you're safe. (Trichinosis dies at 137°F.)

With this everyday loin, Dufresne serves sautéed romaine and smoked mashed potatoes. ("A dash of smoked sea salt or liquid smoke will do the trick," he advises.) He adds crunch to the dish with a mix of panko bread crumbs, orange zest, and chopped parsley.

"Dishes need textural contrast, and this simple mix brings it to any food it touches."

The nouveau BBQ recalls all the flavors of my youthful days in North Carolina—smoke, vinegar, salty crunch—and the roast is juicy on the inside, caramelized on the outside, and shot through with a hammy intensity.

His early reservations aside, Dufresne has reinvented the pig loin.

starchy root vegetable and then smoking it for 45 minutes over a mix of alder and cherry wood. At the last second, he deep-fries the yucca into crisp, dice-sized cubes and scatters them next to a mini-tower of pressed and pickled kale—the "collard greens" of our luxe barbecue plate.

For the Sixpack version, he roasts the brined pork in a sauté pan on the stove top and then finishes it off in a 400°F oven for 10 minutes. It is perhaps the most popular way of cooking meat and fish in restaurants, and a technique all home cooks

THE TROTTER AND SHANKS

TURNING FORGOTTEN FLESH INTO MEMORABLE MEALS

As a young girl in a small northern Italian village, Lidia Bastianich grew up with her grandmother, Rosa, rearing suckling pigs. Little Lidia would name the pigs, feed them, and play with them until late November, when her grandfather and the local men would hold down the pigs as the butcher drove a blade through their hearts.

"For a week you'd hear squealing pigs," she tells me. "The slaughtering would set the whole town in motion. The women would catch the blood in buckets and make blood sausage right away. The legs would be salted to make prosciutto. The hog head was turned into cotechino, and the hooves and trimmed meat were put into a huge vat of sauerkraut. The loin was cured and preserved in fat. The organs were eaten right away, cooked with bay leaves and onions. The bladder was the only thing people didn't eat. That was given to the kids, who would hang it to dry, and then blow it up and make it into a soccer ball."

Bastianich is the grandmother most of us dream of, the one with an encyclopedic knowledge of the immense comforts of *la cucina italiana*, the one who would not only try to stuff you silly, but do it with prime stuffing. As an award-winning chef, she spends more time on public television than Big Bird. Her programs and books have been instrumental in bringing Italy's true regional cooking to the American culinary forefront—no chicken parm or meatball hoagies for her.

Nobody understands the alchemy of turning cheap, humble cuts of meat into dishes worthy of obsession quite like the Italians do.

"The flavor comes from muscles that were heavily used: the shoulder, the shank, the foot. They have more tendons, more gelatin, more fat," says Bastianich.

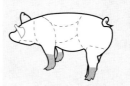

THE SHANKS AND TROTTERS
LIDIA BASTIANICH, FELIDIA

Cost per pound: $2.99/$1.42
Best for: Slow cooking, either by braising in liquid or dry roasting
Recipe relatives: Beef short ribs, lamb shanks, pork shoulder

1. Connective tissue and gelatin make these parts some of the most flavorful on the pig, but it takes slow, steady cooking to turn the flesh fork tender. When braising foods, the cooking liquid becomes your sauce. To concentrate the flavors, remove the meat and simmer the liquid until it's thick enough to coat the back of a spoon.
2. Bastianich cooks the pork in tomato sauce, creating two separate dishes: (1) tender, braised pig's foot and shoulder, and (2) pasta accompanied by pork-perfume tomato sauce.
3. Braised food may be fork tender, but it lacks texture. To add a crispy exterior to the pork, Bastianich finishes the shanks in a 500°F oven for 10 to 15 minutes, until the skin is deeply bronzed.

Sunday sauce. The pork infuses the sauce, which we serve first to dress a big bowl of pasta. Then we eat the meat separately with vegetables."

It's a perfect example of the Italian way of getting the most out of your ingredients. Can't put your hands on trotters? Shoulder and sausage will do, but you'll miss out on all that lip-smacking natural gelatin that seeps into the sauce.

For the shanks, we travel to the north of Italy. The dish—*stinco arrosto*—reflects a typical Italian treatment for large hunks of meat. Today it's shanks, but Bastianich's simple braising method is a reliable formula for handling any tough cuts.

"Start by searing the pieces of meat until they're nicely caramelized. That's what flavors the broth. Then add roughly chopped onions, carrots, and celery. Cover the meat partway with stock, maybe a bit of wine. Build flavors with dried mushroom and herbs. A few hours of slow cooking over a low flame or in the oven, and the meat will fall off the bone."

Beef short ribs, lamb shanks, chicken legs: All will submit enthusiastically to this low-and-slow approach, which renders the cheapest cuts of meat into restaurant-quality fare. Add the extra little steps that Bastianich and Nicotra employ—boiling

Together, she and her longtime culinary soul mate, Fortunato Nicotra, executive chef at Bastianich's acclaimed East Side haunt, Felidia, slow cook these tricky parts into submission. The trotters are paired up with a chunk of pork shoulder and dropped into a giant pot of simmering sauce made of onions, garlic, olive oil, and canned San Marzano tomatoes.

"It's a traditional southern Italian

down the braising liquid to make an intensely porky sauce, roasting the shanks dry under the broiler to create a golden, crackling crust—and you'll trade in your chops and your loin (and your dinner reservations) in favor of these humble bits.

THE BELLY

BEYOND THE BACONATOR

Is there a better combination of taste and texture than perfectly cooked bacon? Americans don't think so. Bacon is a $2 billion-a-year business, popping up across every culinary platform imaginable—bacon salt, bacon-and-chocolate cupcakes, bacon-infused spirits, Wendy's Baconator. There are even spray bottles of bacon-flavoring. (Mist your vegetables with essence of pork belly!)

I understand it all. If pig murder were a crime and I found myself on death row, my last meal would be a BLT: thick slices of heirloom tomato, a pile of peppery arugula, and a weave of crisp but chewy homemade bacon (yes, the warden would make a special exception and allow me to cure bacon in my cell). So when Seamus Mullen tells me he's planning to roll the 10-pound hunk of Berkshire belly into pancetta—a kind of spiced, unsmoked, European-style bacon— my mouth begins to water reflexively.

Mullen spent years apprenticing in kitchens across Spain, where pork is treated with the utmost reverence. I'm thinking of the massive *jamones*—the cured hams—that hang from the rafters of every Madrid bar (at least the good ones). And the legendary black pigs of Andalusia, living on their diet of acorns and developing elegant, buttery flesh that

can fetch $125 a pound or more when salted and dried.

"The pig is sacred; it's ubiquitous," says Mullen. "I was in a small bar in Sevilla recently and I counted up their legs. They had at least $50,000 of inventory hanging above them." A life's savings in cured pork! No doubt, it's holding its value better than my 401(k) is.

So what's with all the dangling ham?

"Spain has a hot climate for keeping meat in the summer, which is why Spaniards

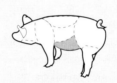

THE BELLY
SEAMUS MULLEN, BOQUERIA
Cost per pound: $2.99
Best for: Slow roasting, curing
Recipe relatives: Lamb belly, pork cheeks

1. Belly means bacon, of course, but it's also great for slow roasting. Brine it for a day, and then cook it for 3 hours in a 250°F oven until it's tender. Finish with 10 minutes of broiling to crisp the skin. Serve as is, or turn the tender, crispy hunks into the centerpiece of an enlightened BLT.
2. For every meat, 60°F and 60 percent humidity are ideal conditions for curing. A bit of air movement is important, too. Basements and closets usually work great. Mullen recommends placing a tray of salt water beneath the pancetta to create moisture in the air and to kill off bacteria.
3. Mullen browns pancetta chunks in a pan as a base for beans, and then folds in cooked white beans, chopped chard or spinach, and manchego cheese. Add a fried egg, and you've got an amazing meal.

turned to curing. And nothing works better with salt and cures than pig. The great cured hams of Spain were born out of necessity. That necessity created a flavorful style and a tradition of eating that is built into the culture."

Mullen pays tribute to that culture every day as chef at his two Boqueria restaurants in lower Manhattan. He might not have pig legs dancing up in the rafters, but he does have an entire walk-in cooler dedicated to curing the pork he butchers in the restaurant's basement. I count 47 large sausages and hams, some as fresh as 2 days, others as old as 18 months, hanging from stainless-steel racks. The sour tang of fermentation is thick in the air.

Some of these sausages—the salami-like *fuet*; the smoky, paprika-spiked chorizo—take considerable time and talent to produce; homemade pancetta, on the other

A few hours of slow cooking, and the meat will fall off the bone.

hand, is within the grasp of even the clumsiest cook. Mullen rubs the belly with a mixture of salt, garlic, black pepper, juniper berry, and dextrose, a corn-based sugar commonly used for curing. The pork sits in the mix for 4 days. Then it's rinsed, rolled tight, and hung to cure for 3 weeks.

"When it's ready, it gives off a nice, funky, porky aroma."

Mullen uses the pancetta in a dozen different ways: to wrap around scallops, to fold into stewed beans and pasta sauces, to envelop sweet dates stuffed with blue cheese and a single Spanish almond. Every application is gorgeous—well worth the 3-week wait. But more than anything, I want it sliced thin, sautéed till it's crisp, and piled on lightly toasted bread.

THE ORGANS

THE MAKING OF HAUTE DOGS

When I find Michael Psilakis at Anthos, his high-end Greek restaurant in midtown Manhattan, I'm freighted with organs. Not surprisingly, so is he; a mound of flaccid innards are heaped on a cutting board in the upstairs prep kitchen. This is the place for guts: It was a five-course offal tasting menu—including brain tortelloni, prosciutto-wrapped kidney, and goat consommé with poached eyeballs—that won him a ravenous following at his first Manhattan restaurant. Five years later, Psilakis boasts four restaurants, dozens of awards, and a Michelin star in his burgeoning portfolio.

He walks me through the humble castoffs that are the foundation of his success: "I think the majority of the issues people have with offal are cerebral. It has nothing to do with the palate experience. Sweetbreads [thymus and pancreas glands] are great beginner organs. It's all about texture; they'll assume whatever flavors you throw at them. The heart is a muscle, so if it's cleaned and cooked properly, you wouldn't know it's organ meat. The liver and kidneys are more challenging, since there's a big iron, mineral flavor."

We start with heart. The pig heart is sliced into hunks the size of matchboxes and then marinated overnight in olive oil and fresh rosemary and oregano. We take the meat to a blazing hot grill and char the slices for a few minutes on each side. Psilakis then fans the slices out onto a plate and dresses them with his take on a Greek salad: olives, capers, feta cheese, roasted red peppers, fresh lemon juice, and dill. The meat is soft and tender and has a faint mineral tang, which is accented perfectly by the salty-sweet punch of the garnish.

"If I blindfolded you, you would think you were eating steak," he says.

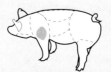

THE ORGANS
MICHAEL PSILAKIS, ANTHOS
Cost per pound: $1.40
Best for: Quick-cooking techniques like pan roasting or grilling
Recipe relatives: Chicken liver, calf liver, beef heart

1. "Heart is really mild. When it's grilled, it tastes just like beef." For the price, it's one of Psilakis's favorite cuts. (It's also one of the most nutritious proteins on the planet, loaded with B vitamins and iron.)
2. Psilakis works hard to balance salty and acidic flavors. For salt, he uses classic Greek ingredients, like feta, olives, and capers; for acid, plenty of fresh lemon juice and vinegar.
3. Psilakis makes kokoretsi, which is a traditional Greek sausage packed with six different organs and crisped up on the grill.

"Steak's easy to get right," says Psilakis, "but when I see organs on a menu, I know a chef's bringing his A game."

THE CURE FOR SOW BELLY

Bacon is one of the world's most delicious foods, but supermarket strips are too often anemic, pale, and pumped full of additives. Cut out the middleman and the chemical soup, and start curing delicious belly at home. This Italian-style treatment from Seamus Mullen, chef/partner at New York City's Boqueria restaurants, replaces the smoking process with a long, spice-heavy cure, which yields intensely porky, deep-flavored bacon.

6	cloves garlic, crushed to a paste
2	teaspoon pink curing salt (available at butcher-packer.com)
½	cup kosher salt
2	tablespoons brown sugar
4	tablespoons crushed black peppercorns
2	tablespoons juniper berries
2	tablespoons crushed fennel seeds
4	dried bay leaves, crushed
1	teaspoon fresh grated nutmeg
5	sprigs fresh thyme
1	pork belly (5 to 7 pounds), skin removed

1. Combine the garlic and spices, rub them all over the pork belly, and place the belly in a sealable plastic bag to store in the refrigerator. Turn the bag every day to distribute the curing mixture. After a week, check to see if the belly is firm; it should have the firmness of a lemon. If it doesn't, return it to the fridge and check it every day until it does.

2. Rinse the belly thoroughly under cold water and pat it dry with paper towels. With the skin side down, roll it, like a bedroll, as tightly as possible. Use butcher string to tie off the belly in 1-inch intervals, leaving enough string at one end to hang the pancetta in a basement or closet.

3. After 3 weeks, the pancetta should take on a sweet, pungent, porky smell; that means it's ready to go. It's not meant to be eaten raw, so get into the kitchen and cook it up! The raw pancetta will last up to a month in the fridge.

The pork practitioners sample each other's creations. From left: Fortunato Nicotra, Michael Anthony, Lidia Bastianich, Seamus Mullen, Akhtar Nawab, Michael Psilakis, and Peter Daversa.

The man has a point, but his simple salad could make anything—grilled chicken, roasted fish, shoe leather—taste good. Even calf or chicken liver (both widely available in supermarkets, and both among the healthiest parts you'll find on any animal) would shine on a platter like this.

Psilakis is by no means alone in his affection for innards. For decades now, most organs have disappeared into the dark corners of our food chain, with some of the most affordable, nutrient-dense animal parts turned into pet food and hot dogs. But chefs are changing that, finding ways to take a $2 calf liver, say, or a $5 bag of brains and turn it into a dish worthy of critical acclaim and a $20 price tag.

Now that he's won me over with heart, I'm ready to explore more deeply. We make *kokoretsi*, a traditional Greek sausage, using no fewer than six organs. He starts by poaching kidney, brain, sweetbreads, liver, heart, and spleen in their own baths of simmering stock. Then they're chopped into small chunks, bound together with ground pork shoulder, and wrapped in caul—the fatty membrane that serves as packing material for internal organs—and finished with a tight sleeve of interwoven small intestine. The sausage is grilled until it's crisp, and then sliced and served with a drizzle of oil, a squeeze of lemon, and a few leaves of parsley and dill. The balance of smoke, acidity, and meatiness would make a believer out of even the most cautious omnivores.

Psilakis learned to cook organs at his mother's elbow.

"I've been butchering whole animals since I was a kid. Greek cuisine is ultimately a peasant cuisine, so there's a specific use for every part. To waste anything would be disrespect to the animal that gave its life to feed you. Americans look at the odd parts as scrap. The Greeks look at it as a prize, because there's only one heart, there's only one liver."

THE HEAD

EVERYTHING BUT THE EYELASHES

Of course, there's the whole matter of the head. Speckled with blood and spinal fluid, an 18-pound pig head isn't exactly the type of comestible you can carry around with you, for snacking. So it was back to the Gramercy Tavern for me; Michael Anthony, the restaurant's executive chef, knows a lot about head-to-tail cooking.

His all-or-none approach to food is part of a larger story. Even as our global economy wobbles about, attempting to regain its footing, there are chefs, farmers, and concerned eaters working to replace heavily processed foods with first-rate ingredients. Maybe you've heard the buzzwords: *farm-to-table, sustainability, locavorism?* It's a culinary spirit that's being manifested everywhere from farmers' markets to the Obamas' White House garden. The spirit is alive even in vats of simmered hog head.

Anthony lives by the dictum "thou shalt not waste even that nasty bit." He makes the most of his meat by turning to one of the oldest dishes on earth: headcheese. This unfortunately named dish involves stewing the whole head—along with vegetables and fresh herbs—in a pot of water. Donning rubber gloves, we peel away the delicate facial muscle, cartilage, and fat and press it all into a mold. Then it goes into the freezer for cooling. When the gray sludge is set, the pig's natural gelatin will hold the whole thing together.

Hungry yet?

"Most people aren't, when they hear about it," admits Anthony.

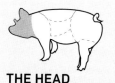

THE HEAD
MICHAEL ANTHONY, GRAMERCY TAVERN

Cost per pound: $2.99
Best for: Braising, curing
Recipe relatives: Cow head, goat head

1. You can make any tough cut of meat—head, trotter, shank, shoulder—tender and tasty by simmering it in a pot of water or stock laced with onions, carrots, celery, and garlic cloves.
2. Bubble until the facial muscles and cartilage pull away. Remove the bones, reduce the liquid, and then pour the natural gelatin and tasty meat into a mold. Yuck? No, yum.
3. "It just needs a new name," says Anthony. "If you called it something other than headcheese, I think most people would love it." It's "pork terrine" on the Gramercy Tavern menu; sounds good, doesn't it?

But when the headcheese cools and he slices off a chunk and tops it with a few crystals of coarse salt, I'm floored: It's the best single bite of pig I've experienced in 2 weeks of relentless hog consumption. The seasoning is perfect, the texture smooth and creamy, and the flavors extracted from the jowls and ears and snout are as rich and deeply satisfying as Kobe beef.

Up from the depths of disgust comes pure deliciousness.

Consider it: This quavering slice is the first bite of food customers will receive in their $88 prix fixe meal at Gramercy Tavern. So I ask Anthony how he has the nerve to serve headcheese to his guests.

"We don't tell them what it is unless they ask."

THE SHOULDER
PETE DAVERSA, HILL COUNTRY

Cost per pound: $2.72
Best for: Slow cooking, smoking, sausage making
Recipe relatives: Leg or shoulder of lamb, beef brisket, pork shank, turkey leg

1. The shoulder isn't fancy, but it is the most versatile part of the pig. It's used for chops, ground for sausage, or cooked whole for barbecue or other tasty treats.
2. "To break down the fat and connective tissue," says Daversa, "shoulder needs a long, slow cook." Learn how on page 121. One thing it doesn't need, according to Daversa, is a bunch of sauces or magical spice rubs. "If the pork is good and you cook it right, all you need is salt and pepper."
3. Don't have a smoker but still want the smoke? Place hickory or oak chips inside a foil packet and toss it directly onto the grill. Even 15 minutes of smoke at the beginning or end of the cooking process will lend big flavors to your food.

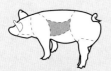

THE CHOPS
AKHTAR NAWAB, ELETTARIA

Cost per pound: $5.27
Best for: Pan roasting, grilling
Recipe relatives: Lamb chops, strip steak

1. Nawab immediately brines the chops in the same mixture that Dufresne uses, but he adds three shallots, 10 cloves of garlic, five pieces of star anise, and a tablespoon each of coriander seed, fennel seed, and black peppercorns. "Brining is key. It permeates the meat with flavor."
2. For moist chops with a crackling crust, Nawab cooks them over medium-high heat (not smoking, though) in a cast-iron skillet, basting them constantly with butter spiked with a blend of Malaysian and Szechuan peppers, and fresh thyme branches.

AN APOTHEOSIS OF PORK

I have eaten pig for 22 days straight. I can feel the smoke of the belly and the gelatin of the trotters seeping through my pores. I'm having pork sweats. All told, I've eaten 27 preparations of my animal. And yet when I step on the scale, the needle stops at 152 pounds, the same as when I tucked into that first hunk of loin 3 weeks back.

With the 230-pound beast reduced to a pile of skin, bones, and fat trimmings—along with the 6-pound pancetta hanging in my closet—there was only one sensible thing to do: cook it all again. Reconstruct the pig, literally, with the help of the crew of chefs who so generously worked their way through the animal to begin with.

Around 11 p.m., with the dining room at Akhtar Nawab's Greenwich Village restaurant Elettaria clearing out, the chefs stream steadily in, carrying sheet trays and pans. They stretch out across the open kitchen and begin to assemble pieces of our porcine puzzle: steamed ribs and smoked shoulder, offal sausage and pancetta-spiked eggs, Sunday sauce, braised trotters, and a brick of headcheese. Eager to help out, I pour glasses of homemade bacon-infused

bourbon. Soon, the table is cluttered with creations. The feast continues.

In my freezer, tightly wrapped and carefully labeled, are the last pieces of uncooked or uncured meat from my pig. First, the tail, which I'll keep as a trophy—a curly reminder of these porcine adventures. There's a surprising amount of muscle that keeps that tail moving. I've learned by now that it'll be tasty indeed. And there is, perhaps, the biggest prize of them all: an 8-pound rib roast, held together by big, meaty bones and capped with half an inch of pearl-white fat. I haven't defrosted it yet; I'm just not ready to say good-bye. But when I am, I'll do it justice. ■

BUDDY, CAN YOU SHARE A PIG?

Chances are you can't accommodate a whole hog carcass in your kitchen. But splitting a pig among fellow porkaphiles or ordering a quarter hog to stash in the freezer is a savvy move for the discerning omnivore. "It's 25 to 30 percent cheaper to buy pork in bulk," says Patrick Martins, cofounder of Heritage Foods USA, which connects consumers with farmers raising rare breeds of meat. "It also gives you a chance to cook with new cuts." You can buy these purebred pig varietals as quarter hogs and in pork variety packs.

BERKSHIRE

The most widely available of the purebred hogs is a perfect entry point for people looking to taste true pork for the first time. "It's not too fatty, not too lean. Not too strong, not too timid," says Martins. "It's like the Labrador of the heritage breeds." heritagefoodsusa.com

RED WATTLE

This rare pig from New Caledonia (a South Pacific island) delivers a serious piggy punch. "It's darker and extremely porky," says Martins. "It's the way people used to expect pigs to taste." heritagefoodsusa.com

OSSABAW

Named for the island off the Georgia coast where they were deposited by the Spanish over 400 years ago, these small pigs have since made their way to the mainland and onto many a four-star chef's menu. "It's packed with fat and a porky intensity it gets from lots of movement," says Martins. cawcawcreek.com.

MANGALITSA

This curly-haired Hungarian breed nearly went extinct last century, but it has since become one of the most prized porks on the planet, primarily for its melt-in-your-mouth deposits of creamy fat. woolypigs.com

The Scoop on Protein

Your ultimate power source is simple and satisfying. Learn to fuel up the right way.

If you are what you eat, what does that make a vegan? A string-bean, milquetoast kind of a guy? Of course not, and renowned strength coach Robert dos Remedios, a vegan, is strong evidence to the contrary. Really strong.

But most men eat animal products. And we really do become what we eat. Our skin, bones, hair, and nails are composed mostly of protein. Plus, animal products fuel the muscle-growing process called protein synthesis. That's why Rocky chugged eggs before his a.m. runs. Since those days, nutrition scientists have done plenty of research. Read up before you chow down.

TRUTH #1

You Need More

Think big. Most adults would benefit from eating more than the recommended daily intake of 56 grams, says Donald Layman, Ph.D., a professor emeritus of nutrition at the University of Illinois. The benefit goes beyond muscles, he says: Protein dulls hunger and can help prevent obesity, diabetes, and heart disease.

How much do you need? According to Mark Tarnopolsky, M.D., Ph.D., who studies exercise and nutrition at McMaster University in Hamilton, Ontario, highly trained athletes thrive on 0.77 gram of daily protein per pound of body weight. That's 139 grams for a 180-pound man.

Eating most of your protein at dinner shortchanges your muscle-growing potential.

Men who work out 5 or more days a week for an hour or longer need 0.55 gram per pound. And men who work out 3 to 5 days a week for 45 minutes to an hour need 0.45 gram per pound. So a 180-pound guy who works out regularly needs about 80 grams of protein a day.

Now, if you're trying to lose weight, protein is still crucial. The fewer calories you consume, the more calories should come from protein, says Layman. You need to boost your protein intake to between 0.45 and 0.68 gram per pound to preserve calorie-burning muscle mass.

TRUTH #2

It's Not All the Same

Many foods, including nuts and beans, can provide a good dose of protein. But the best sources are dairy products, eggs, meat, and fish, Layman says. Animal protein is complete; it contains the right proportions of the essential amino acids your body can't synthesize on its own.

It's possible to build complete protein from plant-based foods by combining legumes, nuts, and grains at one meal or over the course of a day. But you'll need to consume 20 to 25 percent more plant-based protein to reap the benefits that animal-derived sources provide, says Dr. Tarnopolsky. And beans and legumes have carbs that make it harder to lose weight.

So if protein can help keep weight off, is a chicken wing dipped in blue-cheese dressing a diet secret? Not quite: Total calories still count. Scale down your fat and carbohydrate intake to make room for lean protein: eggs, low-fat milk, yogurt, lean meat, and fish.

But remember, if you're struggling with your weight, fat itself is not the culprit; carbs are the likely problem. Fat will help keep you full, while carbs can put you on a blood-sugar roller coaster that leaves you hungry later.

TRUTH #3

Timing Is Everything

"At any given moment, even at rest, your body is breaking down and building protein," says Jeffrey Volek, Ph.D., R.D., a nutrition and exercise researcher at the

University of Connecticut. Every time you eat at least 30 grams of protein, Layman says, you trigger a burst of protein synthesis that lasts about 3 hours.

But think about it: When do you eat most of your protein? At dinner, right? That means you could be fueling muscle growth for only a few hours a day, and breaking down muscle the rest of the time, Layman says. Instead, you should spread out your protein intake.

Your body can process only so much protein in a single sitting. A recent study from the University of Texas found that consuming 90 grams of protein at one meal provides the same benefit as eating 30 grams. It's like a gas tank, says study author Douglas Paddon-Jones, Ph.D.: "There's only so much you can put in to maximize performance; the rest is spillover."

TRUTH #4

Workouts Require Fuel

Every guy in the gym knows he should consume some protein after a workout. But how much, and when? "When you work out, your muscles are primed to respond to protein," Volek says, "and you have a window of opportunity to promote muscle growth."

Volek recommends splitting your dose of protein, eating half 30 minutes before the workout and the other half 30 minutes after. A total of 10 to 20 grams of protein is ideal, he says. And wrap a piece of bread around that turkey, because carbs can raise insulin; this slows protein breakdown, which speeds muscle growth after your workout. Moreover, you won't use your stored protein for energy; you'll rely instead on the carbs to replenish you.

You're doing this because resistance exercise breaks down muscle. This requires a fresh infusion of amino acids to repair and build it. "If you're lifting weights and you don't consume protein, it's almost counterproductive," says Volek. Protein also helps build enzymes that allow your body to adapt to endurance sports like running and biking.

TRUTH #5

Powders Are for Everyone

Everyone—not just muscleheads—can benefit from the quick hit of amino acids provided by a protein supplement, bar, or shake. Your best bet is a fast-absorbing, high-quality kind such as whey protein powder (derived from milk): "It appears in your bloodstream 15 minutes after you consume it," Volek says.

Whey protein is also the best source of leucine, which is an amino acid that behaves more like a hormone in your body. "It's more than a building block of protein; it actually activates protein synthesis," Volek says. Whey contains 10 percent leucine while other animal-based proteins have as little as 5 percent.

Casein, another milk protein sold in supplement form, provides a slower-absorbing but more sustained source of amino acids, making it a great choice for a snack before you hit the sack. "Casein should help you maintain a positive protein balance during the night," says Volek. Building muscle while you sleep? Thanks to protein, anything's possible.

Check

Your Oil

What you don't understand about cooking oil can hurt you.
Use our guide to upgrade your diet—and your health.

They called it Formula 47, after the total cost in cents of a burger, fries, and shake, circa 1960. Formula 47 was a blend of rendered beef fat and vegetable oil, which, when used to fry shoestring slices of Russet Burbank potatoes, imparted a flavor so rich and appetizing that it helped the restaurant selling the fries to become the world's dominant fast-food chain: McDonald's. But that story turned into a cautionary tale whose lessons extend into every man's kitchen. Health advocates blamed Formula 47 fries for raising customers' cholesterol, so the Golden Arches switched to what people assumed was healthier—100 percent vegetable oil. The new oils were good fats that had been altered—hydrogenated—for flavor retention and longer shelf life. But that made them even more damaging to cardiovascular health than the saturated fats had been thought to be.

Some public-health experts now blame the trans fats in hydrogenated oils for tens of thousands of premature deaths. According to a recent study review by the Harvard school of public health, trans fat may increase your risk of a host of chronic diseases and also promote weight gain. So McDonald's and others have once again reformulated their frying medium, using vegetable-oil blends that are free of trans fats.

In short, oils aren't as simple as they seem. Like McDonald's, if you cook with the wrong oil, you might be sabotaging your health. To protect your body, ease your mind, and please your palate, too, follow these rules.

Rule 1
Don't Rely on Vegetable Oil

Corn, soybean, and other vegetable oils have high levels of omega-6s. These polyunsaturated fats aren't bad when they're balanced with plenty of omega-3 fatty acids, like the ones found in fish. But that too often isn't the case in the typical American diet.

"We now consume 20 to 1 omega-6s to omega-3s," says Jonny Bowden, Ph.D., author of *The 150 Healthiest Foods on Earth*. "Our inflammatory factory is overstaffed, and our anti-inflammatory factory is understaffed."

A high intake of omega-6 fats relative to omega-3 fats increases inflammation, which may increase your risk of heart disease, diabetes, and cancer, according to a 2008 review of studies by the Center for Genetics, Nutrition and Health. There are plenty of other choices.

Rule 2
Expand Your Tastes

Not all fats are created equal. Experts say the most nutritious way to go is with a few different cooking oils to help balance your intake of omega-3 and omega-6 polyunsaturated fats, as well as saturated and monounsaturated fats.

"That's what most of the world has done. Old Mediterranean cultures had olive oil on salad, fish at night, and then cow or goat butter or cheese, and they were more or less accidentally coming up with the one-to-one-to-one ratio," says K.C. Hayes, Ph.D., a fats researcher at Brandeis University, in Massachusetts.

Here's an easy way to balance your diet: Match fats to the cuisine you're cooking. Making homemade spaghetti sauce? Use a drizzle of olive oil to sauté the onions. Try coconut or peanut oil when you're whipping up an Asian stir-fry. Start a French-style omelet by melting a pat of butter. The greater the variety of nonhydrogenated fats you incorporate into your diet, the better. A moderate intake of all types of nonhydrogenated fat is best, according to the American Heart Association.

RULE 3
It's Okay to Use Butter

Here's great news. "The health scare surrounding saturated fat and cholesterol was overblown," says Walter Willett, M.D., chairman of the department of nutrition at Harvard University. A 2010 review of 21 studies, published in the *American Journal of*

Clinical Nutrition, found no conclusive evidence that dietary saturated fat is associated with an increased risk of coronary heart disease, stroke, or cardiovascular disease.

According to a review in the *European Journal of Nutrition,* a diet high in fat from dairy products like butter might raise levels of large LDL cholesterol, which is considered relatively harmless, while having no effect on levels of potentially harmful small LDL cholesterol.

Margarine, the once-sainted substitute, usually contains at least 80 percent vegetable oil, and that oil often contains trans fat. Butter also has trace amounts of naturally occurring trans fats, but not enough to cause concern. The point is that you can use butter; just don't go overboard, a caution that applies to any fat. Try whipped butter on your toast: You'll take in about a third less calories. Butter is known to be an excellent source of conjugated linoleic acid, which may be a cancer-fighting nutrient, according to Ohio State scientists.

That doesn't mean you want to kick traditionally healthy oils, like canola oil and olive oil, out of your kitchen. Just know that butter and other nonhydrogenated natural fats are not as bad as nutritionists once thought them to be. But there's one caveat.

Rule 4
Go Easy in the Kitchen

Oils typically contain 100 to 125 calories per tablespoon—all of them from fat—so use sparingly. Cook smart. Usually 1 tablespoon of any oil is enough to coat the pan you're using. Any more is overkill.

WHICH FAT IS BEST?

Favor the left side of this chart; use those on the right sparingly.

CANOLA OIL

OMEGA-6 TO OMEGA-3 RATIO: 2:1
FAT FACTS: Near-perfect omega ratio
WHEN TO USE IT: This should be your go-to option for everyday cooking. Canola oil can withstand relatively high heat, and its neutral flavor won't dominate a recipe.

OLIVE OIL

OMEGA-6 TO OMEGA-3 RATIO: 13:1
FAT FACTS: Loaded with disease-fighting antioxidants
WHEN TO USE IT: Extra-virgin has a robust flavor and should be saved to dress salads, vegetables, and cooked dishes. For cooking, regular or light olive oil is fine.

BUTTER

OMEGA-6 TO OMEGA-3 RATIO: 7:1
FAT FACTS: Might fight cancer; won't adversely affect cholesterol
WHEN TO USE IT: It's a logical choice for baked goods and adds a rich note to sautés and sauces.

PEANUT OIL

OMEGA-6 TO OMEGA-3 RATIO: n/a
FAT FACTS: Might boost your HDL (good) cholesterol
WHEN TO USE IT: Because of its high smoke point, peanut oil should be your choice for wok cooking, stir-frying, and pan-searing meat or fish.

SESAME OIL

OMEGA-6 TO OMEGA-3 RATIO: 138:1
FAT FACTS: Contains anti-oxidants and high levels of good fats
WHEN TO USE IT: Use the dark variety, made from toasted sesame seeds, as a condiment over Asian noodle dishes. Save the light variety for high heat cooking.

VEGETABLE OIL

OMEGA-6 TO OMEGA-3 RATIO: varies
FAT FACTS: Avoid. Beware of it in processed foods.
WHEN TO USE IT: Leave it on the store shelf. Sure, it's cheap, but you're better off with canola oil.

The label "vegetable oil" can mean many things. It usually refers to soybean or corn oil, or a blend that may also include sunflower or canola oil. None of these blends is preferable to canola oil, developed in Canada from a hybrid of the rapeseed plant.

MARGARINE

OMEGA-6 TO OMEGA-3 RATIO: 11:1
FAT FACTS: Avoid, unless it's a spread with healthy fats
WHEN TO USE IT: Never use margarine that contains trans fat. Butter is better, or find a healthier version, such as Smart Balance Buttery Spread with Flax Oil.

Change the World (and Your Life) One Apple at a Time

Wondering what organic can do for you—a whole lot as it turns out.

The average guy walks into the average grocery store, and he faces a choice.

Well, actually, 47,000 choices of products, many with labels touting their health benefits. Low-fat. High fiber. Natural. Free range. No high-fructose corn syrup. Organic.

Most of the label language is marketing crap. Some of it is more important than you know.

Organic brands are taking up more and more shelf space, especially in produce sections. Initially, the classier (i.e., pricier) the store, the more organic labels were sprouting among the arugula. But Walmart has now cleared space for them, too. And unless the average guy treats money like so many cabbage leaves, he also notices some unaverage prices on those organic items. He's likely to wonder: Could these foods possibly be worth it? And if I have a cartful, will women like me more?

The answer to the first question is yes, which means the second one probably merits an affirmative as well. Smart women are sensitive to health issues, and the organic movement is all about health.

The founder of Rodale, the publisher of this book, J. I. Rodale launched *Organic Farming and Gardening* magazine in 1942—and with it the organic movement in America. Rodale was a "locavore" before there was such a word; he believed in supporting local farmers and buying local foods. He devoted his life to his father's mission of improving our health and environment through food and how it is grown. Both men knew that organic foods and farming methods were healthier and better for the environment. But in the mid-1960s, they still hadn't proved it to the world. Many people considered them crazy, in fact, or at least highly eccentric. So they set out to prove, unequivocally, the wisdom of their ideas.

Before J. I. Rodale died, he began what is now the longest-running scientific study comparing synthetic-chemical agriculture with organic methods. He bought land, hired scientists who were willing to put up with the ridicule of their peers, and made a commitment to keep going as long as necessary. Over the years, the government finally did help fund and support the research.

Some brave and industrious researchers have since joined the movement. They've been willing to buck the tide of the first and now the second "green revolution"— a hype-driven phrase for chemically and genetically altered foods—to demonstrate the advantages of organic farming and the foods it produces. (In both cases, the "green" in these revolutions stands for more money for chemical companies.)

All that sounds well and good, but let's bring it down to the most basic level— right to your very own shopping cart. By choosing the foods labeled organic, you may. . .

1. Cut your risk of diabetes
2. Decrease global warming (whether you believe it exists or not!)
3. Reduce the chances that your children will be autistic
4. Save the oceans from dead zones
5. Build more muscle and burn fat
6. Increase your chances of siring healthy offspring (sons in particular)

Do we at least have your attention now? We're motivated to eat the best foods. You are, too. Consider these points before your next grocery-store visit, and see if we can't convince you that those great foods are in the organic aisle. Why?

The Average Guy's Guide to Totally Above Average Food

Organic foods are safer. If you want to protect yourself and your loved ones from harm, you'll choose organic. No food system will ever be 100 percent safe: Processing facilities and home kitchens can be unsanitary, and there's the chance of wind transferring pesticides and pollen from genetically modified crops to organic farms.

But organic foods are safer because they are produced without dangerous chemicals and preventive antibiotics. Organic producers also eschew cheap but risky practices (to say nothing of disgusting ones), like feeding dead cows to living cows or dumping human sewage sludge onto farm fields. Yes, you still have to wash your hands and organic produce before you cook. But you'll be that much further along in assuring food safety if you start with organics.

Your kids might be healthier if they eat organic foods. Children are more likely than adults are to experience health complications from pesticides, according to the Environmental Protection Agency. Because their organs are still developing, children might not be able to excrete harmful chemicals from their bodies. Plus, pesticides can block the absorption of nutrients that children need to grow.

In one study published in the journal *Environmental Health Perspectives,* researchers found that when children ate their regular diets of conventionally grown foods, their urine had detectable levels of organophosphorous pesticides. But after eating organic diets for just 5 days, their urine concentrations of those compounds fell to undetectable levels. (Returning to their original diets only spiked their levels again.) Allergies, asthma, autism, ADHD, diabetes, and childhood leukemia have all been linked to exposure to chemicals. And that includes the fertilizers and pesticides you use on your lawn.

Organic farming is better for the environment. Growing foods organically prevents thousands of toxic chemicals from entering the environment and poisoning our soil, our wells, our wildlife, our children, and ourselves. Organic farming produces better-quality soil than conventional farming does, a USDA study revealed. What's more, the organic plots in the study also yielded more crops. Growing foods organically also restores the earth's ability to process and store carbon, so it significantly reduces the atmospheric problems causing the climate crisis. Even more important, restoring the earth's ability to store carbon will help us all keep breathing.

Organic foods might have more nutrients. Studies show that some organic foods have more disease-fighting antioxidants than chemically farmed (a.k.a. conventionally farmed) foods do. A 2007 study from the University of California at Davis may provide the best evidence to date: The researchers grew organic and conventional kiwifruit on the same farm, for the same amount of time. After harvest, they discovered that the organic kiwis contained more antioxidants, including vitamin C, than the conventionally grown ones.

The theory: Because the organic kiwis weren't grown with pesticides, which fight off environmental hazards, the fruit had to produce more antioxidants naturally in order to survive. What's more, research also shows that organic dairy foods contain more conjugated linoleic acid, which is a powerful cancer-fighting nutrient.

Why You Should Worry about Chemicals in Your Food

There are plenty of reasons why it pays to spend extra for organic foods, starting with the taste. But the picture isn't complete without exploring the substantial downsides of the chemicals we've been using for the past 100 years to grow our food, maintain our idea of landscape perfection, and make our lives easier and "cleaner" and our food "cheaper."

Most of us probably think the world's biggest problems, aside from the global economic collapse, have to do with energy and energy dependence. The debates over global warming, the climate crisis, and environmental destruction have focused almost entirely on energy usage—how we drive our cars, heat our homes, and power our affluent, well-lit lifestyles. We haven't made the full connection: The way we grow our food has an impact on the climate crisis and our health crisis.

Nature, when it's given optimal circumstances (mainly, when we leave it alone) heals itself. Regeneration is necessary to repair the damage we have already done to

ourselves and to the environment. And in any case, chemicals are not necessary for growing food. Virtually every food in the world has been successfully grown and made organically in modern, productive, and regenerative ways—from fine wine and white flour to apples, cherries, the most delicious gourmet beef, olive oil, and even lard.

You think there's no problem inherent in continuing to eat the way our world has been eating? There's plenty of scientific evidence to the contrary.

Pesticides might harm your brain. Exposure to some widely used pesticides—diphenyl, paraquat, and maneb—can damage nerve cells and deplete your brain's supply of the feel-good chemical dopamine. This could potentially lead to Parkinson's disease,

Key to the Produce Section

Here are the best and worst picks in the most pesticide-laced section of the supermarket.

THE DIRTY DOZEN

People who eat the 12 most contaminationally grown fruits and vegetables consume an average of 10 pesticides a day, according to the Environmental Working Group. Those who consume the least contaminated produce ingest fewer than two pesticides a day. Of course, the optimal number is zero.

You should always buy the following 12 foods organic

PEACHES · SWEET BELL PEPPERS · **APPLES** CELERY · **NECTARINES** · STRAWBERRIES **CHERRIES** · KALE · **LETTUCE** **IMPORTED GRAPES** · CARROTS · **PEARS**

THE CLEAN 15

If money is an object (and when isn't it), you can save money by buying some conventionally grown produce if necessary.

The following foods are relatively pesticide-free

ONIONS · **AVOCADOS** · SWEET CORN **PINEAPPLES** · MANGOES · **ASPARAGUS** SWEET PEAS · **KIWIS** · CABBAGE **EGGPLANTS** · PAPAYAS · **WATERMELON** BROCCOLI · **SWEET POTATOES** · TOMATOES

according to a recent British study review.

Pesticides might lower your sperm count. Nearly 100 different pesticides are thought to disrupt your body's hormonal balance, which could reduce fertility, British scientists say. And even trace amounts in food may be enough to damage sperm. That's because low doses of toxins don't trigger a chemical cleanup in your body and can still harm reproductive cells.

Chemicals in animal feed may cause cancer in humans. Chemical farmers often lace feed for their pigs and poultry with arsenic. It promotes growth in livestock, but it might also cause a number of cancers that affect humans, including prostate cancer, according to a recent Johns Hopkins University study. The government sets dosage thresholds, but feed formulations are considered confidential and monitoring is limited.

There are other problems with feed as well. Growth-promoting hormones added to cattle feed not only toughen the meat but also may be linked to hormone-dependent cancers, according to a recent Spanish study.

Pesticides may weaken your immune system. Certain pesticides may inhibit the growth of immune cells, a recent Italian study found. This weakens your body's ability to fight off invaders, and may also allow cancer cells to proliferate unchecked, the study says.

Nonorganic meat may upset your intestinal balance. Chemical farmers may legally administer antibiotics to livestock before disease strikes. This allows drugs to accumulate in meat—which, once consumed, may alter the natural bacteria in your bowels and increase your susceptibility to pathogens, according to researchers in Spain.

Agricultural chemicals could be making you fat. Synthetic chemicals may cause obesity in adults by altering hormone levels or by changing the way certain genes work, according to a recent French study. Plus, it's a vicious circle: The more fat your body has, the more toxins you store.

Pesticides may cause you to develop allergies. Certain agricultural chemicals, such as the widely used insecticide chlorpyrifos, may cause your immune system to overreact to harmless antigens. This may trigger an allergic reaction, Italian researchers say.

Small doses of chemicals can be just as dangerous as large doses. Most of the government regulations on chemicals are based on estimated safe amounts of exposure. Doctors and scientists are finding, however, that small doses—especially over time—can be just as toxic as large ones.

Genetically modified organisms have never been tested on humans, and now results from animal studies are showing kidney and liver failure. In a recent study in the *International Journal of Biological Science*, rats that ate a diet of genetically modified corn (which we ingest in large doses every day) had internal damage to their organs, especially the liver and kidneys. The only way to ensure you're not eating any of these widespread, potentially harmful organisms is to seek out food with the USDA Organic label.

What Does "Organic" Mean?

Organic: Products given the USDA Organic stamp of approval must be made up of at least 95 percent organically produced ingredients. The other 5 percent can be nonorganic, but only if the ingredients are not commercially available in organic form and are on the USDA's list of approved substances for such use. Any food labeled USDA Organic was grown without the aid of genetic engineering, ionizing radiation, or sewage sludge (yes, it's what you think it is), and without pesticides disallowed for organic agriculture by the USDA. If it's meat, the animal was raised without antibiotics and growth hormones and fed an organic diet. The USDA classifies organic foods as 100 percent organic only if all the ingredients and processing aids are made organically.

Made with organic ingredients: The USDA defines a product as being "made with organic ingredients" if the food contains at least 70 percent organic ingredients. (Hey, it's better than nothing.) In addition to this, you can be assured that the product wasn't made with methods that are not approved in organic agricultural practices, like the use of sewage sludge or ionizing radiation.

Natural: Foods labeled "natural" aren't necessarily organic. Except for meat and poultry, no official standards legally define "natural" for producers or consumers. Nevertheless, the term often refers to foods with no preservatives or artificial ingredients. There is no independent confirmation of that; it's just a word that can be used on any food label. Organic foods follow standards defined by the USDA, and compliance is independently verified by inspectors.

Local: The local-food movement has been very important in revitalizing small farms and communities and bringing fresh, seasonal food to many more people. However, as a means of saving the planet and improving health, it goes only so far. Local chemical farming contaminates communities and actually increases their carbon footprint and energy usage. Local organic farming cleans up local communities and decreases their carbon footprint and energy use.

Studies show that being organic is much more critical than being local when it comes to a food's carbon footprint. In one study commissioned by PepsiCo, an independent researcher determined that the most significant component of the carbon footprint for Tropicana orange juice (a PepsiCo product) wasn't transportation or manufacturing but the production and application of fertilizer to grow oranges.

And for Dessert, Heal the Planet

By selecting organic products, you can bring about positive change to the planet. And that's a lot to do over dinner. Consider these benefits.

We can feed the world with organic food and farming. Contrary to the propaganda churned out by biotech and chemical corporations, organic farming can feed the world. Transferring our chemically dependent agricultural system to other nations is a sure way to bring about global environmental collapse. The energy expenditure, the toxicity of the chemicals, and the soil degradation would be catastrophic. Instead, we need to export the knowledge we've gained about successful modern organic farming and help others adapt these practices to their climates, regions, and cultures.

Organic living can stop the climate crisis (whether or not you believe it exists). When you combine the impact of protecting the beneficial mycorrhizal fungi in the soil (which absorb and neutralize carbon) and eliminating all the toxic chemicals (and their packaging and the energy spent producing them), the carbon problem in our atmosphere is practically solved. We still need more renewable energy, but restoring the earth's ability to sequester carbon is a good place to start. And you'll do it while eating.

It's not too late to change—and be healthier and happier. People who switch to organic foods reduce their pesticide intake. Further, research by University of Colorado neuroscientist Christopher Lowry, Ph.D., found that certain strains of soilborne bacteria not only stimulate the human immune system but also boost serotonin levels in mice. Serotonin is essential to fighting depression. Perhaps if we all farmed and gardened the organic way, we would not need the antidepressant drugs that are being pissed out into our water supply.

It's simple: Go organic.

The 20 Best Organic Foods for Men

Here's your Earth-healing, palate-pleasing, diet-improving shopping list for healthier, tastier meals all day long.

Breakfast

BEST EGGS
Eggland's Best Organic

Scrambled, fried, or poached, these heart-healthier eggs cook up flavorful and fluffy.
One large egg: 70 calories, 6 g protein, 0 g carbs, 4 g fat

BEST CEREAL
Kashi Whole Wheat Biscuits, Cinnamon Harvest

One serving is nearly 20 percent of your daily fiber, and it doesn't taste like the box it came in.
2 oz: 180 calories, 6 g protein, 43 g carbs (5 g fiber), 1 g fat

BEST MILK
Stonyfield Organic Reduced Fat

It's creamy, without the calories of whole milk.
1 cup: 130 calories, 8 g protein, 13 g carbs, 5 g fat

BEST COFFEE
Stumptown Coffee Roasters Organic French Roast

"Direct trade" means the roasters buy directly from growers and then ship this dark, rich coffee to you.
1 cup: 2 calories

Lunch

BEST FROZEN MEAL
Amy's Roasted Vegetable Tamale

It's satisfying enough to stave off hunger, but sanely portioned to prevent a gut bomb.
Per meal: 280 calories, 9 g protein, 46 g carbs, 7 g fat

BEST BREAD
Bread Alone Bakery Organic Whole Grain Health Loaf

Sweetened with honey and topped with sesame and sunflower seeds, it's the perfect slice for sandwiches.
1 slice: 140 calories, 5 g protein, 27 g carbs (4 g fiber), 2 g fat

BEST LUNCH MEAT

Applegate Farms Organic Roasted Turkey Breast

Try some of this lean, luscious protein rolled and slathered with pesto.
2 oz: 50 calories, 10 g protein, 1 g carbs, 0 g fat

BEST DELI CHEESE

Applegate Farms Organic Mild Cheddar Cheese

Serve your next grilled cheese without a side of hormones.
1 slice: 85 calories, 5 g protein, 0 g carbs, 6 g fat

BEST CONDIMENT

Annie's Naturals Organic Dijon Mustard

It has no calories, tons of flavor, and goes great with our pretzel pick. (See "Best crunchy snack.")

After Your Workout

BEST RECOVERY DRINK

Organic Valley Reduced Fat Chocolate Milk

Stocked with the protein your muscles need to rebuild quickly.
Per cup: 170 calories, 8 g protein, 24 g carbs, 5 g fat

Dinner

BEST MEAT

Full Circle Bison Ranch Organic Grass Fed Buffalo (Rib Eye)

This steak outranked all the organic beef brands we sampled.
3 oz: 150 calories, 25 g protein, 0 g carbs, 5 g fat

BEST ORGANIC SPICE

McCormick 100% Organic Cayenne Red Pepper

After you hit your steak with salt and pepper, ratchet up the heat with a shake of this. (0 calories)

BEST COOKING OIL

Spectrum Organic Canola Oil

Use this for medium-to-high-heat cooking.
1 Tbsp: 120 calories, 0 g protein, 0 g carbs, 14 g fat

BEST BEER

Samuel Smith Organic Ale

Consider this balanced, full-bodied ale your new warm-weather brew.
12 oz: 150 calories, 2 g protein, 15 g carbs, 0 g fat

BEST WINE

Scribe 2008 Pinor Noir

Alice Waters of Chez Panisse, in Berkeley, California, gives it the thumbs-up. We second.
3.5 oz: 84 calories, 0 g protein, 2 g carbs, 0 g fat

Snacking

BEST SWEET SNACK

Newman's Own Organics Champion Chip Double Chocolate Mint Chip Cookies

Indulge your chocoholism without overeating.
4 cookies: 160 calories, 2 g protein, 21 g carbs (1 g fiber), 8 g fat

Best Brands

Amy's

Just because you eat organically doesn't mean you should sacrifice your favorite foods. Amy's delivers big on flavor while sticking to its organic guns. Look for Amy's oatmeals, soups, chili, frozen entrées, and cakes (yes, cakes!) nationwide.

Cascadian Farms

This company calls northern Washington home, where it produces more than 75 organic products—from frozen fruits and vegetables to granola and cereal.

Newman's Own Organics

The Towering Inferno was good, but Paul Newman just may cement his legacy with organic cookies. Try the Oreo alternatives, and pick up his popcorn, tea, and Fig Newmans while you're at it.

Diamond Organics

Bookmark this company (diamondorganics.com) as your mail-order source for organic products you can't find at the supermarket. Beef, chicken, dairy, produce, mushrooms—they're at your doorstep.

BEST FRUIT SNACK

Peeled Snacks Muchado-About Mango

Only one ingredient: dried organic mangoes.
Per bag: 120 calories, 2 g protein, 28 g carbs (2 g fiber), 0 g fat

BEST FIERY SNACK

Eden Organic Spicy Pumpkin Seeds

Seasoned with soy sauce, garlic, and cayenne, these put spicy chips to shame.
¼ cup: 200 calories, 10 g protein, 5 g carbs (5 g fiber), 16 g fat

BEST CRUNCHY SNACK

Newman's Own Organics Honey Wheat Mini Pretzels

Not too sweet. Amazing with peanut butter.
20 pretzels: 110 calories, 2 g protein, 22 g carbs (3 g fiber), 1 g fat

BEST YOGURT

Stonyfield Oikos Organic Greek Yogurt with Honey

Sweetened naturally (and organically) without added preservatives.
5.3 oz container: 120 calories, 13 g protein, 18 g carbs, 0 g fat

PROVE IT.

Alaska King Crab
Omega-3s: 389 mg*
Protein: 16.4 g

Swordfish
Omega-3s: 898 mg
Protein: 21.6 g

Rainbow Trout
Omega-3s: 1,051 mg
Protein: 20.6 g

Mussels
Omega-3s: 736 mg
Protein: 20.2 g

FIGHT FAT WITH FAT

Fish isn't just good for your heart; it's good for your gut, too. That's because **omega-3 fatty acids help you feel full longer,** report scientists from Iceland. In the study, dieters who ate salmon felt fuller 2 hours later than those who either didn't eat seafood or had cod, a fish with little fat. The researchers found that eating foods high in omega-3s (such as the ones above) increased blood levels of leptin, a hormone that promotes satiety.

Hate fish? Take a fish-oil capsule every day—one that has 500 milligrams of the omega-3s DHA and EPA. It offers the same benefits as the salmon.

* Information is based on 3-ounce servings.

DRINK AWAY CANCER?

Sure, we know, you are what you eat. But perhaps what's even more important is what you drink. In a prime example, two popular beverages can decrease your risk of cancer.

Green tea may slow prostate cancer progression, according to research from the Louisiana State University Health Sciences Center. In the study, prostate cancer patients were given daily doses of a drug made mostly from the catechins in green tea. After about 5 weeks, the men had lower levels of the molecules that advance the disease. The catechins may block these harmful molecules from being transcribed by your DNA, say the scientists. More research may determine if drinking the tea has similar benefits.

Also, drinking a daily cup of coffee may decrease your risk of mouth, throat, and esophageal cancers by 50 percent, say Japanese researchers. The scientists think that cafestol and kahweol, two antioxidant-like compounds found in coffee beans, might stymie the growth of DNA-damaging carcinogens.

SAVE YOURSELF WITH CHOCOLATE

Taking your medicine never tasted so good. Scientists in Italy determined that the ideal dose of dark chocolate is a 100-calorie serving every 3 days. That's based on a study of nearly 5,000 people that found that the **antioxidants in chocolate lower chronic inflammation by an average of 17 percent**—enough to cut your risk of heart disease by 26 percent.

The bad news: "Eating more chocolate didn't seem to provide additional benefits," says study author Licia Iacoviello, M.D., Ph.D.

Your prescription: a total of about 2 ounces a week.

Almost three-quarters of Americans know that trans fats increase their risk of heart disease.

TAKE THE TRANS FAT TEST

Pop quiz: What are the biggest dietary sources of trans fats? If you know the answer, you're in the minority. **Only one in five men can name up to three foods that contain trans fats,** according to the *Journal of the American Dietetic Association.* Yet 73 percent of Americans know that this food component—most often found in french fries, cookies, pastries, crackers, and muffins—increases their risk of heart disease. Beware: The culprit is also known as partially hydrogenated oil. To find out which foods and restaurants are harboring trans fats, go to MensHealth.com/eatthis.

HARD TRUTH

99.9

Percentage of people who don't look at nutrition information in restaurant chains when it's available, according to the *American Journal of Public Health*

CRACK DOWN ON CHOLESTEROL

Smart snacking could help you shelve the statins. Just one or two servings of pistachios a day can lower LDL (bad) cholesterol by up to 12 percent, report Penn State University scientists. The lipid-lowering effect is likely due to the nuts' content of heart-healthy monounsaturated fats, phytosterols, and fiber, says study author Sarah Gebauer, Ph.D. Try pistachios as an afternoon snack or as a salad topping.

Pistachios too expensive? Try walnuts instead. Australian researchers recently found that **eating walnuts might lower your LDL and also boost your HDL (good) cholesterol, too.** When people with type 2 diabetes added a handful of walnuts to their prescribed diets, they had higher HDL and lower LDL levels after 1 year. Researchers aren't sure of the exact mechanism behind this beneficial effect, but it may have to do with the synergy among the heart-healthy fats and other compounds found in the nuts. Shoot for 8 to 12 nuts a day, the same amount the study participants ate.

PUMP UP THE PROTEIN

If you hate to diet, it might be that you're just eating the wrong foods. University of Illinois researchers found that people who ate higher amounts of protein were more likely to stick to their diets for 1 year than those who ate more carbohydrates instead.

The reason: "Protein is more satiating than carbohydrates are, so people weren't as hungry as those in the other group," says study author Donald L. Layman, Ph.D. "They also had more energy and didn't feel as tired."

Turns out, the dieters who best stuck to their eating plan consumed a diet that provided 40 percent of its calories from carbohydrates and 30 percent from protein.

BE A BLUE BLOOD

Here's some sweet news: **Blueberries might help lower blood-sugar levels and insulin resistance,** researchers in Canada found. In a small study, overweight men at risk for heart disease and diabetes drank 1 cup of wild blueberry juice every day for 3 weeks. Their blood sugar dropped by roughly 10 percent, and their insulin resistance also fell, compared with that of control-group participants who drank a placebo.

Study coauthor Marva Sweeney, Ph.D., says the benefits might come from the effect on the pancreas of the fruit's high levels of anthocyanins. (The pancreas regulates blood sugar by producing insulin.)

Frozen wild blueberries offer the same benefits as juice. Farmed blueberries also contain anthocyanins, but in lower amounts.

BREAK AN EGG

Here's more proof that yolks are good for you: A new study shows that **you can benefit all day from eating eggs at breakfast.** University of Connecticut researchers found that men who ate eggs as their first meal took in fewer calories over 24 hours than those who ate bagels. The reason? Protein is more satiating than carbs, say the scientists.

EAT THIS MAGICAL FOOD

If you're not a legume lover, consider this: In the National Health and Nutrition Examination Survey, scientists found that **people who consumed beans were 23 percent less likely to have large waists** than those who said they never ate them. The bean eaters in the survey also tended to have lower systolic blood-pressure measurements, says researcher Victor Fulgoni III, Ph.D. Of course, it's not really magic—legumes are rich in belly-filling fiber as well as potassium, which helps fight hypertension. Aim for half a cup of cooked beans 3 or 4 days a week.

FILL UP WITH FRUIT

Turns out, an apple a day might also keep the extra weight away. Penn State researchers discovered that people who ate a large apple 15 minutes before lunch took in 187 fewer calories during lunch than those who didn't snack beforehand. (The apples had around 128 calories.) What's more, they reported feeling fuller afterward, too.

Sure, the fruit is loaded with belly-filling fiber, but there's another reason apples help you feel full: They require lots of chewing.

YOU ASKED.

Is high-fructose corn syrup (HFCS) all that unhealthy??

A: "Several studies have shown no real difference between the biological effects of HFCS and sucrose (table sugar)," says Mary Ellen Camire, Ph.D., a professor of food science in the department of food science and human nutrition at the University of Maine. "But to keep off the pounds, watch your intake of all refined or concentrated sugars."

Q: What one heart-healthy food should I eat every day?

A: "Variety is key, so there's no single food," says Prediman Krishan (P. K.) Shah, M.D., the director of the division of cardiology and the atherosclerosis research center at Cedars-Sinai Medical Center in Los Angeles and a professor of medicine at the UCLA school of medicine. "But there are two kinds you should eat daily: inflammation-fighting cruciferous vegetables, such as broccoli, brussels sprouts, and kale (eat half a cup); and blood-pressure-lowering berries, such as blueberries, blackberries, and strawberries (half a cup)."

Q: Is there any nutritional difference between instant and steel-cut oatmeal?

A: We give steel-cut oatmeal the edge. It's made from oat grains (a.k.a. groats) that have simply been chopped up. Instant oatmeal consists of groats that are first chopped and then flattened with rollers so they'll cook faster—except faster isn't always better for your body.

"The enzymes in your gastrointestinal tract take a longer time to penetrate the unrolled groats in steel-cut oatmeal," says David Jenkins, M.D., Ph.D., a nutrition and metabolism researcher at the University of Toronto. "This results in a slower uptake of glucose, and that makes steel-cut oatmeal better, especially for people who are at risk of diabetes."

Steel-cut oats contain 8 grams of soluble fiber per 1-cup serving, which is twice the amount in instant rolled oats. So while both types can slash your risk of heart disease by up to 40 percent, steel-cut may get you there sooner.

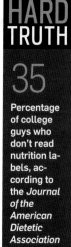

HARD TRUTH

35

Percentage of college guys who don't read nutrition labels, according to the *Journal of the American Dietetic Association*

YOU ASKED.

Q: What's a good snack to bridge the gap from 5 p.m. to dinner?

A: "Celery sticks smeared with almond butter will provide a balance of carbs and protein to take the edge off your appetite and steady your blood sugar," says Jonny Bowden, Ph.D., C.N.S., a board certified nutritionist and the author of seven books on nutrition and health. "Another good 250-calorie combo: an apple with peanut butter. In fact, any pairing of fruit with a handful of nuts works. Don't like nuts? Pair an apple with string cheese."

Q: I'm no good at the smell test. How can I tell if my leftovers are okay to eat?

A: Taking a big whiff won't do you any good anyway.

"The bacteria that can make you sick settles in well before sour smells develop and mold becomes visible," says dietician Sarah Krieger, M.P.H., R.D., a spokeswoman for the American Dietetic Association.

Your best strategy is to write dates on your leftovers, she says, and pitch Tuesday's shrimp fried rice by Friday. The limit for pretty much all leftovers is 3 to 4 days. After that interval, you risk becoming sick from *E. coli*, salmonella, and staphylococcus aureus. Exceptions to the bacterial-growth rule are salads with vinegar-based dressings; the dressings contain acids that make it difficult for germs to thrive. In theory, this could extend fridge shelf life. However, those same dressings also make your food soggy after just a day or two.

Q: Can I overdose on omega-3 fish oil?

A: "Yes. Too much fish oil can dampen your immune responses and interfere with blood clotting," says Dr. Bowden. "I recommend 1 gram of fish oil twice a day, totaling roughly 1,000 milligrams of DHA and 300 milligrams of EPA. Some supplements bump up the EPA levels, which is also fine. But don't take more than 2 grams a day without consulting a physician."

However, ignore the myths that omega-3 supplements depress a man's testosterone. Low testosterone has many causes, but omega-3s aren't among them. On the contrary— fatty acids are essential for normal testosterone production. Talk to a hormone specialist.

Q: Is it okay to drink a six-pack of diet cola every day?

A: "I wouldn't drink more than four cans," says Dr. Camire. "Colas contain phosphoric acid to provide tartness and stabilize the brown coloring, but too much phosphorus can leach calcium from your bones. People who drink 100 ounces (eight cans) of cola a day risk depleting their potassium and damaging their muscles."

HONEY
Origin: A fructose-glucose mix regurgitated by bees
Taste: Varies depending on where it's harvested, but no aftertaste
Best for: Everyone

AGAVE
Origin: Nectar from the same Mexican cactus that yields tequila
Taste: Light versions have a floral taste, while dark agave is more like molasses
Best for: Everyone

ASPARTAME (Equal, NutraSweet)
Origin: Two amino acids combined with methyl ester
Taste: Sugarlike, but with a faint bitter aftertaste
Best for: Normal tasters and nontasters

SUCRALOSE (Splenda)
Origin: Chlorine atoms are substituted for hydrogen-oxygen groups in ordinary sugar
Taste: The closest to sugar, with virtually no aftertaste
Best for: Everyone, but especially supertasters

STEVIA
Origin: The dried leaves of a South American shrub
Taste: Ultrasweet, with a licorice-like aftertaste for some people
Best for: Nontasters

SACCHARIN (Sweet'N Low)
Origin: Sulfur and other components combined in a chemically complex stew
Taste: Cloyingly sweet; leaves a metallic aftertaste
Best for: Nontasters

Q: **What's the best sugar substitute?**

A: In theory, the perfect product would have the sweetness of sugar without the hit to your waistline. Splenda, stevia, Sweet'N Low, and Equal are effectively zero calories, yet they're hundreds of times sweeter than sugar. By compar-ison, honey and agave are only slightly sweeter and are more caloric. So if your goal is weight loss, the first four win. As for which of those is best, only your tongue can tell.

"People differ in their number of taste buds," says Steven Witherly, Ph.D., a professor of food science at California State University at Northridge.

"Supertasters are the most sensitive to sweet and bitter tastes and typically dislike fudge and broccoli; nontasters are the least sensitive, and normal tasters are in the middle."

Use the menu above to find a match for you. If you're worried about safety, research still hasn't proved that artificial sweeteners cause cancer in humans.

Q: Are there any benefits to eating hybrid fruits?

A: If you count rousing your taste buds and adding some antioxidant oomph to your diet, then yes. "The best hybrids combine the qualities of two or even three fruits," says Jim White, R.D., a spokesman for the American Dietetic Association. "You're eating a wider variety of nutrients." Supplementing your favorite fruits with the hybrids here can also help you nail your five-a-day produce quota, a target that 80 percent of men miss. Oh, don't worry, hybrids are not genetically altered Frankenfruits but simply the products of crossbreeding.

PLUMCOT
FIGHTS AGING

A 50-50 cross between a plum and an apricot, the intensely sweet plumcot is packed with age-fighting antioxidants called anthocyanins and immune-boosting carotenoids.
Season: May through October
Serving size: 1 fruit
Calories: 76
Fiber: 2 g
Vitamin A: 550 IU
Vitamin C: 16 mg

TUSCAN MELON
PROMOTES EYE AND SKIN HEALTH

Boasting three parents, this fruit is a combination of the sweet cantaloupe, the aromatic Charentais melon, and the juicy muskmelon. The Tuscan melon is rich in vision- and skin-fortifying vitamin A (delivering 166 percent of your RDA), and it's also high in vitamin C.
Season: May through September
Serving size: ¼ melon
Calories: 50
Vitamin A: 5,000 IU
Vitamin C: 48 mg

MINNEOLA TANGELO
HELPS PREVENT CANCER

A pomelo-mandarin orange love child, the tangelo has more flavanones (antioxidants associated with lower risks of various cancers) than an orange, yet it's just as sweet and juicy. But like the grapefruit and uniq fruit, the tangelo can interact with prescription drugs, such as statins. (Visit MensHealth.com/druginteraction/ for a list.)
Season: November through March
Serving size: 1 fruit
Calories: 70
Vitamin A: 200 IU
Vitamin C: 60 mg

UNIQ FRUIT
BOOSTS HEALING

A grapefruit-tangerine hybrid, the uniq grows wild in Jamaica. One fruit serves up 93 percent of your RDA for vitamin C, which helps heal cuts. The tart, juicy uniq also contains folate, which can guard your sperm against DNA damage.
Season: November to July
Serving size: 1 fruit
Calories: 90
Fiber: 4 g
Vitamin C: 84 mg

LIMEQUAT
PROTECTS YOUR HEART

Snacking on three of these bite-size nuggets provides about 20 percent of your daily fiber, which may help tamp down your blood pressure and cholesterol levels and lower your risk of type-2 diabetes. Eat them as you would kumquats, skin and all.
Season: July through November
Serving size: 3 fruits
Calories: 60
Fiber: 6 g
Vitamin C: 63 mg

Q: What kind of bread is the most nutritious?

A: First off, ignore the advertising copy on the front. Flip around to the ingredient list. Is the first ingredient a whole grain? Does each slice have 2 or more grams of fiber? Do "inulin" or "polydextrose" show up? The correct answers are yes, yes, and no.

"With whole grain, nothing is stripped away," says White. That means you're noshing on natural fiber, not inulin or polydextrose, two additives used to artificially boost fiber. The breads here meet the criteria, and they could also help you build muscle, lose weight, and beat heart disease.

Ignore the advertising copy on the front. Flip around to the ingredient list.

ARNOLD GRAINS & MORE: DOUBLE OAT HEARTY OATMEAL BREAD
The third ingredient listed is rolled oats, which means that like oatmeal, this hearty, home-baked style bread can help lower your LDL (bad) cholesterol more than wheat alone can. *110 calories, 5 g protein, 3 g fiber**

SARA LEE: 45 CALORIES & DELIGHTFUL 100% WHOLE WHEAT WITH HONEY
With half the calories of most whole-grain loaves, this smooth-textured, slightly sweet bread is good if you're looking for strategic ways to shed pounds. *45 calories, 3 g protein, 2 g fiber*

FOOD FOR LIFE: WHEAT & GLUTEN FREE BROWN RICE BREAD
An infusion of juice concentrate (pineapple, peach, pear) gives each dense slice a fruity flavor. And since it's made with a whole grain that isn't wheat or bran, it's safe for the more than 2 million Americans with celiac disease (a.k.a. gluten intolerance). *110 calories, 2 g protein, 2 g fiber*

MARTIN'S: 100% WHOLE WHEAT POTATO BREAD
By combining whole wheat with nonfat milk, Martin's has made a sweet-tasting bread that delivers a unique combination of muscle-building protein and stomach-filling fiber. *70 calories, 6 g protein, 4 g fiber*

GENESIS 1:29: SPROUTED GRAIN AND SEED BREAD
Look past the Bible branding and enjoy a coarse, nutty-tasting bread that contains enzymes, unique proteins that can help in digestion and nutrient absorption. *80 calories, 4 g protein, 3 g fiber*

* All nutritional facts are per slice.

3

Muscle Up Fast

The 5-Second Muscle Test

Forget how much weight you lift.
What's critical is, how fast are you?

A crucial but often overlooked aspect of weight training is the pace at which you lift. Bill Hartman, C.S.C.S., uses this simple test to spot weaknesses and help men increase the amount of weight they can hoist. Take the test as you perform a squat or bench press.

The Test

Do a typical warmup. Estimate a weight you can lift only once, and lift 60 percent of that for 5 reps. Then lift 70 percent (3 reps) and 80 percent (1 rep). Now do your 1-rep max, noting the time it takes to lower and raise the weight.

Your Score

If you take more than 5 seconds . . . You might lack explosive strength. Work on lifting faster to increase the elasticity of your muscles and tendons. Perform the following workout once or twice a week for 4 to 6 weeks.

1. Using half of your 1-rep max weight from the test, time how long it takes you to lift that weight for 5 reps. Add 1 second to that time. That's your target time. For example, if your 1-rep max is 200 pounds, you'd lift 100 pounds for 5 reps. And if those 5 reps take you 7½ seconds total, your target time is 8½ seconds.

2. Add weight to the barbell in 5- or 10-pound increments, and try to perform 5 reps with each weight within a time faster than your target time. For example, you'd do 5 reps of 110 pounds, then 120 pounds, and so on. Rest 60 to 90 seconds between sets.

3. Perform as many sets of increasing weight as possible. When you can no longer perform 5 repetitions faster than your target time, the exercise is over for the day.

If you take less than 5 seconds . . . Your muscles and tendons already move fast, so increase the amount of weight you can lift. To do that, follow the workouts in this chart on separate days. They focus on lowering reps and adding weight. Rest 2 to 5 minutes between sets.

* This indicates the percentage of your 1-rep maximum from the test. If your max was 200, your first lift in Week 1 is 65 percent of 200, or 130 pounds.

Week	Workout 1 *sets/reps*	Workout 2 *sets/reps*
1	65%* 4/6	72% 4/6
2	70% 4/6	77% 3/6
3	75% 3/6	82% 5/4
4	80% 4/4	87% 5/3
5	85% 4/3	90% 4/2
6	92% 2/2	95% 4/1
7	85% 3/2	OFF
8	Retest your 1-rep max	Retest your 1-rep max

Strong Shoulders Ahead

Use these exercises to eliminate shoulder pain and strengthen your entire upper body.

Walk into any gym in America, and you'll find one common scene: men complaining about their shoulders.

"Man, I used to be stronger," they moan. "More shredded, more this, more that. But my shoulders, man, my shoulders!" Strains and pains force guys to avoid exercises like the bench press, leading to decreased muscle and a steady whine that never goes away.

The secret isn't to avoid your pain. Instead, add moves that strengthen your joints.

At trainer Bill Hartman's Indianapolis facility, he's used the exercises on the next pages with terrific results—no "coulda been a contender" complaints about hurt shoulders. Follow his routine, and you'll see less shoulder strain and more serious muscle on your arms, chest, shoulders, and back.

Perform the following workout routine as part of your total-body workout or your upper-body day. Complete all the sets in each sequence (1A and 1B, for example) before moving to the next number in the program. For added variety, you can substitute one of the extra options listed to help fix your shoulders and build the ultimate upper body.

A

Floor Press

3 or 4 sets of 6 to 8 reps
(can also be done with a barbell)

Grab a pair of dumbbells and lie faceup on the floor with your knees bent and feet flat. Start with the dumbbells above your shoulders and your arms straight. Lower the weights until your upper arms touch the floor, and then press the weights up to the starting position. That's 1 rep.

Benefit: This movement restricts shoulder extension; that's the stretching of the muscles in front of your shoulders when you lower the weights to your body. Too much stress on the front of your shoulder makes the area unstable and leads to injury. This is a good sub for the bench press when your shoulders are acting up, or just to periodically reduce strain.

Other options:
Dumbbell bench press/Dumbbell incline press

A

Lean-Away Lat Pulldown

2 or 3 sets of 10 to 12 reps

Sit at a cable tower or lat pulldown machine using an underhand grip about one and a half times wider than your shoulders, and lean back about 30 degrees. Pull the bar down to your lower sternum, making sure you pull your shoulders down and back as you follow through with your arms. Return to the starting position in a smooth, controlled motion.

Benefit: The angle of your body reduces demand on the rotator cuff, promoting a more stable shoulder joint. Also, a 30-degree lean-away can increase activation of your lats.

Other option:
Underhand closed-grip pulldown

A

Cable Face Pull

2 or 3 sets of 12 to 15 reps

Attach a rope to the high pulley of a cable station and grab each end so your palms face each other. Step away until your arms are straight out in front of you and you feel tension in the cable. Now pull the middle of the rope toward your eyes by bending your elbows, squeezing your shoulder blades together, and flaring your upper arms out to your sides. Then slowly straighten your arms in front of you.

Benefit: You'll work the smaller muscles in your upper back, maintain shoulder rotation and strength, and improve trapezius strength, all of which enhances stability of your shoulder blades and shoulder joints.

Other options:
Pushup/Inverted row

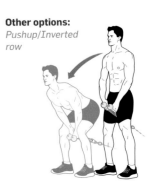

B

Medium-Grip Barbell Row

3 or 4 sets of 6 to 8 reps

Grab a barbell with an overhand grip with your hands about shoulder-width apart, and hold it in front of your thighs with your knees slightly bent. Bend at your hips, lower your torso about 45 degrees, and let the bar hang straight down from your shoulders. Pull the bar up to your torso, pause, and then slowly lower it.

Benefit: Too many men focus on "mirror muscles," such as the chest and arms. Exercises that use the muscles in your back provide balance to your training plan, and they help maintain the natural movement of your shoulders to help you avoid weaknesses and pain.

Other options:
Medium-grip cable row/ Dumbbell row

B

Scaption

2 or 3 sets of 10 to 12 reps

Stand with your feet shoulder-width apart and hold a pair of dumbbells at arm's length by your sides, your palms facing each other and elbows slightly bent. Without bending your elbows, raise your arms until they're parallel to the ground while keeping them at a 30-degree angle to your body. Pause, and then lower your arms back to the starting position.

Benefit: The muscles around your shoulder joint and shoulder blade are activated so you can build more muscle and strengthen your shoulders at the same time.

B

Side-Lying External Rotation

2 or 3 sets of 12 to 15 reps on each side

With a dumbbell in your right hand, lie on your left side with a rolled towel under your right elbow. Bend your left arm and rest your head on your left hand. Flex your right elbow to 90 degrees and rest the weight in front of your stomach. Don't bend your wrist. Keep your upper arm at your side as you rotate your right forearm to raise the weight until it's above your body. Slowly return to the starting position.

Benefit: Because you're on your side, you activate the rotator-cuff muscles on the back of your shoulder; these help maintain shoulder position during activities. The exercise also reduces the risk of tendinitis in your rotator cuff. And it limits shoulder impingement, a painful condition that occurs when the front of your shoulder blade exerts pressure on the muscles or tendons of your rotator cuff as you lift your arm.

A Rock-Solid Chest

Build a bigger, stronger upper body without lifting a weight.

Face it: The bench press is irreplaceable. No guy should completely eliminate the exercise from his workout. But the truth is, you can build lots of muscle in your chest and arms—and boost your bench—without lifting a barbell or dumbbell, or using a machine.

We're conditioned to think that using weights is the only way to develop a strong, muscular chest. But at the gym Juan Carlos Santana owns, the Institute of Human Performance in Boca Raton, Florida, they do the opposite of what you learned. They use no weights, no spotters, and no bench—which means you can do their entire program at home.

We're talking about pushups. You'll shred fat, boost strength, stimulate new growth, and carve eye-grabbing pecs by blasting through 60-rep pushup sets. The bench press is popular. But after this routine, you'll wonder why you ever tried anything different.

PUSH YOUR GROWTH

Follow these three steps to add layers of new muscle in just 8 weeks. The first step builds your endurance, the second increases strength, and the final step adds explosiveness and speed so you can pack on more size.

Before starting the program, you should be able to do 20 consecutive pushups. If you can't, then build your strength with this 3-week prep: Three days a week, do 3 sets of pushups, resting 3 minutes between sets. (A set is as many pushups as you can complete.)

The entire workout uses variations of the standard pushup. For each movement, assume a pushup position (with your body in a straight line from ankles to shoulders) and then lower your chest to the floor. Press your body back to the starting position by straightening your arms. To add difficulty, perform the exercise with your hands on a medicine ball.

1. WEEKS 1 AND 2

Perform these exercises 2 or 3 days a week in the order shown, with at least 1 day of rest between workouts. Complete 3 sets of each pushup type, resting 1 to 2 minutes between sets. Aim for sets of 10 to 15 reps; if you can't reach that goal, do as many reps as you can.

A
Wide Pushup
Do a standard pushup, but with your hands wider than shoulder-width apart.

B
Alternating Shuffle Pushup
Start in pushup position. Move your right hand to the left until your two hands are next to each other. Now slide your left hand farther left until your hands are shoulder-width apart again. Do a pushup and repeat the process, this time moving to the right and doing another pushup. That's 1 rep.

C
Diamond Pushup
Do a pushup with your hands close enough for the tips of your thumbs and index fingers to touch, forming a diamond shape.

2. WEEKS 3, 4, 5, AND 6

Perform these exercises 2 days a week. Complete 4 sets of each pushup type, resting 1 to 2 minutes between sets. Aim for 10 to 15 reps in each set. For these pushups, you'll need a 4- to 8-inch-high box or step.

A
One-Arm Pushup
Do a pushup with your right hand on the floor and your left hand on the box. Switch arms and repeat. That's 1 rep.

B
Crossover Box Pushup
Do a one-arm pushup with your left hand on the box. Then, from the starting position, lift your right hand and place it beside your left hand on top of the box. Then move your left hand down to the floor so your hands are shoulder-width apart again. Perform a pushup. That's 1 rep.

C
Hands-on-Box Diamond Pushup
Perform a diamond pushup, but with both hands on the box.

3. WEEKS 7 AND 8

Complete the exercises in step 2 as a circuit, performing one exercise after the other with no rest. Try to perform 10 reps of each exercise. Do this twice a week, and allow 3 or 4 days of rest.

The Best Ab Workout You've Never Done

Use this cutting-edge core routine to sculpt your six-pack.

If it weren't for dead guys, we'd probably never have started doing crunches. That's because for years, much of our knowledge of the way muscles work was based on the study of human cadavers.

By looking at the anatomy of corpses, modern scientists figured that the function of our abdominal muscles must be to flex the spine. Which is exactly what you do when you perform a crunch, a situp, or any other move that requires you to round your lower back. As a result, these exercises were popularized as the best way to work your abs.

But the reality is that your abs have a more critical function than flexing your spine: Their main job is to stabilize it. In fact, your midsection muscles are the reason your torso stays upright instead of falling forward due to gravity. So your abs actually prevent your spine from flexing.

The upshot is that if you want better results from your core workout, you need to train your abs for stability. And the best part? You'll hardly have to move.

Your Hard-Core Training Plan

Fair warning: This workout might not feel like your usual ab routine. Because the exercises focus on spinal stabilization instead of spinal flexion, they don't create the same type of abdominal-muscle soreness you might feel from traditional core moves. But that doesn't mean they're not working. Men using this program see faster progress than ever. So don't worry—this workout will make your core strong and stable, and it'll also make your abs pop. For the best results, do the workout that matches your training level—beginner, intermediate, or advanced—twice a week. Simply perform the exercises that follow in the order shown, using the prescribed sets, reps, and rest.

Three Abs Myths, Busted

If you listened to all the flawed abs advice out there, you'd be doing upside-down crunches until you passed out. Here's the absolute truth.

Myth #1

High-rep workouts make your abs grow.
Reality: Your progress will plateau if you do the same exercises, regardless of reps.

You need to intensify your workouts to teach your abs to stabilize your body weight. Add either more-challenging variations of body-weight exercises, or weighted abdominal exercises once the unweighted versions become too easy. Matt McGorry, C.F.T., a trainer at Peak Performance in New York City, recommends the triple plank. This combo—a front plank followed by a left-side plank and a right-side plank—forces you to contract your abs for long intervals, which helps carve your midsection. Start by maintaining each plank for 15 seconds, and work up to 60 seconds. When you hit that level, start adding sets, and rest only 30 seconds between them. If planks on the floor are too easy, put your feet on a small box.

But don't forget: "No amount of abs work can take the place of a well-planned diet and a total-body workout," McGorry says. Abs don't start showing when you build them; they show when you've built all the muscles in your body and cut the fat around your midsection.

Myth #2
Abs workouts involve a lot of movement.
Reality: Exercises that require steadiness are best.

When you bend your spine during crunches or situps, you risk injuring it, says Stuart McGill, Ph.D., a professor of spine biomechanics at the University of Waterloo, in Ontario. Doing those exercises isn't the best way to target your abs anyway, because you repeatedly bend the disks in your back and aren't forcing your abs to resist motion. That's why McGill suggests exercises that encourage spinal alignment and stability, such as planks. Your abs do all the work to keep you stabilized and lower your risk of back injury. (If you have back pain, see a physician before starting any abs regimen. Some abs exercises can make back problems worse.)

Exercises that prevent movement are especially good for building lateral abdomi-

nal strength, which is what helps your body stay in proper form under pressure (like when you play sports or do squats and deadlifts).

Dr. McGill suggests the suitcase carry: Hold a heavy dumbbell in one hand and then walk increasingly long distances while maintaining perfect posture. This burns more calories than crunches do.

Myth #3
Rotational exercises are best for building your obliques.
Reality: Rotational exercises don't build obliques well, and they can harm the spine in some cases.

Obliques surround and accentuate your abs and protect them from damage when you rotate your body quickly. So while exercises like the Russian twist can help build your obliques, they might not be the best way to build foundational strength, and they can force your spine to rotate under stress, says McGorry.

Instead, use heavy compound exercises—such as squats and deadlifts—to make your obliques work harder to keep your spine aligned. For more challenge, add unbalanced moves—the single-leg lunge, for example, or a deadlift with one dumbbell. These types of exercises require your body to adjust to uneven stress while your spine is in its neutral position, which further stabilizes your core and builds your obliques (as long as you maintain proper form).

Beginner Workout

1
Plank on Elbows

Assume a pushup position, but with your elbows bent and your weight resting on your forearms. Your body should form a straight line. Brace your abs as if someone were about to punch you in the gut. Hold for 30 seconds. Rest 30 seconds; repeat once.

2
Mountain Climber with Hands on Bench

In pushup position with your hands on a bench, brace your abs and slowly lift your left knee toward your chest. Pause 2 seconds, lower it slowly, and then raise your right knee. Alternate for 30 seconds, rest 30, and repeat once.

3
Side Plank

Lie on your left side and prop your upper body up on your left forearm. Raise your hips until your body forms a straight line from ankles to shoulders. Now brace your abs and hold for 30 seconds. Roll over onto your right side and repeat. Rest 30 seconds, and do 1 more set.

Intermediate Workout

1
Plank with Feet Elevated

Use the guidelines for the beginner version of the exercise (left), but with both of your feet on a bench.

2
Mountain Climber with Hands on Swiss Ball

Follow the beginner instructions, but place your hands on a Swiss ball instead of a bench.

3
Side Plank with Feet Elevated

Do this the same way as the beginner version, but with both of your feet on a bench.

Advanced Workout

1
Extended Plank

Do the beginner version, but place your weight on your hands, which should be positioned about 6 to 8 inches in front of your shoulders.

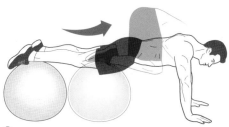

2
Swiss-Ball Jackknife

In pushup position with your feet on a Swiss ball, raise your hips and pull the ball forward. Do 2 sets of 15 reps, with 30 seconds of rest.

3
Single-Leg Side Plank

Do the beginner version, but once you're in position, raise your top leg and keep it raised for the duration of the set.

The Bun Blaster

Too much junk in the trunk?
Here's how to make your gluteus more maximus.

If building a better body were all about the bench press and biceps curls, every man would look like Adrian Peterson. But your body is more than just a collection of individual muscles; it's a single muscular system. So if one muscle is ignored—or worse, shuts down—the rest won't work as well.

When Bill Hartman, P.T., C.S.C.S., evaluates clients at his gym, Indianapolis Fitness and Sports Training, he finds one key area of weakness over and over again: their glutes, or butt muscles.

It's no secret that men typically train only the muscles they can see in the mirror. This one-sided approach is bad for your body and even worse for your glutes, because long hours spent sitting can cause your glutes to "forget" how to fire.

Consider this: Your glutes are perhaps the most powerful collection of muscles in your body. Which means weak glutes negatively impact your entire muscular system.

Use this plan to activate your glutes and maximize your body's potential. You'll increase lower-body strength, decrease your injury risk, and burn more fat.

The Program

Follow these three phases to improve your hip and glute functioning. Some exercises might seem too easy at first, but doing them is essential to properly activating muscles that have been ignored. As you make progress, you'll perform more challenging moves and ultimately improve the various functions of your glutes. Spend 2 to 4 weeks on each phase before increasing the difficulty.

Phase 1

1
Hip Raise

Lie on your back with your knees bent and your feet flat. Lift your hips until they're straight. Hold for 5 seconds, and return to the starting position. Perform 2 or 3 sets of 10 to 12 reps, resting for 30 to 60 seconds between sets.

2
Clamshell

Lie on your side with your knees bent 90 degrees and your heels together and in line with your butt. Open your knees as far as you can, without rotating your pelvis or back. Pause; return to the starting position. Do 2 or 3 sets of 10 to 12 reps, resting for 30 to 60 seconds between sets.

3
Bird Dog

Get down on your hands and knees. With your back straight, fully extend one leg behind you until you feel your glutes tighten; avoid any lower-back movement. Hold the position for 5 seconds and return to the starting position. Do 2 or 3 sets of 10 to 12 reps on each side, resting for 30 to 60 seconds between sets.

Phase 2

1
Hip Raise with Feet on Bench

Lie on your back with your feet on a bench and your legs straight. Then do a hip raise, as in phase 1. Hold for 5 seconds, and return to the starting position. Do 2 or 3 sets of 10 to 12 reps, resting for 30 to 60 seconds between sets.

2
Lateral Walk

Place an exercise band around your thighs. Step to the side, toes pointing slightly outward. Sidestep to the left 20 feet, and then repeat to the right. That's 1 round. Do 1 or 2 sets of 3 rounds, resting 60 to 90 seconds between sets.

3
Cable Pull-Through

Face away from a cable machine, holding a low cable handle between your legs. Bend and reach back between your legs, with your knees bent and back straight. Now stand up, keep your glutes tight, and pause. Do 2 or 3 sets of 12 to 15 reps, resting 60 to 90 seconds between sets.

Phase 3

1
Hip Raise with Feet on Swiss Ball

Perform this exercise just like the first exercise in phase 2, but with your feet on a Swiss ball. Do 2 or 3 sets of 10 to 12 reps, resting for 60 to 90 seconds between sets.

2
Single-Leg Squat-to-Bench

Stand on your right foot and extend your left leg. Lower yourself to a bench by bending your hips and right knee. Stand up without your left foot touching the ground. Do 8 to 10 reps and switch legs. That's 1 set. Do 2 or 3 sets, resting for 60 to 90 seconds between sets.

3
Stepup

Step up with your right leg onto a bench that's 6 inches in front of you. Raise your left knee to hip level without your foot touching the bench. Return your left foot to the floor. Complete 10 to 12 reps on one side, and then repeat on the other side. That's 1 set. Do 2 or 3, resting for 60 to 90 seconds in between.

Small Muscles, Big Results

These hard-to-pronounce muscles get little publicity, but they pack plenty of power.

Where would we be without our supporting cast? Peyton Manning wouldn't have time to throw, captains would be swabbing their own decks, and the Dunder Mifflin paper company's brainstorming meetings wouldn't be considered entertainment.

Success typically depends on behind-the-scenes help, and your body is no different. While your abs and biceps receive all the glory, here's a secret: It's the little-known muscles that make the big ones stand out.

The problem is, working the muscles you can't see—such as the ones deep inside your core, hips, and shoulders—can be a difficult process. But target those areas, and your whole body benefits. You will look better, and you'll also have more strength and suffer fewer injuries.

These five muscles may never earn top billing, but they may rejuvenate your workouts and ignite new growth.

Serratus Anterior

Know it: This muscle, located on the side of your chest along your ribs, attaches to and allows you to rotate your shoulder blade (a.k.a. scapula). It plays a vital role when you raise your shoulder to flex your arm and move it away from your body; that's why it's prominent in boxers but not your average guy. The reason? Blame the bench press. Because of the support provided by the bench, the serratus anterior doesn't receive much direct challenge during this popular exercise, says Mike Robertson, C.S.C.S., a strength coach in Indianapolis.

Test it: Do a pushup without wearing a shirt and have someone look at your back during the move. If you have a winged scapula, your shoulder blade will stick out; this means your serratus is weak, says Robertson. A strong one suctions your scapula in during the movement, eliminating the winged look.

Improve it: Standard pushups strengthen the muscle, but doing pushup variations is the quickest way to correct a weakness, says Robertson. Use a power rack to perform incline pushups on a barbell (see exercise **1**, page 170). Start with your body at the lowest incline that doesn't allow your shoulders to wing, placing the bar relatively high. Perform 3 sets of 8 to 12 repetitions. As you become stronger and learn to control your scapular motion, work your way down the rack until you're doing regular pushups with perfect body alignment.

Piriformis

Know it: This muscle near your gluteal (butt) region helps with thigh rotation and tends to suffer from overuse. Why? Because weak hamstrings and glutes force the piriformis to take on some of the work those big muscles should be doing, says Keith Scott, C.S.C.S., a strength coach based in New Jersey. This creates back and hip pain, and weaker lower-body performance.

Test it: Sit on a chair and cross one leg over the other, with the crossing ankle of one leg resting on the bent knee of the other. If you can't get your top leg parallel to the ground, your piriformis is probably tight.

Improve it: Increase your mobility with windshield wipers: Lie on your back with your knees bent and your feet placed wider than shoulder-width apart on the ground (see exercise **2**, page 170). Press your knees together, and then return to the starting position. Do 2 sets of 10 to 15 repetitions.

Now add some soft-tissue work: Sit on a foam roller with your weight shifted to your right butt, and place your right ankle on your left knee. Roll your right glutes from top to bottom, working any painful areas. Continue for 45 to 60 seconds, and switch sides. Do this daily.

Psoas

Know it: The psoas (so-az) muscle runs through your hips to connect the lower portion of your back to the top of your thigh. It's one of your body's main back stabilizers and hip flexors (the muscles that line your hips and allow you to bring your knees toward your chest). If you sit all day,

By strengthening your stabilizing muscles, you'll improve your bench press.

the psoas becomes rounded like a banana. Then, when you stand up, the psoas pulls on your back, making you more prone to pain and lower-back injury.

"A weak psoas also means you'll end up with assorted knee issues, because other secondary hip flexors take over and cause pain," Robertson says.

Test it: Lie on your back and pull one knee to your chest. Keep your other leg straight. If the psoas is of normal length, your straight leg will rest on the floor. If your leg sits above the floor, your psoas is either stiff or shortened, says Bill Hartman.

Improve it: The only way to strengthen a weak psoas is by bringing your knee above 90 degrees. Sit with your knees bent on a low box or bench (6 to 10 inches high) (see exercise **3**, page 171). Maintaining good posture and keeping your abs tight, use your hips to raise one bent knee slightly higher than your hips. If you lean forward or backward, you're not performing the

exercise correctly. Hold for 5 seconds, and return to the starting position. Complete 3 sets of 5 repetitions per leg.

Also, to help release some of the pressure you might feel, use your thumb to press on your hip flexor; it'll be on your side and a little lower than your belly button.

Tensor Fasciae Latae

Know it: This muscle (also known as the TFL) starts along the outer edge of your hip and can affect lateral movement (abduction), which is movement away from your body. A tight TFL can mean you're at increased risk for lateral knee pain, because it attaches directly to your iliotibial band—tissue that runs vertically along the outsides of your thighs to help stabilize your knees. Weak or tight abductors means you're constantly getting beat off the dribble, or you're late getting to the ball on the tennis court.

Test it: Try old-fashioned leg lifts. Lie on your side with your legs straight, and raise your top leg to about a 40-degree angle. Then lower it. You should be able to lift your leg in a straight line, without your hip or thigh moving forward, says Jeff Plass-chaert, C.S.C.S., a strength coach based in Gainesville, Florida. Make sure you're using hip strength, though. Many people substitute motion from their core and lower back to finish the movement.

Improve it: Stretching the TFL is the secret to improving your performance, says Robertson. To stretch your left TFL, stand with your left hip adjacent to a wall (see exercise **4**). Cross your right foot in front of your left foot. From this position, contract your core and left glute, and then push directly into your left hip. Don't let your hips move backward, and instead make sure your left hip pushes to the side. Hold for 20 to 30 seconds, and then switch legs

Five Functional Fixes

1
Gradually decrease the incline to normal pushup position.

2
Add more juice to your legs with a little squeeze.

so your other side faces the wall. Perform 2 or 3 reps on each leg every day.

Supraspinatus and Subscapularis

Know it: The supraspinatus is one of the small muscles at the top of your shoulder that makes up the rotator cuff; the subscapularis is a large muscle on the front of your shoulder blade. Blame your desk job for weak shoulders: If your upper body is rounded, it's most likely because your chest is tight, which means the opposing muscles in your shoulders are weak. Strengthen the stabilizing muscles, and you'll see improvement on your bench press and in overhead sports like swimming or tennis, as well as in your overall upper-body power.

Test them: Bring your arms straight out in front of you at about a 45-degree angle, your thumbs pointed up—like you're about to hug someone. Have a friend stand in front of you and push your arms downward with moderate pressure. (The friend's hands should be positioned above your wrists on your forearms.) If you feel soreness in your shoulders or can't resist the pressure, you probably need to strengthen your supraspinatus, Plasschaert says.

Improve them: "A lot of people think they need to work the rotator muscles like crazy," says Scott. But a simple move is all you need. Stand holding a light pair of dumbbells in front of your thighs, palms facing each other (see exercise **5**). Keeping your thumbs pointed up, raise your arms up at a 30-degree angle to your torso until just above shoulder height. Hold for 1 second, and lower to the starting position. Do 2 sets of 8 to 10 repetitions. The exercise will help you add pounds to your bench by improving the stability of your shoulders. ∎

3
Don't use your upper body for momentum.

4
For best results, press hard through your hip.

5
Keep your arms straight for the entire move.

The Best New Fitness Gear

Overhaul your physique with this power-boosting, fat-blasting equipment.

Wall Street shouldn't rule your workout, but marketing fitness products is a big business— $5 billion in 2007—so the industry is full of gear meant to deliver fiscal dividends first and physical results second, says Fabio Comana, C.S.C.S., an educational curriculum developer for the American Council on Exercise.

"There are a ton of bad fad products out there that are either ineffective, unnecessary, or dangerous," he says. His fail-safe rule for filtering out the duds? Seek out simplicity.

"Recent research into how the body's muscles and joints move has given us a better idea of what type of equipment is actually effective," says Comana. Read on for our favorite low-tech, high-intensity power tools.

Best Home Gym

FreeMotion EXT Dual Cable Cross

Most home gym machines lock your limbs into one range of motion, limiting potential strength gains. The arms on this machine swivel like shipyard cranes into 108 different positions, recruiting stabilizer muscles and increasing the time muscles stay under tension.

The net benefit is a superior workout, according to a 2008 study published in the *Journal of Strength and Conditioning Research*. Scientists found that compared with users of fixed-form equipment, men who work out on free-form machines saw a 58 percent greater improvement in strength and a 196 percent greater improvement in balance, and they felt 30 percent less pain.

KNEELING CABLE PULLDOWN: Resistance and rotation challenge your core.

"The repetitive motions on fixed-form equipment probably cause muscular imbalances that lead to structural changes and the increase of skeletal-frame stress," says study author Keith Spennewyn, M.S., president of the National Institute of Health Science. "Free-form exercise reduces these factors by training muscles and joints together, the same way they function out in the real world."

The FreeMotion machine isn't cheap, but free delivery and in-home setup sweeten the deal. ($4,000, freemotionfitness.com)

Best Lo-fi Fitness Tool

Iron Woody Woody Bag

The rugged PVC shell of this amped-up sandbag allows you to perform dynamic moves, such as snatches, jerks, and throws, without creating a dust storm in the process.

"We have about 400 athletes a week using them," says Tracy Sibley, director of strength and conditioning at Gardner-Webb University in Boiling Springs, North Carolina. "Even with all that punishment, the bags are nearly indestructible." ($60 to $120, ironwoodyfitness.com)

POWER CLEAN:
This exercise builds total body strength and muscle.

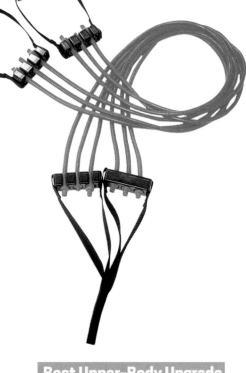

Best Upper-Body Upgrade

JC Predator Band

Elastic resistance bands create constant tension that dumbbells can't match, recruiting more muscle fibers during a movement. The problem is, most bands are more brittle than Eli Manning's ego.

"The Predator Band is one of the only sets that uses dipped rubber tubing comprising several layers, as opposed to the cheaper and weaker extruded rubber made of a single layer," says Grif Fig, C.S.C.S., a coach with the Institute of Human Performance in Boca Raton, Florida.

Tougher guts means these bands can handle more explosive repetitions and be attached to rougher surfaces, such as park benches. We also like the 4-foot, tri-tube design, which makes it easy to switch resistance between sets: Simply snap bands in or out to adjust the difficulty level. ($50, ihpfit.com)

For detailed workouts tailored to each piece of equipment, go to MensHealth.com.

Best Total-Body Tool

Fitness Anywhere TRX Suspension Trainer Force Kit
Designed by a Navy SEAL as a go-anywhere workout, this set of nylon straps creates resistance from two sources always at your disposal: body weight and gravity. Lock the straps onto any elevated fixture—a pullup bar, door, or tree branch—and you'll unlock new dimensions in your training.

"Traditional isolation exercises, such as the biceps curl and side lunge, primarily occur in only one of the three planes of motion," says Todd Durkin, C.S.C.S., owner of Fitness Quest 10 in San Diego. "But with multiplanar training on the TRX, we're able to strengthen muscles and joints as a group, ironing out any muscular imbalances. That makes the moves more effective, realistic, and challenging." ($210, fitnessanywhere.com)

Resistance can be adjusted from 5 percent to 100 percent of body weight by changing the incline of your body.

The fail-safe rule for filtering out the duds: Seek out simplicity.

PLANK SLIDEOUT: The reach forces the abs to step up and support the body weight.

Best Stability Trainer

Valslides

These foam-topped plastic sliders transform hard floors and carpets into ice rinks, intensifying old standbys like pushups, lunges, and squats.

"We can replicate the glute, hamstring, and core-focused exercises that can be done on a 10-foot slideboard in a fraction of the space," says Mike Boyle, C.S.C.S., cofounder of Mike Boyle Strength and Conditioning in Winchester, Massachusetts. "The collegiate and pro athletes we train are always shocked with the workout intensity that can be achieved with two pieces of plastic."

Simple, portable, and versatile, they're ideal travel training tools, turning hotel floors into proving grounds. ($30, valslide.com)

Power Perks

Boost gains with these muscle accessories.

NIKE FREE 5.0

Wearing this flat-soled shoe replicates training barefoot, which engages more muscles during lower-body lifts, such as squats and deadlifts, says Tony Gentilcore, C.S.C.S. ($85, nike.com)

POWERBLOCK U-90

The most compact dumbbell we found, this adjustable short stack's weight is concentrated toward the center for easier control. A urethane coating also makes this the toughest adjustable set we've ever hoisted. ($800, powerblock.com)

POLAR FT80

Rushed rest periods between sets decrease the number of subsequent repetitions you can perform, so this heart-rate monitor chimes in when your body is primed for the next round. ($350, polarusa.com)

Best New Cardio Tool

Art of Strength Ropes Gone Wild

Jump ropes are for playgrounds, right? Not if you're hurling around these python-size cables, which had us sucking wind after a 15-minute session. Instead of hopping over the ropes, though, you guide them through undulating and rotating motions, recruiting your core and taxing your heart and lungs while sparing lower-body joints from treadmill torture.

"Some players love it because it's so challenging, and others hate it for the same reason," says Jason Novak, C.S.C.S., an assistant strength and conditioning coach for the NFL's Tennessee Titans. "But when any of them want a conditioning boost and need to keep their legs fresh, the first thing they go for is one of these ropes."

Be forewarned, however: These 30- to 100-foot manila monsters require plenty of room and a sturdy anchor point. ($85 to $350, artofstrength.com)

DOUBLE WAVE
Muscle perk: Big waves require all-body stabilization.

PROVE IT.

KEEP AN EYE ON THE FINISH LINE

Your heart and lungs aren't the only body parts that benefit from cardio. **Vigorous exercise might prevent vision loss,** two new studies indicate. A 7-year study of nearly 41,000 runners found that men who run regularly have a lower risk of developing cataracts. And in a separate study, 110 men who ran more than 2½ miles a day cut their risk of age-related macular degeneration by as much as 54 percent.

Study author Paul T. Williams, Ph.D., of the Lawrence Berkeley National Laboratory in California, says the next step is to determine how running preserves eyesight. In any case, keep going: Studies have already shown that vigorous exercise lowers blood pressure and cholesterol.

BEAT STRESS AND FAT

Here's a two-for-one deal that's perfect for this troubled economy: **Spend a little time in**

HARD TRUTH

91

Percentage of adults who haven't lifted weights in the past month, according to the *Journal of Physical Activity and Health*

the gym, and you can make your flab and your recession stress disappear. Researchers from Stony Brook University school of medicine found that people with the lowest body-fat percentages remained the most calm and collected when they were dropped into stressful situations.

Study author Lilianne Mujica-Parodi, Ph.D., explains that people with high body fat produce more of the hormone cortisol in reaction to a stressor. The problem is, excess cortisol overexcites your brain, preventing you from calming down and thinking rationally. To send stress packing, choose weights instead of the treadmill; **pumping iron is more effective than cardio at blasting fat.**

STOP YOUR MUSCLES FROM SHRINKING

Injured? A broken arm doesn't have to be a withered arm. Creatine can stop your muscles from shrinking even while you're wearing a cast, according to researchers from St. Francis Xavier University.

"Creatine appears to help muscle-building hormones, even if you're not active," says Darren Candow, Ph.D. Consume 5 grams a day to help save your size while your injury is healing.

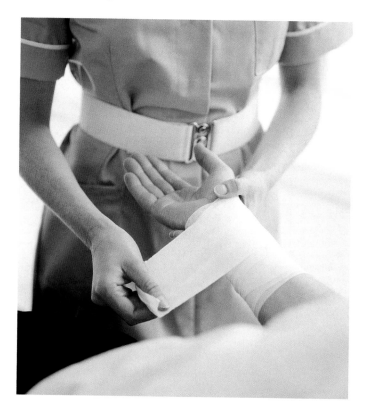

DON'T GET IN A RUT

For the fastest results, **change the number of reps you perform every time you hit the gym.** In a Brazilian study, people who alternated upper- and lower-body training days gained more strength when they rotated among 4, 10, and 15 repetitions each workout. They outperformed those who did the same number of reps every session or even shifted rep counts weekly. That's because **changing the load recruits different muscle fibers, which lets you train your muscles completely,** the researchers say. Best of all? The approach works for both beginners and experienced lifters, making it the perfect way for anyone to bust out of a plateau.

MIX IT UP

A little variety can make a big difference in your workout results. "Life and sports occur in three planes of motion, and working your muscles from multiple directions can help prevent joint problems and muscular imbalances," says Craig Rasmussen, C.S.C.S. Use this guide to increase your strength and limit pain in your shoulders and hips. The best part: **These multimuscle exercises can also boost your metabolism.**

Transverse plane
Motion that's rotational. This plane divides the body into upper and lower halves.
Try these: Single-arm cable row with rotation, cable chop, crossover stepup

SHAKE IT

What you eat before you go to the gym might make a big difference in transforming your body. **Drinking a protein shake before and during weight training may speed fat loss,** say researchers at Syracuse University. They found that people who drank a combination of amino acids and carbohydrates had higher metabolic rates the next day compared with when they ate just carbs.

Sagittal plane
Motion that's primarily forward or backward. This plane divides the body into left and right halves.
Try these: Forward lunge, chinup, close-grip bench press

Frontal plane
Motion that's primarily side-to-side. This plane divides the body into front and back halves.
Try these: Side lunge, dumbbell overhead press, pullup

DODGE DIABETES

Short bursts of exercise can reduce your risk of diabetes, say Scottish researchers. In their study, men sprinted on a stationary bike for 30 seconds, rested for 4 minutes, and then repeated the routine three to five more times. **After six workouts, the men's insulin sensitivity improved by 23 percent.**

"High-intensity sprints prime your muscle fibers to respond better to insulin," says study author James Timmons, Ph.D. If you're not tiring toward the end of each sprint, you're bicycling with too little resistance.

CHEW ON THIS

Clenching your teeth during your workouts could boost your performance. Marquette University scientists found that **athletes who bit down on mouth guards as they jumped were able to leap higher.** The result might be due to what the researchers call motor overflow.

"Signals in the area of your brain that activates your jaw muscles may spill over to the part of your brain that affects activation of other muscles, such as the ones in your legs," says study author William Ebben, Ph.D.

BOOST YOUR BENCH

If your strength has plateaued, you can bust your slump without lifting a weight. Arizona State University researchers found that **doing only the lowering portion of a bench press leads to greater gains than performing a complete rep.**

The key: You must have two experienced spotters, says study author Kyle Carothers, C.S.C.S. Choose the heaviest weight you can lift once, and then have your spotters—one at each end of the barbell—help you lift the bar off the rack. Lower the weight to a count of three. Then have the spotters raise the bar back to the start. That's 1 rep. Do 4 sets of 8 reps, resting 3 to 5 minutes between sets. Be sure to reduce the total volume of your workout, because you'll experience increased soreness.

CHILL OUT

Scientists have determined that **the best ice pack is a mixture of ice and water.** When applied to calf muscles for 20 minutes, this combo works better than ice cubes or crushed ice, according to a report in the *Journal of Athletic Training*. The icy water conforms well to the muscle, but the real key is that it conducts thermal energy best. Try doubled zip-top bags; they're reusable.

MOVE LESS, GROW MORE?

Sometimes it's better to cut your workout short. Restricting your range of motion can boost your strength, say Australian researchers. They determined that **performing partial reps—such as lowering the bar only halfway on the bench press—allows you to increase the weight you can use.**

The shorter range helps strengthen your "sticking region," the point where you struggle to move the weight, says Ross Clark, Ph.D. The caveat: Full range of motion is still best, so use partial reps as a short-term approach on one exercise for 4 weeks at a time.

YOU ASKED.

Will lifting heavy weights put too much strain on my heart?

A: Depends what's written in your medical records and on the weight plates. Every time you strain to hoist a heavy weight, you instinctively hold your breath, causing the muscles around your spine to contract and give your back greater support.

Problem is, this same exertion creates a spike in blood pressure. For most men, the temporary BP boost isn't dangerous. But if you're older than 45, overweight, a smoker, or have high cholesterol, hypertension, or a family history of cardiovascular disease, there could be trouble. A single bout of heavy lifting—greater than 85 percent of your 1-rep max—on compound exercises, such as the squat, leg press, bench, or deadlift, can lead to an increased risk of heart attack or stroke in men who are already at risk, says Mark Peterson, Ph.D., an exercise physiologist at the University of Michigan. "If you're at all concerned, discuss your heart health and lifting regimen with your physician."

But even if your doc tells you to avoid hefting herculean weights, you shouldn't stop strength training altogether, says Peterson. Numerous studies show that regular lifting sessions (at least 3 days a week) at moderate levels (70 percent to 75 percent of your 1-rep max) can boost your heart health and lower your blood pressure.

Q: I've heard I should eat before I hit the gym, but doing that makes me sick to my stomach when I start lifting. What's going on?

A: "If you feel like you're about to throw up, it's because you are," says nutritionist Alan Aragon, M.S., the Men's Health Weight-Loss Coach.

Here's why: When you begin lifting, bloodflow to the muscles you're working increases, while bloodflow to your GI tract decreases. The change in circulation can trigger reflux. If this happens while you have undigested food in your gut, there's nowhere for it to go except back up your esophagus.

The simplest solution, Aragon says, is to slug a shake: Liquid food can be digested much more quickly. For those times when you want a real meal, make sure you eat 90 minutes to 2 hours before your workout so your stomach has time to break down the food.

"Whatever you do, don't head to the gym hungry," says Aragon. Consuming a combination of protein and carbohydrates—20 to 40 grams of each—before lifting increases energy, helps build muscle, and prevents the breakdown of muscle protein.

Q: For winter, what's a solid indoor cardio activity?

A: Jumping rope, says Mike Mejia, M.S., C.S.C.S., author of *The Men's Health Gym Bible*. It burns calories and improves your stamina, agility, coordination, and balance, all of which help you hit the weights harder and longer.

Try skip pyramids, a challenge that melts away your winter weight. Start with 50 jumps, and don't worry about tracking time. Rest for 30 seconds, and continue the pyramid by adding 25 jumps with each successive set—so you'll do 75, 100, 125, and so on. Rest 30 seconds after you reach each goal.

When you hit 200, reverse the process by decreasing 25 jumps in each set until you're back at 50 jumps. If you step on the rope, just pick up where you left off. And don't bother buying a weighted rope; it won't add bulk. Jumping rope builds muscular endurance, not muscle.

Q: Dumbbell press vs. barbell press— which is better?

A: "The dumbbell bench press is an excellent stimulus for muscle growth while providing a greater range of motion and placing less stress on your shoulders," says David Pearson, Ph.D., C.S.C.S., a professor of exercise physiology at Ball State University and a senior editor for the *Strength and Conditioning Journal* of the National Strength and Conditioning Association. "Men who benefit the most from the barbell press are guys who compete in powerlifting and need to lift maximum weights."

Q: What percentage of body fat is needed to see definition in the ab region?

A: "It varies," says Alexander Koch, Ph.D., C.S.C.S., an associate professor of exercise science at Truman State University. "A six-pack usually won't emerge until total body fat dips below 10 percent, as measured by skin-fold testing or underwater weighing."

Q: Should I do my cardio before I lift weights or after?

A: If you're using the same muscles for weight training and cardio (say, a day of lower-body lifting and jogging), weight training should come first. Weights preserve muscle when you're dieting; cardio does not. But if you're training, say, your arms and jogging, the order doesn't matter much. Start with whichever motivates you.

Q: I've been trying to bulk up for 6 months. Now my back hurts. Is this normal?

A: "No. Adding muscle shouldn't cause back pain," Koch says. " You've probably strained something or developed a muscle imbalance. See your doctor."

Q: I always gorge after a workout. Bad habit?

A: Postworkout is the best time to have the largest meal of your day—as long as it's a reasonable size and not a full-on gorge, says Aragon. That's because you've just reduced your body's fuel reserves, and food can help aid your recovery. Also, when your body is in this state, incoming calories and nutrients stand a better chance of being taken up by muscle tissue instead of being stored in fat tissue.

If your goal is to curb uncontrollable hunger, make sure you're filling up on beef, poultry, or fish. Solid foods are more filling than liquid foods, and protein is the most filling of all the macronutrients. Pair some of that meat with whole-food, high-fiber carbohydrate sources, such as beans, because fiber can also help you feel fuller faster.

Q: Every time I do shrugs, I strain my neck. Help!

A: "Drop the weight—and your ego," says Mejia. "Most men shrug a lot of weight, thinking it makes them look stronger, but their neck muscles may not be prepared for the heavy load. Reduce the weight by 50 to 60 percent of what you're currently lifting and see if your pain goes away. And keep a close eye on your form. Perform the exercise slowly, and don't roll your shoulders. Your traps are designed to pull your shoulders up and down.

"Prepare for heavier shrugs by doing neck extensions, which can strengthen your weak link. Lie facedown on a bench with your entire head off the bench. Hold a light (5- to 10-pound) plate behind your head, elbows flared out to your sides, and then slowly move your head up and down. Perform 2 sets of 12 to 15 reps once a week at the end of your upper-back workout."

Q: My forearms hurt during biceps curls. How can I stop the pain while still working on my arms?

A: When men curl too much weight (and most men do), they end up flexing their wrists to assist with the movement, says Alwyn Cosgrove, C.S.C.S., the owner of Results Fitness in Santa Clarita, California. This, in turn, places tremendous stress on your forearms, causing the muscles to contract under loads that are way too heavy.

"It creates discomfort and severely limits your performance," he says.

The prescription? Don't do any more curls until you can perform at least five pullups. These will strengthen your biceps muscles by forcing them to handle heavier loads than you can curl. And while you're pumping your biceps by doing pullups, you can still do hammer curls. This variation of the standard dumbbell curl takes the stress off your wrists because your palms face each other. Hammer curls strengthen the brachioradialis, which is often the weakest muscle in your arm. Keep in mind, however, that hammer curls target less arm muscle overall, so after you've built up your forearms, continue with traditional barbell or dumbbell curls.

Q: My dominant arm is stronger than my other arm. What's the best way to balance them out?

A: Your body is hardwired to balance muscle power quickly and efficiently, so the fix is relatively simple.

First step: Drop the barbell, says Cosgrove. "When you use a barbell, your 'good' arm always moves more of the weight." Perform dumbbell exercises instead—curls, rows, shoulder presses, and bench presses—one arm at a time. Choose a weight that you're able to lift eight times with your weaker arm, and do as many repetitions as you can. Then, using the same weight, duplicate the reps with your dominant arm, even if you know you can lift more.

Not only will you be putting more strain on the side that needs it, but you'll also trigger a physiological phenomenon that makes exercising your stronger arm actually build muscle in the weak arm. Yep, believe it. When you work your arms separately, you allow your body's natural muscle-balancing system to kick in and reapportion nerve stimulation where it's required. Once your dumbbell reps are equally challenging for both sides, add barbells back in. It may seem like you'll risk reproducing the original imbalance all over again, but Cosgrove says that as long as you don't completely ignore dumbbell training, your strength should stay symmetrical.

Q: **I can lift a lot on the leg press but very little on the squat. What's wrong?**

A: Most guys excel on the leg press because it's a guided movement, says Mejia. The squat is different; it challenges your legs, but it requires balance and coordination and involves strong upper-body muscles. Your core strength influences how much weight you can carry, because when you squat with a heavy weight on your back, your core muscles must keep your spine stable and protected.

Strengthen your core and add weight to your squats by performing exercises such as Romanian deadlifts, planks, or woodchoppers. After about a month of consistent training (3 days a week), go back to the squat. You'll be amazed at your improvement.

4

Look Better Instantly

Dress It Up

Look commanding by following Barack Obama's model: traditional, clean, and impressive.

Here's How the President Does It

—And how you can look presidential, too.

LOOK MODEST, AND STILL STAND OUT

In sober times, there's one smart way to look: "He's modern, but without appearing too fashion-forward," says Clinton Kelly, cohost of TLC's *What Not to Wear*. Whether you're at your job or in the White House, you want to show confidence but not cockiness.

FIT YOUR KNOT

The wider the opening between collar points on a dress shirt, the larger the tie knot between them should be. Obama's Windsor knot fills out that space, and his tie's clean dimple shows attention to detail.

START AT THE TOP

When you buy a suit jacket, make sure the shoulder pads sit securely on your shoulders. If they dip or droop, the jacket is too big. That will affect the chest and waist of the jacket, which should outline your frame without hugging it.

BUTTON IT RIGHT

A two-button jacket, like the one shown here, creates a V shape that elongates the torso; a three-button can make you look stocky.

EXTEND THE SLEEVES

Shirt sleeves should protrude half an inch past the jacket sleeves.

"That touch of white at the wrist pulls a look together," Kelly says. It can be hard to find shirts that work perfectly with your jacket, so reverse engineer it: Bring your own dress shirt to the tailor so he can make sure they work together.

SHOW SOME COLOR

A black suit should be accented with something bright, such as a red tie like Obama's. Color shows optimism, says political consultant Brian Kirwin— something you always want to embody, regardless of your job.

THE SUIT FITS THE MAN

Buy for your body type: American-made suits are typically cut bigger and boxier than their European counterparts. Find an affordable suit, and then spend some of your savings on a trip to a tailor—as Obama clearly does. It matters.

"If you don't have fit, you don't have style. End of story," Kelly says.

> "If you don't have fit, you don't have style. End of story."

PRIZE ON THE EYES

The enduring popularity of aviator sunglasses makes them prime targets for counterfeiting (and hipster abuse). But there's a reason pilots wear only the real thing: When you spend half your day flying directly into the sun, you can't afford substandard glare protection or flimsy design.

"A poorly made pair is at best uncomfortable and at worst dangerous," says optician Deb Lochli of the Vision Council. Examine the finer points of these well-heeled aviators—made civilian-friendly by swapping mirrored lenses for a graduated tint—and ground the $10 impostors for good.

Five Keys to Great Glasses

1 UV PROTECTION

Shady manufacturers can legally claim their wares "block most UV rays" or "absorb UV rays," but that means nothing. **The amount of protection from damaging UVA and UVB rays** is what really matters. Before your eyes fry, use them to look for labels that claim "99 (or 100) percent UV protection," "UV 400," or "meets ANSI UV requirements."

2 LENS MATERIAL

To check the optical quality of glasses, Lochli says, cover one eye and hold the pair at arm's length while looking at a straight edge, such as a doorjamb or tile floor. Slowly move the lens in all directions; the line shouldn't bend or ripple, especially near the edge of the lens. A good lens will also be securely attached to the frame.

3 TINTS AND COATINGS

The gradient tints on the sunglasses shown here make you look like you're perpetually staring down a sunset, but they provide a functional edge, too. The darker tint toward the top blocks incoming light from above, while the lighter tint at the bottom affords clarity for driving or reading.

4 TEMPLES

A pair of aviators is only as solid as its temples. Titanium, carbon, and magnesium frames withstand abuse best. Some pairs also have plastic or rubber sleeves on the temples' ends for increased comfort and security. Sensitive skin? Look for a nickel-free finish, which is hypoallergenic.

5 HINGES

Do they spring open, snap closed, and flex when gently bent outward? Those are signs of quality you want. Whether you're in a jet or a Jetta, the hinges should help the glasses grip your head while playing nice with your ears.

The DNA of Jeans

Jeans are the workhorses of our wardrobes—
the fabric of America. Here's how to flaunt your jeans.

A well-fitting pair of jeans can play up your assets. They're the ultimate clothes staple—the item around which many outfits are based. Yet few men give them more than a few seconds thought. It's time to give these hardworking winners their due.

WEAR JEANS TO WORK WELL

Don't compromise your reputation. Casual Fridays can be tricky.

A COTTON BUTTON-DOWN SHIRT IS A NATURAL FIT WITH JEANS.

A DARK WASH WITH A MEDIUM-TO-SLIM FIT IS JUST THE TICKET.

A WELL-FITTED JACKET TOPS OFF THE LOOK.

"If you don't dress properly, your credibility will be undermined, even on casual days," says Ron Herzog, CEO of Fortune Personnel Consultants, an executive search firm in New York City. "Your boss may not admonish you, but he'll make a mental note that may cost you a promotion."

Here's how to keep your style and professional image intact.

Don't confuse casual workdays with Saturday night. "You want to look just as put together and professional as if you were wearing a suit," says Eric Jennings, fashion director for menswear at Saks Fifth Avenue. So avoid holes, frays, and distressing.

Don't wear jeans that are too loose or too tight. Baggy may be comfortable, but it's also sloppy, while tight jeans scream high school. Your work jeans should match your maturity and fit as well as your trousers do, says Herzog.

Don't confuse your jeans with formal wear. "Some men look like they put on a suit and tie to go to work, and then just took off the suit pants and replaced them

ACCESSORIZE YOUR DENIM SIMPLY AND ELEGANTLY

New York–based designer John Varvatos earns high marks for his sharp tailoring and vintage-inspired jeans, but he's also an expert at adding the right accessories to casual looks.

"Jeans are the most authentic American product out there, so whatever you add to them should be authentic as well," Varvatos says. Here's how to pair the right finishing touches with denim.

Look natural. Aim for a natural-looking finish on your accessories, with subtle distressing that will age better over time. The more you wear a great brown leather belt, the more it takes on its own personality. The same goes for a leather bag, bracelet, or pair of boots. Those are pieces you'll want to keep in your closet forever.

Know when to quit. Do what's right for your personality. "That means knowing how you feel about an accessory when you look in the mirror," Varvatos says. "If you don't feel it matches your style, then you probably shouldn't wear it." And remember that a little can go a long way. If you have any reservations about the number of accessories you're wearing, take one off before you step out the door.

Save your neck. Think of a scarf as punctuation on your look—subtle, declarative, or simply the piece that holds everything together. It's functional, yet adds a layer of sophistication and complexity without being too fussy, Varvatos says. If you're unsure about how to make it work, ask your girlfriend or a salesperson.

Be bold. So many men's personal styles are evolutionary, not revolutionary, Varvatos says. "Don't be afraid to stir things up. Your style will never progress if you're not open to experimenting with accessories," he says. "As you boost your confidence, you may even develop a signature style that others will notice."

with a pair of jeans," says Jennings. So no French-cuff shirts or silk ties, please.

Do stick to a dark wash with a straight, medium-to-slim fit. This look is universally flattering and not overly casual, says stylist Marcy Carmack, the creator of chicwardrobesolutions.com. "Go for simple," says Carmack. "Some designer jeans look too 'fashiony.'"

Do pair jeans with wingtip brogues to dress up the denim without looking too fussy. Suede desert boots are a cool, slightly more casual option. If you can get away with sneakers at your office, make sure they're clean and simple, with a sleek profile. ■

Be a Blast from the Past

Meet the new blue blazer—versatile, functional, and thanks to this season's new cuts and styles, sophisticated enough for any occasion.

"The old rules of dressing no longer apply for so many people. Guys wear 'dress denim' now," says Michael Jarvela, vice president of men's design at Gap. "So there's a return to all the classic pieces,

LOOK 1

After hours.

Keep the heavy coat in the closet as long as you can. Adding a few layers under a denim jacket will keep you warm and allow you to make subtle adjustments as you move between indoors and out. Start with a fine-gauge cardigan, which will help maintain a sleek profile.

"Denim jackets look best when they're fitted to the body," says Dean Micklewhite, senior vice president of men's design at Express. "Oversized, chunky sweaters add way too much bulk and make the whole outfit uncomfortable." A wool scarf can offer another level of warmth and help punch up the look.

LOOK 2

Date.

Sport coats are great for the office, says Jarvela, "but you want to freshen the look on dates," he says. A denim jacket breaks from convention and comes alive when paired with midweight cotton trousers. Mixing patterns, like this checked shirt and striped tie, will surprise her. But stay true to the rules of proportions: A dark, fitted denim jacket looks best with broken-in trousers.

including denim jackets." Pulling it off with style, though, means combining the right jacket with the right casual and dressy elements. Look for one with a simple, dark rinse that's smooth and not broken in, Jarvela recommends. Then use it to create perfect combinations, like the four we've built here around a single jacket.

LOOK 3

Work.

A denim jacket under a wool coat or other outerwear adds an unexpected, youthful edge to a traditional work uniform.

"You can break from convention, but still toe the corporate line," says Jarvela. The darker and less distressed the wash, the easier it is to mix with refined dress shoes and tailored wool trousers. A washed or light denim jacket works only with casual looks.

LOOK 4

Weekend.

Sync up your denim jacket with corduroys, cargos, or even jeans. Just make sure your jacket and jeans are several shades apart; otherwise you're wearing a denim suit. Dark, rigid jeans, for instance, should be paired with a beat-up, light-colored jacket.

"Either the shades need to be significantly different or the wash needs to be, if the denim values are similar," says Jarvela.

"When I design things, the sense of accomplishment doesn't compare to anything else."

HERE ARE SOME EXAMPLES OF THE WAY JEREMY RENNER PUTS HIS OWN STAMP ON HIS THINGS AND HOW YOU CAN, TOO.

BOOTS
"My boots are old, hammered, and feel great," he says. For instant comfort, try a handcrafted pair from Esquivel.

LUGGAGE
Why buy something that's easy to lose in a crowd? Renner's bag of choice is a beat-up '70s carry-on: "One look, and you know whose it is."

Build a Wardrobe That Works

From the roles he plays to the clothes he wears, actor Jeremy Renner creates his own blueprint.

It's hard to work in 100°F heat, sweating fluids faster than you can replenish them. Now try it while wearing a 75-pound blast-resistant suit that renders even the simplest of movements exhausting.

"There was no acting; we were reacting," Jeremy Renner says about filming the new Iraq War drama *The Hurt Locker*. To play a hotshot U.S. Army bomb expert, Renner spent 3 months sweating it out in Jordan.

"The flies in my mouth aren't CGI flies. Those were real bugs we tasted as we lay in a hot sandstorm eating sand sandwiches all day. That wind whipping our faces wasn't from a fan. That was real wind pummeling us."

Not that he's complaining. The 38-year-old Modesto, California, native doesn't shirk

difficulties in his career. He's drawn to antiheroes. He played the famous flesh eater in *Dahmer*, and an old-school outlaw in *The Assassination of Jesse James by the Coward Robert Ford*, among others. Complex, flawed characters are more challenging, he says. And when you take on projects that might have scared off others, people take notice. They rely on you and trust you with even harder work. It's career gold.

The problem is, big projects linger in your mind. You can't help taking them home, and neither can Renner. So he's found a mental escape by immersing himself in another kind of craft: working with his hands. Between gigs, he built a car from the ground up, fusing a Porsche 914 frame with Porsche 911 running gear

WORKWEAR
"Functionality is key," he says. That's why classics like this Dickies shirt are great. It's durable, has pockets, and softens with age.

CAR
A Jaguar shows off your cash. Renner's 1970 silver Dodge Charger shows off his attitude. "It sounds like it can eat you for breakfast," he beams.

CARGO PANTS
On construction sites, Renner needs the carrying capacity of cargo pants. This pair holds your essentials with style.

and a 350 Chevy engine. He also runs a small construction and design business with his best friend, remodeling homes or building them from scratch. He and his crew have transformed ho-hum spaces into Mid-Century, Spanish Colonial, or French Normandy dream houses.

"It's the only tangible art I do," he says. "I sleep well at night knowing I've built an incredible lifestyle for someone."

Renner applies the same build-it-yourself approach to what he wears. Rather than abiding by the trendy uniforms of L.A., he prefers blending new and old—like wearing a pair of vintage boots and a lived-in T-shirt under a designer jacket.

"Any tool can go into a Gucci store and purchase a really fine suit," he says. ■

FRAGRANCE
Cologne adapts to every body differently, so find one that works for you and stick with it. Renner's been using this one for 17 years.

JACKET
Casual, outdoorsy styles are Renner's favorite types because they fit his lifestyle, but he still wants added details to make them stand out. "I like a military twist or an element of tailoring," he says. This jacket-length wool coat from Oliver Spencer is an ideal midweight layering piece for the fall.

WATCH
Renner collects vintage watches, but for day to day, he prefers something rugged and bold.

This Chicago rapper's denim is both his offense and defense. This self-reliance applies to his wardrobe as well. His clothes boost his confidence and look great because of that. Take his denim: Common picks his jeans to suit his moods. Light or dark, distressed or clean, he makes them part of his personality.

"I just know when they fit and when they look good on me," he says. In a way, his jeans are his weapons. "When you have style, it doesn't matter what other people are saying," he says.

The Chicago native's slick, confident look is one reason denim giant Diesel tapped him to be the face of its new fragrance, Only the Brave. Details are important, Common says, and the right scent can be a good indicator of a man's taste.

"To women, if a man smells good, that's a great sign," he adds. "It's an appetizer. It can't describe everything, but it can give you a hint of who he is."

Likewise, jeans speak volumes about your personal style, he says.

"If I like the style and the way they fit and feel, I'll wear them all the time. They're subject to my everyday abuse," says Common, whose latest studio album is *The Believer*. "Because of that, they develop character that reflects my personality. My jeans say I'm **down-to-earth but stylish**—with flavor."

Uncommonly Cool

Common knows how to master his worlds. Whether he's onscreen— he starred in *Terminator Salvation*— or onstage, the Grammy-winning rapper relies on his faith in himself to pull it off, and to pull it off with style.

American Classics, Renewed

Homegrown labels acknowledge their roots while looking ahead.

Claiborne

John Bartlett, the well-known designer who took the creative helm of Claiborne's men's collection, is stationed in New York City as he develops the Claiborne by John Bartlett collection. But, he says, "I keep the heartland in mind when I'm creating."

That means balancing style and approachability for this classic American label. The hallmarks of the Claiborne brand—affordability and comfort—remain intact, with a few contemporary upgrades. Trimmed-down silhouettes still offer a democratic fit, and a greater use of natural fabrics keeps the brand user-friendly; many garments can be thrown right in the wash. As Bartlett designs new pieces, he says foremost in his mind is his core audience: "The men who want to look like themselves—only better."

A FALL LOOK FROM CLAIRBORNE BY JOHN BARTLETT

THE NEW FEEL OF J.CREW ACCESSORIES FOR MEN

J.Crew

If the name J.Crew still conjures up images of preppies playing touch football, it's time to click Refresh. Several years ago, the company began refashioning its line with a style-savvy fit and palette. Just duck inside its new men-only outposts in Manhattan or check out its catalog and Web site: It appears that the J.Crew designers have produced clothes they want to wear but are hard-pressed to find. Examples: a trench coat with plenty of attitude but minimal bulk; khakis that fit well but still let you run for the bus; a tailored cashmere cardigan that will only improve with age.

This new approach includes a few carefully curated outside brands, from Thomas Mason dress shirts to Red Wing work boots to Baracuta windbreakers—stuff you might wish some stylish forebear (Steve McQueen, perhaps?) had bequeathed to you.

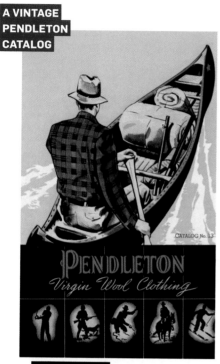

Woolrich

When Woolrich was founded in 1830 by John Rich, its target customers were the men in contact with a young nation's raw outer edge. A new line, John Rich & Bros., evokes that pioneer spirit for urban dwellers in (surprise!) Europe, and it finally reached our shores.

"In Europe, 'outdoorsy' means anything you do once you walk outside," says Andrea Canè, the creative director for WP Lavori, Woolrich's licensee in Italy. The collection, for work or weekends, is inspired by the company's iconic wool check and arctic parka (created during construction of the Trans-Alaska Pipeline System) but recalibrated for city living, with trim wool blazers and modern logger-style pants.

Pendleton

Durable, reliable: That's Pendleton. But when Vans came out with a shoe line using Pendleton plaids, the century-old company began to refocus on younger customers, says Jim Buckner, division manager for menswear. Soon Nike created a collection around the Pendleton print, and Hurley made a streamlined version of the Pendleton board shirt worn by the Beach Boys on the cover of their 1962 debut album. Now Pendleton is partnering with edgier brands Comme des Garçons and Opening Ceremony.

"Some people call it urban; some people call it street," says Buckner. "We're just calling it Pendleton from a new perspective."

THE CLASSIC
WOOLRICH FABRIC
IN AN UPDATED STYLE

Banana Republic

Despite its origins as a borderline kitsch purveyor of all things safari, Banana Republic is now known as a resource for stylish basics (the perfect white shirt, a classic pair of khakis). In the past few years, head designer and creative director Simon Kneen has imparted a subtle contemporary spin. For fall, that translates into splashes of color amid the traditional grays and whites; tailored jackets paired with jeans and cords; and chunky sweaters and scarves. Its new fragrance, Republic of Men, blends classic notes, such as sandalwood, with unexpected ones, like basil.

"We offer a lot of great essentials," says Kneen. "And we're very good at them—in part because we're so good at putting energy and innovation into the process." ■

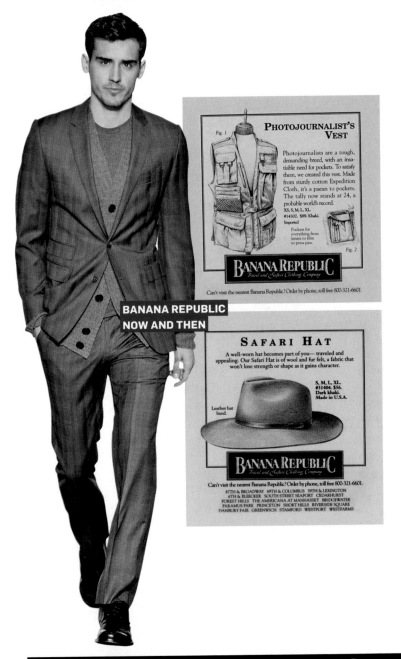

BANANA REPUBLIC NOW AND THEN

Five Shoes That Make You Shine

Footwear is expensive, and closet space is tight (especially if her shoes are in there). The solution: Buy styles that look great in both casual and formal settings. Here are some in-between picks.

CHUKKA BOOTS

Their large width and grooved rubber soles play well with many styles, but watch your trouser shape. Wear nothing slimmer than a straight leg with these shoes, or your pants won't appear to be in proportion with the footwear's bulk, says Lloyd Boston of Fine Living Network's Closet Cases. "Anything narrower could give you a moon-boot look," he warns. **WEAR THEM WITH** cargo pants and a T-shirt, or chinos, a button-front shirt, and a tie.

Kenneth Cole Reaction Flow Theory ($120), Macy's West stores

OXFORDS

These shoes can be classy, but beware of bulk: If their soles are more than a quarter of an inch thick in the front, they're too sporty for dressy looks. "Chunky indicates that you're a plodder," says Sarah Whittaker, a Georgia-based image consultant. "A sleeker shoe looks more lightweight. That's better. It implies that you can move with the times."
WEAR THEM WITH loose chinos and informal trousers.

Aldo Clytorigi ($90), aldoshoes.com

HYBRIDS

They have the conservative look of leather shoes but the soles of sneakers, which gives them a place at the office or the bar. Just don't push it: Your hybrids may be more sophisticated than your favorite pair of Chucks, but they can't complement tailored clothing. Nor are they supportive enough for even a quick pickup game.
WEAR THEM WITH jeans, corduroys, or flat-front pants.

Hogan ($375), (888) 604-6426, Hogan store, 134 Spring Street, NYC

MODERN WINGTIPS

Don't bury these classic beauties beneath baggy pants legs. You want them to stand out. "Slim-leg dress pants will bring the eye down to the cool details of this shoe," says Boston.
WEAR THEM WITH slightly distressed denim and a suit vest. In warmer temps, be adventurous and pair them with tailored shorts. No, really. It's the new refined casual.

Johnston and Murphy Matheson ($250), (888) 792-3272, johnstonmurphy.com

LOAFERS

A loafer's opening sits low on your ankle, so pair the shoes with fine-gauge socks and medium-width pants. The shoes' sleek lines will complement a dressed-up look. For casual outings, though, wear loafers without socks or with minisocks that aren't visible outside the shoe. They'll create an instantly casual vibe.
WEAR THEM WITH nearly anything, from denim to double-breasted suits.

Donald Pliner Firm ($375), (888) 307-1630, donaldjpliner.com

Ultimate Age Erasers

Looks. Energy. Health. Time erodes them all, unless you follow these simple instructions to slow the clock.

Think there's no limiting time's toll? Well, you're right. If you don't lift a finger, time will take everything you have. But nearly 70 percent of aging factors actually fall within your control.

"People just accept that they're going to start looking and feeling older, but they really don't have to," says Steven Austad, Ph.D., an expert on aging at the University of Texas at San Antonio. You can outrun Father Time—at least for a while.

Here's an arsenal of age-defying weapons—distilled from experts and visits to key "fountain of youth" labs—that will help you look, feel, and stay in your prime.

Look Younger

A man typically greets those first wrinkles with an anxious frown, which in turn produces more wrinkles. Indeed, the effects of age first show up on our faces, especially around the eyes. In a recent study in *Ophthalmology*, 47 young adults had their eye movements tracked as researchers presented them with images of older adults. When asked to determine the ages of the people in the photos, the study participants focused on the eye region, particularly the brow and lower lids.

If you want to fool the kids, the best thing you can do for your skin is to wear sunblock with an SPF of 30, says Cameron Rokhsar, M.D., a dermatologist and laser surgeon. The best block is Anthelios. It's the only sunscreen that contains mexoryl, a powerful drug that protects your skin against UVA rays. But that's just the start.

SCRAPE OFF THE YEARS

Reach for the razor every morning.

"The low-grade friction from shaving stimulates collagen production and smooths the skin," says Kenneth Beer, M.D., a dermatologist in West Palm Beach, Florida. "That's one of the reasons men typically have far fewer wrinkles than women have."

So even though a survey of 60 women at Northumbria University found that light stubble was considered sexy, you should limit the Clooney treatment you give her to only a few days a month. (Besides, those same women also said that clean-shaven men looked 5½ years younger than those wearing beards.)

Men's Health Age Eraser Awards

We surveyed 5,000 readers to find out who's done the best job keeping Father Time on hold.

30s

1. MARK WAHLBERG (38):
His home gym includes a boxing ring and weights—terrific tools for fighting old age.

2. DEREK JETER (35):
Playing 150 ball games a year, plus cover-worthy grooming, helps Jeter stay draft-pick young.

3. TOM BRADY (32):
Quarterbacking tends to add years to your body, but Brady keeps the linemen scrambling, not sacking.

SOOTHE YOUR EYES

As you age, your cell-renewal process slows: A 20-year-old's outermost layer of skin sheds every 2 weeks. By age 50, that cycle takes twice as long. Your skin also gradually loses collagen, which is the spongy protein beneath the epidermis. Both factors produce wrinkles and sagging, particularly around your eyes, where the skin is thinnest.

"Wrinkles there instantly make you look older," says Rokhsar. He recommends using Retin-A (tretinoin) or retinol, citing studies showing that it creates new collagen. Try L'Oreal Paris Men's Expert Vita Lift Anti-Wrinkle & Firming Moisturizer ($10, lorealparisusa.com).

TRIM THE MANE

If you're starting to thin out, befriend a barber. In the early stages of hair loss, you can actually make your hair appear fuller by having it cut short, according to John Allan, the founder of a chain of grooming and lifestyle clubs. Upright and feathered hair tends to look thicker, while longer hair will part and reveal the scalp you're trying to hide.

And a less shaggy cut will age well with you, Allan says. "Many men actually have better hairstyles—and look better—in their 40s than they did in their 20s," he says.

WAKE UP YOUTHFUL

Chronic sleep deprivation could quickly add years to your face. Here's why: The extraocular eye muscles are exercised during rapid eye movement (REM) sleep and could atrophy when not used, says sleep researcher David Kuhlmann, M.D.

This may contribute to the circles beneath your eyes after a poor night's rest.

If you can't sleep, then don't go low-carb at dinner. A 2008 Australian study found that men who consumed carbohydrates before bed had significantly longer REM sleep cycles than when they ate a low-carb meal. The carbs help create acetylcholine, a neurotransmitter that promotes REM sleep.

Feel Younger

Don't want to lose your marbles later? Lose some calories now. German researchers recently found that eating less can reduce markers of inflammation and insulin

resistance, which are suspected risk factors for cognitive decline. Older study participants who cut 30 percent of their daily calories for 3 months were able to improve their memory on a word-recall test. Here are more ways to keep your youthful edge.

ENJOY A HEARTY LAUGH

One of the greatest differences between a child and an adult is that the child has no worries, says sports psychologist Terry Orlick, Ph.D., the author of *In Pursuit of Excellence*. You can counteract stress—and roll back psychological aging—with laughter. Even the anticipation of a good laugh decreases the stress chemicals cortisol and epinephrine by 39 and 70

Men's Health Age Eraser Awards

40s

1. WILL SMITH (40):
Sustaining two careers—music and acting—have kept Smith's mind razor-sharp, like his look.

2. DANIEL CRAIG (41):
A British company launched an ice pop in the shape of the Bond star's physique this year. The ladies ate it up.

3. BARACK OBAMA (48):
Yes he's busy, but he still works out 6 days a week. He'll look just as good 4 years—or 8 years—from now.

percent, respectively, say researchers at Loma Linda University.

Laughter is also great for the heart. When participants in a University of Maryland study watched stressful film clips, they experienced vasoconstriction—a narrowing of the blood vessels—while the blood vessels of those watching funny films expanded by 22 percent.

EXPLORE OPPOSITES

Your brainpower naturally starts to slide as you become older. You can help slow that decline by simply deviating from your daily patterns whenever possible—jog backward for a few hundred yards, or brush your teeth with your nondominant hand. This can increase bloodflow in your brain and recharge your neurological connections, according to Daniel Amen, M.D., author of *Magnificent Mind at Any Age.*

Additionally, research by Gary Small, M.D., director of the UCLA Memory and Aging Center, found that "brain training" exercises focusing on memory techniques (for instance, remembering to pick up stamps and eggs by visualizing an egg with a stamp on it) can reset a 45-year-old's cognitive ability score to that of a 30-year-old.

KEEP IT UP, WAY UP

There's no better way to feel like a 20-year-old than to have sex like one. But plaque buildup affects bloodflow in the small arteries of a man's penis sooner than anywhere else in his body, according to Steven Lamm, M.D., an internist and the author of *The Hardness Factor*. That's one reason the angle of a man's erection falls to 100 degrees by age 45, down from 130 degrees in his 20s.

Dr. Lamm's recommendation for a gravity-defying erection? Edox. Research shows that this supplement's two ingredients, pycnogenol and the amino acid L-arginine aspartate, increase the production of nitric oxide, which is a vasodilator that relaxes blood vessels in the penis, allowing increased bloodflow and harder, longer-lasting erections.

Stay Younger

If you want to see your 85th birthday, limit your alcohol to two drinks a day. This may make you less likely to die of cardiovascular disease, according to Japanese researchers. And make one of those drinks red. A recent review in *Alcoholism: Clinical and Experimental Research* suggests that resveratrol, a compound commonly found in red wine, might prevent or delay the onset of chronic disease. As you savor your pinot, swallow these other stay-young secrets.

LOSE THE BELLY, WITH BREAKFAST

Developing a big, round gut as you age will not only make you look bad but also weigh heavily on your manhood. According to a landmark 2007 study in the *Journal of Clinical Endocrinology and Metabolism*, men with a 5-point increase in body-mass index—about 30 extra pounds—had testosterone levels comparable to men who were a full decade older.

Eating the right breakfast—one with lots of protein—will keep your belly at bay, according to multiple studies of the subject. Yet 19 percent of men in their 40s skip this meal altogether.

"I've seen guys drop serious weight just by eating protein at breakfast," says Louis Aronne, M.D., the director of the comprehensive weight control program of the West Chester Medical Group, in New York. People on weight-loss diets who break eggs for breakfast, lose 65 percent more weight than those who down a bagel with the same number of calories, according to a study in the *International Journal of Obesity*.

MAINTAIN YOUR MUSCLES

If you don't use your muscles, you'll lose them. And over time lost muscle is likely to be replaced by fat, according to a *Journal of the American College of Nutrition* study. That's particularly problematic, because a pound of fat takes up 18 percent more space on your body than a pound of muscle does. So even if you maintain your weight as you age, your waist might still balloon.

Spinach can help with muscle maintenance; recent test-tube research from Rutgers University found that a hormone in spinach increases protein synthesis. Spinach is also rich in vitamin K, potassium, and calcium.

BUILD A LONGER-LASTING TICKER

If you want to stay young, make your heart stronger. With proper conditioning (high-intensity activities such as cycling and rowing work best) you can increase your heart's stroke volume and your body's oxygen uptake. This allows your heart to pump blood more slowly and efficiently.

"The average human life span is about 3 billion heartbeats," says Michael Lauer, M.D., of the National Heart, Blood, and Lung Institute. If you lower your heart rate, you increase your life expectancy. ∎

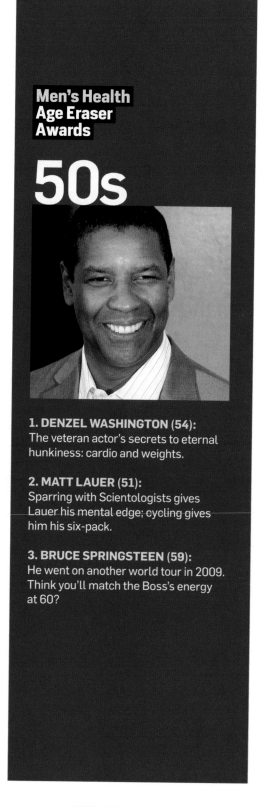

Men's Health Age Eraser Awards

50s

1. DENZEL WASHINGTON (54):
The veteran actor's secrets to eternal hunkiness: cardio and weights.

2. MATT LAUER (51):
Sparring with Scientologists gives Lauer his mental edge; cycling gives him his six-pack.

3. BRUCE SPRINGSTEEN (59):
He went on another world tour in 2009. Think you'll match the Boss's energy at 60?

PROVE IT.

CLEAN UP YOUR ACT

When it comes to **attracting women,** men worry about the wrong things. Or at least that's the conclusion of a new survey by the research firm Synovate, which asked 250 women to identify **what makes a man desirable** and then polled 250 guys on what they thought mattered most.

Turns out that while you're sweating over your abs, a sculpted six-pack isn't even in her top five:

	WOMEN SAY...	MEN SAY...
1	Good hygiene	Confidence
2	Confidence	Good hygiene
3	A great smile	A great smile
4	Strong fashion sense	Defined muscles
5	A macho look	Strong fashion sense

ACE THE EYE EXAM

Don't underestimate the power of your eyes to make or break your appearance. A new study in *Ophthalmology* found that when people were told to evaluate photos of faces for age and tiredness, they focused mostly on the eyes. The top tells: crow's-feet, droopy lids, dark circles, and puffiness.

And while only cosmetic procedures can fix the first two, a few nights of strategic sleep can erase the others. Because puffiness is often caused by fluid buildup during sleep, prevent it by raising the angle of your head with an extra pillow, says study author Peter Rubin, M.D. To eliminate the circles, catch more z's; fatigue causes your blood vessels to dilate and show through the thin skin under your eyes.

GET YOUR OWN WAY

The Stones sang that you can't always get what you want, but there is an easy way to **improve your odds.** Scientists say that expressing disappointment might be your best negotiating tactic. In a new Dutch study, people making deals with self-centered opponents were significantly more likely to get their way when they acted disappointed than when they showed irritation or wore a poker face. Disappointment signals that **you might walk away,** so people might make concessions to prevent the negotiation from falling apart, says study author Gerben Van Kleef, Ph.D.

SWISH THIS

Bad breath might not be so bad: A recent Australian study review concludes that mouthwashes containing alcohol may damage oral tissue, leaving it vulnerable to carcinogenic compounds. More research is needed to prove a cause-and-effect connection, but if you want to play it safe in the meantime, switch to an alcohol-free rinse.

DIAGNOSE YOUR DERMIS

Gone are the days when men scrubbed their faces with Lava soap. Today, smart skin care means matching the cleanser to your mug, says David Bank, M.D., a dermatologist in private practice in Mt. Kisco, New York. Use Dr. Bank's guide here to figure out which of the four face types you have, as well as the best way to keep your skin clean.

COMBINATION

Calling cards: People with combo skin have oily T-zones (forehead, nose, and chin) and dry-to-normal cheeks. Each area requires a different kind of care.
Perfect product: Look for a gentle wash that can degrease your T-zone without drying your cheeks, such as pHisoderm Deep Cleaning Cream Cleanser.

NORMAL

Calling cards: Normal skin has a nice glow but isn't shiny, thanks to its balanced combination of oil and water.
Perfect product: This skin type reacts well to pretty much any kind of product, because it's not easily irritated. A safe bet is a mild cleanser that contains soap, such as Purpose Gentle Cleansing Bar.

OILY

Calling cards: If your face feels slick or sticky by lunchtime even though you haven't broken a sweat, then you have oily skin.
Perfect product: Choose a cleanser with 2 percent salicylic acid, which reduces excess oil and prevents it from building up in your pores. Try Neutrogena Oil-Free Acne Wash.

DRY

Calling cards: Dry skin feels tight right after washing. This is because the cells on the outer layer of your skin don't work properly, so you lose more water than you can absorb.
Perfect product: Harsh detergents can be aggravating; try Cetaphil Gentle Skin Cleanser, which doesn't strip oils from your skin.

DON'T FADE TO GRAY

A team of German and British researchers have discovered that our hair follicles produce high amounts of hydrogen peroxide, a natural bleaching agent. Normally, this hydrogen peroxide is broken down by an enzyme called catalase, but as you age, enzyme production drops off, giving the hydrogen peroxide a chance to alter the hue of your hair. The finding may help scientists someday develop a drug that can reverse the process.

TAKE HEART

Engineers are developing a new robotic device that can repopulate a balding person's head faster and with less pain than before. Currently, surgeons have to remove small strips of scalp from the back of your neck or behind your ears to harvest hair follicles to be transplanted to bare areas. But with the robotic system, doctors will be able to extract and implant those follicles without snipping skin. The technology may be just 2 years away.

JOIN THE ANTIFUR CROWD

Take off the gorilla suit. Women are most attracted to men who keep their chest hair in check, reveals a new study in the *Archives of Sexual Behavior*. The finding might stem from women's evolutionary belief that hairless men are healthier, says study author Barnaby Dixson, Ph.D.(c).

But don't worry—you don't need to go bodybuilder-bare. If you're sporting a pelt on your pecs, just buzz off the excess with a trimmer like the Remington Body and Back Groomer ($40, remington-products.com).

SKIP THE MILK MUSTACHE

Dairy has plenty of health benefits, including appetite control, but consider cutting your consumption if you're acne prone. Drinking milk can fuel breakouts, according to a review from George Washington University researchers. Certain hormones in cows' milk may stimulate overproduction of oil and skin cells, which can lead to clogged pores, says study author Hope Ferdowsian, M.D., M.P.H. Ease off any form of dairy (milk, yogurt, cheese) and watch to see if your skin clears up. Be patient; it can take up to 6 weeks to notice a difference.

HARD TRUTH

66

Percentage of male cosmetic surgery patients whose goal was to stay competitive at work, according to the American Academy of Facial Plastic and Reconstructive Surgery

Women are most attracted to men who keep their chest hair in check.

BANISH BREAKOUTS

If acne-fighting medications haven't solved your skin woes, flip the switch: Red-light therapy can banish breakouts. When Italian researchers shone red light on the faces of people with moderate acne, the subjects' complexions improved by 50 percent after just a month of twice-a-week treatments.

Magic? It's more like physics: The specific wavelength of red light annihilates the bacteria that breed in clogged pores, says study author Piergiacomo Calzavara-Pinton, Ph.D. Check with your dermatologist for availability.

YOU ASKED.

I blush a lot. What can I do about it?

A: The problem with blushing is that it's an embarrassing phenomenon. Let's face it, blushing isn't very manly, and feeling yourself blush only causes you to blush more.

"People stare at you, so naturally it gets worse," says Michelle Magid, M.D., a clinical assistant professor of psychiatry at the University of Texas Medical Branch.

In order to stay out of the red zone, you need to interrupt the cycle. One way is with imagery training.

"Try to block out the people around you and imagine a place that is calm and soothing," says Dr. Magid. "Picturing yourself in a less threatening place can reverse the physiological response from embarrassment."

Sure, going to your "happy place" might feel a little silly, but it is really an effective diversionary tactic. Here's another one: Take four slow, deep breaths. Each time you exhale, focus on releasing the tension throughout your body. Concentrate on the muscles in your shoulders, forehead, stomach, and chest. Relaxing the body will relax the mind, which can break the cycle.

Q: I'm 25. is there any reason I should wait to have Lasik?

A: "No. By the time you reach your early 20s, your eyes are mature," Kimberly Cockerham, M.D., who has a private practice and is an adjunct clinical associate professor of ophthalmology at Stanford University school of medicine. She has a grant to investigate vision-enhancing nano-technology implants.

"Refractive surgery can fix nearsightedness and farsightedness," Dr. Cockerham says. "And it's especially worth having if you play any kind of sport where contacts or glasses can hinder performance."

Q: I've always heard that you should never pop a pimple because it'll leave a scar. Is that true?

A: Picture a dandelion. When you give it a yank, you rip off only what's above the ground. The root remains, and so does the problem. The truth is it's the same with a pimple.

"When you look in the mirror and squeeze it, the top pops out, giving you a feeling of accomplishment, but the bottom squirts pus deeper into your skin," says Stuart Kaplan, M.D., an assistant clinical professor of dermatology at UCLA's medical center. "This causes more inflammation, creating a larger pimple that you're just as likely to go after again. And if you keep messing with it and your scabs, you run the risk of scarring."

But popping your zits isn't the only way you can end up pockmarked: Scrub your face with a washcloth and you may rip off the thin layer of skin surrounding the pimple. So either leave the pimple alone or ask a dermatologist to extract the pus with a syringe.

"We then inject a drop of cortisone to prevent inflammation," says Dr. Kaplan. "The pimple flattens out within a day."

Q: Can pitted acne scars from my teen years be removed, or at least diminished?

A: "Yes, although most guys who've had acne have more than one type of scar and may need more than one treatment method," says Adnan Nasir, M.D., Ph.D., an adjunct clinical assistant professor at the University of North Carolina at Chapel Hill and the medical director of dermatology research at Wake Research Associates. "These can range from scar-reducing creams to cosmetic procedures such as dermabrasion, lasers, and surgery. Seek out a physician with experience in this area."

Q: What feature do women most judge me by? Eyes, smile, pecs maybe?

A: So much for flex appeal. It's your choppers the ladies are checking out, according to a recent University of North Carolina study. Males with perfectly aligned pearly whites are associated with qualities such as dominance, strength, and social competence.

To brighten your teeth, see your dentist about a set of custom-fitted or moldable whitening trays and a hydrogen peroxide whitener. If your teeth are crooked, think about porcelain veneers.

Q: Do any chewing gums with teeth whiteners really work?

A: Don't stake your smile on them. Most whitening gums contain either a mild abrasive, such as baking soda, or a cleanser, such as sodium hexametaphosphate, but neither ingredient will brighten your teeth dramatically, says Edmond Hewlett, D.D.S., an associate professor of restorative dentistry at UCLA's school of dentistry.

"At the most, a whitening gum will help prevent the buildup of everyday stains, such as those from coffee, tea, or red wine," Dr. Hewlett says.

Then again, regular gum will help do this, too: Any chewing action stimulates your mouth to produce more saliva, which makes it difficult for stains to take hold on your teeth. For true whitening, ask your dentist about having a peroxide gel applied using custom-fitted trays, says Dr. Hewlett. Or try over-the-counter moldable trays that use hydrogen peroxide.

Q: Is brushing my teeth after every meal a good idea?

A: Only if your goal is to brush everything off your teeth—including the enamel. You see, many foods and beverages are acidic, which isn't a problem unless you immediately add a brush to the equation.

"The acid temporarily softens your enamel, and brushing too soon may abrade it away," says Dr. Hewlett.

The best way to avoid dental damage is to wait at least an hour after eating or drinking before you brush. This will allow enough time for your saliva to neutralize the acid imbalance.

If your mouth feels funky between meals, keep a pack of Johnson & Johnson Stim-U-Dent Plaque Removers on hand. These specially designed toothpicks let you scrape the gunk out from between your teeth.

Q: What's the most stylish, spine-healthy bag for work? Mine is a pain in the neck.

A: Because you said "stylish," a backpack is out, even though it is the safest way to lug your load.

"The twin straps distribute weight evenly," says Scott Bautch, D.C., a spokesman for the American Chiropractic Association. "But a messenger-style bag worn across the chest is a close second."

Choose a messenger-style bag made of a durable material, such as waxed cotton, ballistic nylon, or leather, says *Men's Health* fashion director Brian Boye. "Jack Spade and Bally offer sophisticated versions."

Of course, your back won't benefit if you fill your new bag with heavy "necessities." The contents should total no more than 15 percent of your body weight, says Bautch.

Q: Is deodorant with silver ions the best way to combat body odor?

A: It depends on how much you sweat. Silver compounds act as antibacterials, something the pioneers (who dropped silver coins into milk to keep it fresh) figured out.

"The silver ions in deodorant attack the bacteria that thrive in sweat and cause body odor," says Val Edwards-Jones, Ph.D., a professor of medical microbiology at Manchester Metropolitan University, in England. Traditional deodorants made with the antibacterial triclosan manage stench in the same way.

The verdict's still out on which is most effective. But here's the rub: Neither silver-laced deodorants nor those with triclosan reduce the amount you sweat, which is critical to reducing odor if you perspire a lot. So if you don't sweat much, an antibacterial deodorant should keep the stale smell at bay.

But to KO the BO that's caused by heavy sweating, tag-team a deodorant plus an antiperspirant with aluminum zirconium or aluminum chloride. Apply an extra-potent variety, such as Certain Dri or Gillette Clinical Strength, the night before. Then after your morning shower, swipe on an antibacterial deodorant.

Q: Do 2-in-1 shampoo-plus-conditioners really work?

A: If you're Mr. Multitasker and believe even your grooming products should do two jobs at once, then yes, a shampoo/conditioner might be worth trying. When you suds up with a 2-in-1, cleansing agents called surfectants bind to the dirt and excess oil in your hair and pull them off as you rinse. While those surfactants are streaming off, the conditioner is kicking in.

"The conditioner portion is bound in molecules that act as cages," says Paradi Mirmirani, M.D., an assistant professor of dermatology at the University of California at San Francisco. "As the hair is rinsed, the conditioner releases, coating the hair."

Dr. Mirmirani says these products work best on hair that's not too oily or too dry, and even then should be used only a few times a week. For dry hair, use a 2-in-1 and follow it up with a separate conditioner, which will have a higher concentration of moisturizers.

Live Longer, Live Better

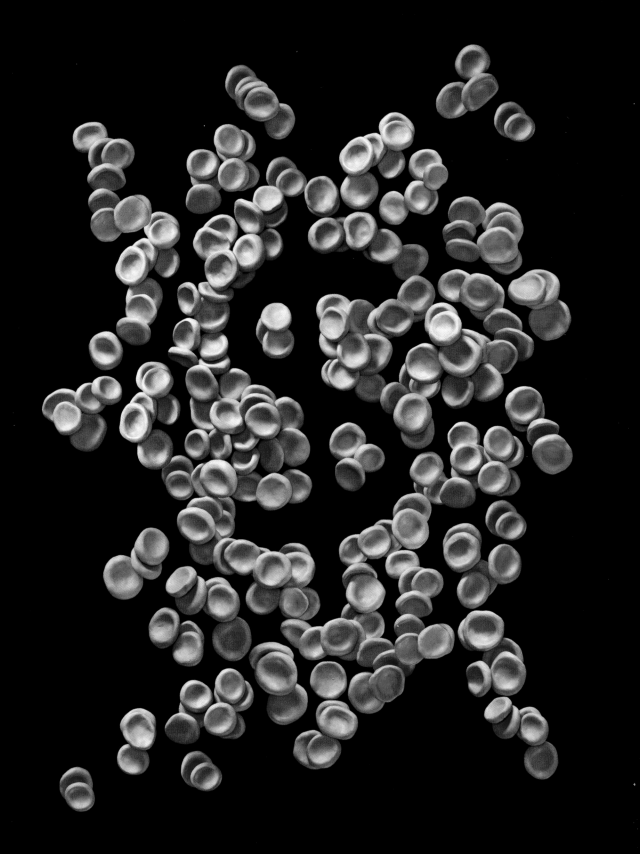

Five Tests That Could Save Your Life

Outlive the recession by spending your health-care dollars where it counts.

There are health tests we need, and those we don't. Pelvic ultrasound? Sounds ultrasuspicious. Occult blood test? Only if it comes with an exorcism. Urinalysis? Great, now I'll be kicked off the tour ...

It's tough to know which of these are truly essential, especially when they're packaged with dozens of other tests and called an "executive health exam." And yet thousands of men sign up for these screenings—at an out-of-pocket cost of up to $10,000 apiece—based on the sales pitch that a test might uncover a hidden health condition.

Of course, 10 grand might be worth it if all that random screening actually did any good. But a seminal study by the Rand Corporation found that patients who had the most screenings over 5 years were no healthier than those given less medical attention. This isn't to say executive health exams are scams. They can be quite valuable—if you know which of the procedures are worthwhile. So we asked our experts to create an à la carte menu to bring to your GP. Think of these as the best tests for a recession.

CARDIAC CT ANGIOGRAPHY

These colorful 3-D images allow radiologists to calculate one of your most important heart numbers: your coronary artery calcium score, which is a measure of how much plaque is piling up in your arteries. A 2007 study of more than 10,000 people published in the journal *Atherosclerosis* reported that calcium scores alone can predict heart attacks, while a 2003 study found that a high calcium score is associated with a tenfold increase in heart-disease risk. This is compared with a less-than-twofold increase in risk from traditional risk factors such as diabetes and smoking.

The test has one significant downside: The radiation exposure from your average cardiac CT is equal to 600 chest X-rays,

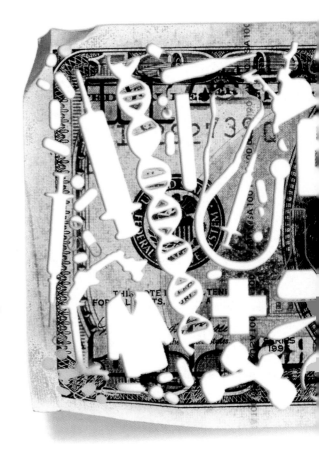

according to a study in the *Journal of the American Medical Association*. This produces a 1-in-5,000 risk of cancer, another study reveals.

Who needs it: Men with some of the risk factors for heart disease whose physicians may be on the fence about starting treatment.

"In these medium-risk cases, cardiac CT scans and calcium scoring can provide the extra level of information that we feel we need," says Gerald Fletcher, M.D., a professor of cardiology at the Mayo Clinic. The lower the calcium score, the lower the

risk. If you reach 112, your physician might recommend aspirin or statins.

Cost: $350 to $900. Most insurance companies will reimburse you if you've previously had an abnormal stress test or chest pain.

BONE DENSITY SCAN

Think osteoporosis affects only old ladies? Fact is, men begin losing bone mass at age 30. That's why it's important to assess the state of your skeleton now with a dual energy X-ray absorptiometry (DEXA) scan,

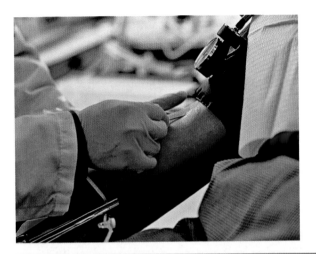

TESTING, TESTING

Medical tests are no fun, so why take them twice? People often end up with inadvertently skewed results, but some simple prep work will ensure that your numbers are accurate.

PSA EXAM

What it does:
Screens for prostate-cancer warnings

What throws it off:
Sex. Or specifically, ejaculation. So watch only Cartoon Network the night before.

The fix: Go celibate for a full day before the exam. Ejaculation can raise normal PSA levels for 6 to 24 hours, say researchers at the Washington University in St. Louis School of Medicine.

COLONOSCOPY

What it does:
Checks for colon cancer and other bowel problems

What throws it off:
The pretest laxative doesn't always work, says Mark Welton, M.D., of the Stanford Cancer Center.

The fix: Help the laxative by walking, which encourages waste to move faster. About 41 percent of patients who walk have a good chance of a clean bowel, compared with 25 percent of those who don't walk, a Korean study shows.

LIPID PROFILE

What it does:
Estimates your risk of developing cardio-vascular disease

What throws it off:
Food and any drink other than water. Some docs also allow coffee during the prescribed 12-hour fast.

The fix: Drink your java black; cream and sugar can alter your triglyceride levels for several hours, which throws off the test. An intense exercise bout can also have that effect. So take it easy at the gym the day before.

TREADMILL STRESS TEST

What it does:
Measures your heart fitness and identifies signs of possible heart disease

What throws it off:
Any interference between skin and electrode. (That's why your chest hair is promptly Bic'd.)

The fix: Be careful how you clean your-self in the morning. Skip body lotion or powder, both of which can weaken an electrode's read on your heart's electri-cal signals. (And you'll leave in need of another shower anyway.)

BLOOD PRESSURE

What it does: Helps monitor your risk of heart disease, stroke, and other ailments

What throws it off:
Anxiety over a visit to the doc can spike systolic blood pres-sure by 5 points and diastolic by 3.5 points.

The fix: Hit the bath-room. Urination reduces blood pres-sure. Then take slow, deep breaths for 30 seconds; that can drop systolic blood pressure by an aver-age of 6.4 points and diastolic by 2.3 points, say Japanese researchers.

which uses low-radiation X-rays to gauge bone mineral density. (It can also measure body fat percentage.)

"DEXA scans allow us to identify people at high risk for fracture so they can start treatment to strengthen their bones before a fracture occurs," says Murray J. Favus, M.D., director of the bone program at the University of Chicago Medical Center. Your doctor might suggest adding strengthening workouts to your exercise program and supplementing your daily diet with up to 1,000 milligrams of calcium and up to 400 IU of vitamin D.

Who needs it: Anyone with any osteoporosis risk factors: inactivity, smoking, a family history of the disease.

Cost: $250 to $300. To increase the odds of your insurance covering the scan, make sure your doctor notes any risk factors.

VO2 MAX TEST

With the VO2 max test, you hop on a treadmill or stationary bike and give your maximum effort while wearing a mask that captures your every breath. By analyzing the amount of oxygen you consume, the test determines how efficiently your body extracts and uses oxygen from the air. This makes it the gold standard of fitness markers, as well as a strong indicator of your overall health.

"Blood pressure, cholesterol—those are what we call 'remote markers.' The best predictor of your longevity is going to be your fitness," says Walter Bortz, M.D., a longevity researcher at Stanford University.

Who needs it: Anyone who wants their blood to pump. If your score is under 18 ml/kg/min, talk to your doctor about increasing the intensity of your workouts.

Click, and Feel Better

Here are three ways that surfing can improve your health.

MAPMYRUN.COM:
Reinspire your running routine with this database of user-generated routes and trails. After a run, trace your route, and then enter your time into

the site's workout calculator. It will break down your average speed, pace, and number of calories burned.

YOUR DISEASERISK. WUSTL.EDU:
Honestly, who cares which character on *Lost* you'd be? Take an online quiz that matters. With this one, you assess your risk of diabetes, cancer, heart disease, osteoporosis, and stroke through quick self-tests sanctioned by the Washington University in St. Louis School of Medicine. If your risk is high, go to MensHealth.com/healthfor disease-specific info. And see your doctor.

NUTRITIONDATA.COM:
Enter your favorite snacks into this site's search bar and it'll spit out a fullness graph, which is a helpful comparison between how full a food will make you feel versus its nutritional content. Plug in a Snickers bar and see what happens. So much for satisfaction.

Cost: $110 to $160. The test is available at physical therapy, rehab, or cardiopulmonary centers. Insurance providers won't cover it.

VIRTUAL COLONOSCOPY

By definition, something "virtual" usually can't compare to the real thing. But with a virtual colonoscopy, you avoid the two downsides of a traditional colonoscopy—sedation and the risk of a perforated colon—while still benefiting from the one big upside: test results you can stake your life on.

"Virtual colonoscopies have the same sensitivity for detecting large polyps, which are the precursor lesions of colon cancer," says Judy Yee, M.D., a professor of radiology at the University of California at San Francisco. Though the CT scanning technology of a virtual colonoscopy can miss some smaller polyps, a University of Wisconsin study found that these are usually benign anyway. And don't sweat the radiation; you'll receive about 5 to 8 millisieverts, an amount that isn't considered dangerous, says Dr. Yee.

Who needs it: People ages 50 and older, especially those on blood thinners, because an "oops" with a regular scope could cause dangerous internal bleeding. The exception: If your family has a history of colon cancer, you should be screened at least 10 years before the age your relative was when he or she was first diagnosed, Dr. Yee says. People who are overweight or inactive, drink or smoke heavily, or have an inflammatory bowel disease should also consider early screening.

Cost: $500 to $1,000. Many health-care plans now recognize the effectiveness of virtual colonoscopies and increasingly cover them.

NUTRITIONAL EVALUATION

While it's not a test per se, putting your diet under the microscope could result in a leaner body and a longer life.

"The benefits of meeting with a dietitian are accountability, moral support, and troubleshooting if your progress stalls," says Alan Aragon, M.S., the *Men's Health* weight-loss coach.

In a 2008 Kaiser Permanente study, people with diabetes who received nutritional counseling were nearly twice as likely to lose weight as those who had no guidance. To find a registered dietitian who can see beyond the food pyramid, Aragon recommends going to the American Dietetic Association's Web site (eatright.org) and clicking on "Find a Nutrition Professional." Then call the R.D. and ask how he or she stays up on the latest research, which should include reading journals such as the *American Journal of Clinical Nutrition* or the *Journal of Applied Physiology*.

Who needs it: Anyone who should lose weight or simply wants to know how they can eat to beat disease.

Cost: $40 to $75 a session. Your insurance company might reimburse you if you have a condition that can be improved with diet changes. Ask your doctor for a referral. ■

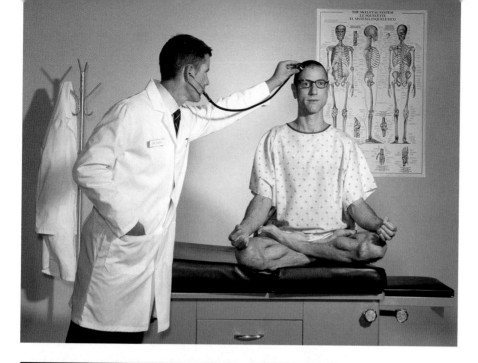

Your Physical, Demystified

Blood-pressure check? No mystery there. Same for the trip to the scale —which is way off, of course. But what's with the penlight and little rubber mallet? Here's what your doctor's looking for when he . . .

. . . asks you to say "ahh."

He's looking for swelling or discoloration in your mouth and throat, which might indicate oral cancer. This test also checks if your palate and uvula— the punching bag at the back of your throat— contract at the same time. If they don't, your glossopharyngeal and vagus nerves may not be working properly.

"This can signal problems such as a stroke, brain tumor, or multiple sclerosis," says David Deci, M.D., a professor of family medicine at the University of Wisconsin.

. . . shines a penlight in your eyes.

Your doc is testing your optic nerves, which transmit visual information to your brain, as well as the oculomotor nerves that control your eye muscles.

"If your pupils don't dilate or dilate too much, that could indicate nerve damage," says Dr. Deci. That damage could involve the specific nerves or be centered in your brain, possibly as a result of a stroke or reduced bloodflow.

. . . taps and presses on your abdomen.

This helps detect an enlarged—and potentially infected—organ. "When I tap over your liver or spleen, the sound is dull. It becomes more resonant as I move off the organ, helping me gauge its size," says David Simel, M.D., chief of medicine at the Durham Veterans Affairs Medical Center. Your doc may also press in as you take a deep breath. This pushes your diaphragm down, shifting your liver and spleen so they're easier to feel.

. . . hits your knee with a small mallet.

This classic reflex test exposes nerve or metabolism problems. If you have lower-back pain, for example, and your leg barely budges when your doctor taps your knee, then some of your spinal nerves may be damaged, says Dr. Simel. An X-ray may be the next step. A karate kick could indicate an overactive thyroid. In that case, flooding hormones can make your reflexes more forceful.

Bad Habits to Break

Your brain loves consistency—the good kind and the bad.
Here's how to shake five of your most vexing gremlins.

A friend offers you a smoke while you're tailgating at the game. You have one every now and then, and you're not hooked, so sure, thanks. Besides, it *does* look good with your drink. This, my friend, is your brain battling a bad habit—and losing. As we continually perform a behavior—smoking socially, say, or texting while driving—neural pathways in our brains form new patterns, according to a recent MIT review. Once the prompt arrives, your brain shifts into autopilot.

"Situational cues bring out habits that are deeply embedded," says Ellen Peters, Ph.D., who studies risk perceptions at Decision Research, which is a psychological research firm in Eugene, Oregon. "When that habit surfaces, it's hard not to let it overcome you."

The problem, of course, is that these proclivities can endanger your health. So follow our guide to rid yourself, once and for all, of a few distinctly unhealthy habits.

A QUICK DRAG EVERY NOW AND THEN

While regular smokers have a chemical component fueling their addiction, people who smoke only occasionally succumb mainly to social and environmental triggers.

"The most powerful prompt is often being around other people who are smoking or drinking," says Michael Fiore, M.D., director of the University of Wisconsin Center for Tobacco Research and Intervention. In stressful situations, a cigarette can put you at ease: Ten minutes after you take a puff, your brain releases a surge of dopamine, a neurotransmitter that can make you feel relaxed and happy.

• **Why it's bad:** Lighting up even a few times a week is still poisoning yourself.

"There's no lower limit of exposure to tobacco smoke that is safe. Period," says Richard D. Hurt, M.D., director of the Mayo Clinic Nicotine Dependence Center.

In fact, a single cigarette can almost instantly injure the inner walls of your blood vessels. That damage can lead to heart disease and blood clots. Looming in the background, of course, is also the risk of developing a full-blown addiction. Some research suggests that about a quarter of "occasional" smokers go full-time.

• **Break the habit:** When you can't steer clear of the smokestacks, benign substitutes can work wonders, Dr. Hurt says.

For instance, grab a drink stirrer and hold it between your fingers like a cigarette. Set it between your lips while you take out your wallet or phone. This keeps your mouth and hands busy. And carry nicotine gum or lozenges. These can mimic the effects of nicotine from cigarettes, Dr. Fiore says.

YOUR CAFFEINE DRIP

The human body embraces some vices with gusto, effectively launching lifelong habits by punishing you for skipping even a single hit. That's caffeine's MO.

When a caffeine fanatic doesn't get that fix, bloodflow in the brain spikes, according to a 2009 study in *Psychopharmacology*. This expansion of blood vessels results in a headache, while you suffer from symptoms such as fatigue and grumpiness. To avoid this, you visit the vending machines or the office java pot. (Makes us wonder: Why can't fruits and vegetables hook us like this?)

• **Why it's bad:** A constant infusion of caffeine can set your nerves on edge. "High daily caffeine intake may decrease hand steadiness and increase anxiety," says Russell Keast, Ph.D., a caffeine-consumption researcher at the School of Exercise and Nutrition Sciences at Deakin University in Australia. Then there's a 2007 study from Dartmouth Medical School, which found that people who consumed 400 milligrams of caffeine a day (about four 8-ounce cups of coffee) for a week experienced a 35 percent decrease in insulin sensitivity, which may increase the risk of diabetes.

• **Break the habit:** Start by keeping a food diary for a few days to identify all the sources of caffeine in your diet—soda, coffee, tea, energy drinks—and tally the total milligrams you're consuming, says Chad Reissig, Ph.D., a researcher at Johns Hopkins University who studies the behavioral effects of caffeine. (Consult beverage manufacturer Web sites for the actual amounts.) Then reduce your caffeine intake by about 10 percent. This could be as simple as drinking a 12-ounce can of cola instead of the 20-ounce bottle.

Your body can launch a lifelong habit by punishing you for skipping even a single hit.

"You can also mix decaf with your cup of full-strength coffee, and slowly increase the ratio," says Dr. Reissig. Keep dialing back by 10 percent every few days until your craving subsides. The gradual reduction should minimize fatigue and headaches, but plan for them anyway: Go to bed earlier to keep drowsiness at bay, Dr. Reissig says, and carry Advil or Tylenol to treat brain pain.

EVENINGS IN FRONT OF THE TUBE

Grabbing some snacks and firing up the plasma after work is okay once or twice a week. But every night? Yes, bad habit.

"People who are under high levels of stress and who may not have a large network of friends are prone to isolating themselves after work," says Leonard Jason, Ph.D., a DePaul University psychologist who studies the challenges of breaking bad habits. "Eventually, it becomes their default."

• **Why it's bad:** Slumming it on the couch plays havoc with your body and your brain. For one thing, people can consume up to 71 percent more food while they're glued to the tube, so it's no surprise that watching more than 19 hours a week increases your odds of being overweight by 97 percent, according to a 2007 Belgian study. And researchers at Case Western Reserve University found that for every hour of TV beyond 80 minutes that you watch daily, your risk of developing Alzheimer's disease increases by a whopping 30 percent.

• **Break the habit:** If you have a digital video recorder, use it to record shows, and simply start your descent to bedtime later in the evening, Jason suggests. Zipping

"Finding alternatives that you can do with others helps reduce passive TV viewing," Jason says.

through the commercials can cut about half an hour off every 2 hours of couch time. Then, at least three times a week, make after-work plans that specifically involve people—meet friends for dinner, or join a recreational sports team.

CRANKING THE TUNES

This habit sneaks up on you: You listen to your music through your headphones at a higher volume than you should a few times, and your ears become accustomed to it. Then you play it at that level all the time. Eventually, you max out the volume controls on the iPod.

"It's possible to quickly adapt and become accustomed to louder and louder sounds without realizing it," says Robert Fifer, Au.D., the director of audiology and speech-language pathology at the University of Miami's Mailman Center for Child Development.

• **Why it's bad:** Blasting Nickelback at full volume through earbuds for long intervals can cause permanent hearing damage, because your body lacks a self-defense mechanism for loud noise. While you won't feel pain in your ears until the volume exceeds 120 decibels, the damage can begin earlier than that. The cells in your inner ear that process sound begin working overtime to keep up with the onslaught and eventually die off under stress, says Dr. Fifer. The fewer of these cells you have, the more difficult it becomes to hear soft sounds. You may also experience a constant ringing in your ears, called tinnitus.

• **Break the habit:** You have to retrain your brain to perceive lower volume levels as normal and to automatically tune out background noise. Start by turning down the volume on your iPod or car stereo until you can hear other people talking to you; they shouldn't have to shout.

"If you force yourself to listen to music at a lower level, your brain will begin to perceive it as normal after about a week," says Catherine Palmer, Ph.D., the director of audiology at the University of Pittsburgh Medical Center Eye & Ear Institute. Also, think about using Loud Enough earphones ($40, loudenough.com), which reduce your music player's maximum volume by up to 20 decibels.

TALKING AND TEXTING WHILE DRIVING

We keep doing this because while we intuitively know that the combination is unsafe, we assume nothing would ever happen to us.

"If you do it once and nothing happens, your experience tells you that it's okay," says Dr. Peters. "Those repeated safe experiences build up a sense of invulnerability."

• **Why it's bad:** The hard reality is that our habit of talking and texting while driving, which springs from our still-bubbling enthusiasm for our mobile devices, conflicts directly with proof that we suck at it. Look no further than the September 2008 train crash in Los Angeles that killed 25 people; a commuter train's engineer had just sent a text message before the collision with a freight train. Even having a hands-free cell phone conversation while driving slows your reaction time by more than 20 percent, a French study found.

• **Break the habit:** Switching your cellphone ringer to silent when you step in the car is an easy, effective fix. But many people forget to do that, or they forget to turn the ringer up again, so a better strategy is to train yourself not to want to pick up the phone.

"You can teach yourself to have a negative emotional association with cell phone use while driving," Peters says. When your phone rings or beeps with a new text message, visualize what could happen if your attention is distracted; picture yourself plowing into the car ahead of you. Be graphic about it. Then imagine the effect that an accident would have on your family and on the family of the person you hit. Over time, you'll start associating the ringing cell phone with a crash, and you'll have less desire to answer it. ∎

The Doctor Will See You Now

Make sure you're a priority patient every time you call.

If you need to see a dermatologist, let's hope you don't live in Boston. It'll take you 54 days to land an appointment there, compared with a national average of 22 days. Even trying to see a general practitioner is an epic wait in Beantown: 63 days, compared with 20 days nationally.

Sure, Boston is a worst-case scenario: The delays are the result of health-care reform enacted in 2006 that guaranteed coverage for uninsured patients in Massachusetts. But guess what? If similar reforms are adopted nationwide, you could end up cooling your jets for far longer than the current national average, suggest the results of a wait-time study from Merritt Hawkins, a medical recruiting firm.

Today's picture varies wildly from state to state, but you'll have to wait 17 days on average to see an orthopedic surgeon for a bad knee, and an urgent matter is no shoo-in. Battling bronchitis? Fifty-three percent of patients who were feeling sick said they weren't able to see their physician on the same day or the following day, according to a separate study by the Commonwealth Fund, which is an independent health-care research group.

But while it might be harder than ever for you to wrestle your way in—and then secure your busy doctor's undivided attention —it's not impossible. We asked physicians and medical experts for insider tips on ensuring the best access to your M.D.

Score the Appointment

Don't assume that your oozing abscess will shoot you to the front of the line. Receptionists have heard it all before.

"You need to work carefully to convince the gatekeeper that you really do need to see your doctor soon," says Paul Konowitz, M.D., the medical director of HealthAngle. com, an informational site for patients. He suggests providing as much detail as you can and then speculating about what it might mean. If you're feeling dizzy, for example, point out that it's affecting your ability to work and function, that you're afraid to climb stairs, and that you have a family history of neurological problems you're worried about. Once the receptionist has all the information, he or she might help push up your appointment to one of the slots doctors typically reserve each day for urgent visits. If that doesn't happen, you can still jump the line.

Flaunt it if you've got it. "If you have good insurance, that's your in," says Mark Smith, president of Merritt Hawkins. Cigna, Blue Cross Blue Shield, and UnitedHealth Group, for instance, are praised by physicians for

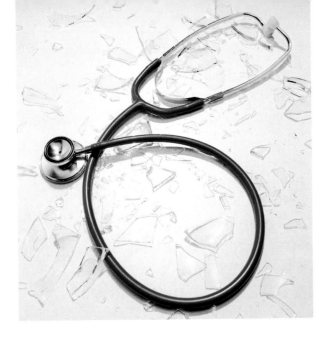

their prompt payment and relatively light paperwork requirements. Mentioning one of them, even in passing, can open doors faster. If you're on a premium plan, tout that, too. You won't need referrals, and extra tests will probably be covered. Finally, if you're willing to pay cash, say so. Doctors' offices love cash customers, says Smith. In fact, some are moving to cash-only practices where upfront, annual retainers ensure immediate doctor access.

Grab an empty spot. Every day, up to 20 percent of patients cancel their appointments, says Gina Minas, R.N., a manager of physician referral and health resources at Northwestern Memorial Hospital. "Always ask if you can be placed on a waiting list."

Go up the ranks. If the receptionist won't squeeze you in, call back and ask for the office manager or the doctor's nurse or personal

Don't assume your oozing abscess will shoot you to the front of the line.

assistant, says Dr. Konowitz. When you reach someone farther up the chain of command, clearly spell out what it is about your problem that the receptionist might not be grasping. The person can always tell the receptionist to bump up your appointment date.

Make Your Doctor Listen to You

Roughly half of doctors' appointments last less than 15 minutes, according to a 2005 survey by the Centers for Disease Control and Prevention. Still, you can have a thorough visit in that time—if you stage-manage things a bit. For starters, keep the pleasantries to a minimum. Don't waste valuable time talking about what you did during your summer vacation.

"There isn't time for the whole catching-up-with-life during your appointment," says Smith. Save the banter for the end of the visit.

Here are other ways to squeeze all the doctoring you can from your physician.

Shoot for the slow times. Friday tends to be the slowest day of the week at doctors' offices, so your visit is likely to be less rushed, says Mark Welton, M.D., chief of colorectal surgery at Stanford University. Regardless of the day, always request the first morning appointment or the first spot after lunch, when the doctor is less likely to be in a hurry, says Anne Chapas, M.D., an assistant clinical professor of dermatology at New York University. "We start on time, but toward the end of the day, things can get hairy," she says.

Prioritize your questions. Fifteen minutes isn't enough time for both an examination and a litany of queries. So make a list of your questions (this is also key to not forgetting them), and put the most important ones at the top, Dr. Chapas says. Skip the yes-no questions in order to reap the most information from the exchange.

"Keep it open-ended, like 'What are some good things I can eat that will help lower my cholesterol?' or whatever your issue is," Dr. Chapas says. If you finish asking those and still have some more time, fire off the remaining questions.

Find out what you're missing. Before you leave, ask your M.D. if there's anything else you should be asking, says Dr. Welton. Are you missing something? Is there anything they're assuming you already know? That will make the doctor think more closely about details of your problem that might not have surfaced during the appointment.

Prep for the Follow-Up

If you're waiting for test results or some other feedback from your doctor, you need to understand how he or she likes to communicate. Some physicians call back at the end of their day; others call only when they have bad news. Some tell the lab to contact you or, more rarely, they send an e-mail or letter themselves. So before you leave your appointment, ask how and when you can expect to receive your news, says Dr. Chapas.

If you've waited an appropriate amount of time and still haven't heard from the office, it's okay to provide a few gentle reminders for the doc to pick up the phone—even three times in one day is fine, says Dr. Konowitz. "Two or three messages on the chart will catch my attention much more quickly than just one."

Still think you'll end up waiting by the phone? Try the following.

Work around the law. Privacy laws prevent your doctor from providing anyone else with your medical information over the phone. That means that a physician can't leave a detailed message on your voice mail or with anyone at your home without your written permission, says Dr. Chapas. Give the doctor your okay ahead of time to leave you a message or to provide your wife with your medical information.

Hold the phone. Some docs check their e-mail more often than their phone messages, says Erin Moaratty, chief special projects officer for the Patient Advocate Foundation. "They can respond to you while they're doing other tasks," she says. Ask your doctor if that's his or her preference, and then grab an e-mail address. Keep your queries short, and refresh your doctor's memory about your condition.

Okay, So the Doctor Really *Can't* See You Now

If you can't muscle your way in to see your doc, find out if there's a physician's assistant in the office. These pros usually have master's-level certification and can provide everything from physical exams and injury treatment to preliminary diagnoses of heart conditions, cancer, and other illnesses.

"PAs can order the studies and follow up with their supervising doctors if they see something," says Jim Delaney, a certified PA in the orthopedic surgery department at the University of Texas Southwestern.

If you're paying cash, consider heading to one of the new mini-clinics at Walmart, Walgreens, Target, or CVS. They are staffed by PAs or nurse practitioners, and fees start at about $20 for a wellness visit.

Your Service Plan

These systems take the garbage out of your body. Here's how to keep them clog-free.

A few times each year, you swing your car into a repair shop for service. Inevitably, the mechanic trots over with your air filter to show you how filthy it is. "See," he'll say, acting as bummed as you are. "Better replace it."

You don't have that luxury with your body, but your lungs breathe in the same stuff your engine does, and your liver and kidneys can become as gummed up as any oil filter. These organs, along with your gastrointestinal tract and lymphatic system, cleanse your blood and sift out waste.

Ignoring them can lead to everything from hypertension to asthma. But while you can't do much for your lymphatic system—it's self-cleaning—you can take steps to keep the other four clear. After all, replacements are very hard to come by.

Filter 1

The Liver

YOUR MULTIFUNCTIONAL MARVEL

Think your liver is just there for you to abuse at happy hour? Well go easy on it, because in addition to processing booze, this 3½-pound gland—the largest in your body—has at least 250 functions. Primarily, it filters bacteria and pollutants from your blood. It also produces bile, a viscous goo that breaks down fat for digestion and absorption.

"These functions begin to suffer when alcohol injures your liver or a poor diet causes extra fat to build up in your liver," says Paul Martin, M.D., the chief of hepatology at the University of Miami. When fatty liver occurs in people who don't drink heavily, it's associated with the same risk factors as those of metabolic syndrome: obesity, diabetes, and high triglyceride levels.

Keep it clear: Hitting the gym for an extra 10 minutes a day helps ensure that your liver stays on top of its responsibilities. In a 2009 study in *Hepatology*, people with nonalcoholic fatty liver disease who increased their exercise by 60 minutes a week for 3 months reduced their levels of four enzymes that indicate liver problems.

"Exercise removes fat from the liver," says study author Jacob George, M.D., a professor of gastroenterology and hepatic medicine at the University of Sydney.

But you can easily undo your gains if you drink too much. While the occasional beer is fine, avoid binges of five or more drinks on a single occasion. And be careful about what you consider to be "a drink." One standard drink contains 0.6 ounce of alcohol, but a 2008 study from the Alcohol Research Group of the Public Health Institute found that in bars, the average glass of wine contains 43 percent more alcohol than that 0.6 ounce. The average draft beer has 22 percent more, and mixed drinks contain 32 percent more. So even if you limit the number of drinks, you could still be imbibing more alcohol than you intended to.

Filter 2

The Kidneys

THE BLOOD BALANCERS

Your kidneys are tireless. Every day they remove 2 quarts of waste and extra water from your blood. This process helps regulate blood pressure by extracting matter from your blood, which lowers your blood volume and, in turn, keeps the stress on your blood vessels and heart in check. The

Your lungs breathe in the ==same stuff your engine does,== and your liver and kidneys can become as gummed up as any oil filter.

kidneys also balance the electrolytes in your body. Too much sodium, for instance, can lead to hypertension, and high potassium can cause abnormal heart rhythms, says Bryan Becker, M.D., a professor of internal medicine at the University of Wisconsin. Signs your kidneys may not be operating at peak performance include pinkish urine, foot or hand swelling, and persistent lower-back pain.

Keep it clear: Coming up short in the H_2O department can lead to cell damage as the kidneys struggle to balance out the fluids in your body. Drink at least 3 quarts of water each day. A steady influx of water also helps to keep kidney stones from forming. These hard masses develop when calcium combines with either oxalate, phosphate, or other chemicals to form small crystals. If the crystals bind together, they can restrict the flow of fluids through your kidneys and cause severe— make that excruciating—pain. In addition to your 3-quart quota, add a glass of orange juice to your daily fluid intake.

Should You Be Tested for Toxic Buildup?

Many different pesticides and industrial compounds can accumulate in your body, but for most people there's usually no need to undergo any testing to find out, says Gabriele Ludewig, Ph.D., an associate professor of occupational and environmental health at the University of Iowa College of Public Health. It's very unlikely that trace amounts of toxins will put you out of commission.

This doesn't mean, however, you shouldn't still be reasonably cautious about what you eat. Think of it this way: "Everything is a poison if you acquire too much of it," Ludewig says. "Simply eating a diverse diet decreases the risk of accumulating too much of any toxin that may be in our food."

JEREMY PIVEN SAYS HE OD'D ON SUSHI.

"Orange juice boosts citrate levels in your urine, reducing the crystallization and lowering the calcium available for binding," says Clarita Odvina, M.D., an associate professor of internal medicine at the University of Texas Southwestern Medical Center.

Filter 3

The Lungs
BAD-AIR BATTLERS

Here's a scary thought: Your lungs are the only internal organs that are continuously exposed to the external environment. Every breath you take brings in whatever debris happens to be floating in front of your face.

To deal with that floating junk, your lungs are lined with hairlike cilia, which sweep out the pollutants, bacteria, and viruses that you breathe in. Your lungs

> Every breath brings in **whatever debris** happens to be floating in front of your face.

also perform the most essential task of extracting oxygen from the air and swapping it for carbon dioxide. Continued exposure to airborne gunk, however, can interfere with these processes, causing inflammation that may trigger bronchitis and asthmalike symptoms.

Keep it clear: Pick some apples. People who ate the most apples were 33 percent less likely to have a chronic phlegmy cough than those who ate the least, according to a National Institutes of Health study. The pectin and antioxidants in the peels can reduce inflammation in your lungs. Also, stay inside when ozone levels are high. This pollutant causes inflammation that can narrow your airways.

"If you're unusually winded after a run, you could be sensitive to ozone," says Norman Edelman, M.D., the chief medical officer of the American Lung Association. Check out daily ozone levels at airnow.gov, and work out indoors when the Air Quality Index is moderate or higher.

Filter 4
The Gastrointestinal Tract
THE FOOD PROCESSOR

You might not know how to deal with that pizza-and-cake dinner you downed, but your body does. Your GI tract runs from your esophagus down into your stomach, small intestine, and colon, and separates what you need—protein, carbohydrates, fat, vitamins, and minerals—from what you don't.

Any problems with absorption, obstruction, or movement can prevent your body from soaking up nutrients, says Brett Neustater, M.D., a gastroenterologist with the GI Group of South Florida. These problems can also cause serious discomfort. Look out for heartburn, bloating, and abdominal pain.

Keep it clear: While occasional flareups are usually harmless, frequent bouts of heartburn (more than twice a week) can scar your esophagus, causing food to stick on the way down. Taking antacids may help with the pain, but they won't prevent the attacks. If you're dealing with chronic heartburn, assess your diet.

"Cut out trigger foods, and then reintroduce them after a week or so in smaller amounts," says Dr. Neustater. Common heartburn triggers include caffeine, onions, chocolate, citrus fruits, garlic, and tomatoes. If your symptoms persist, see your doctor to rule out a more serious problem.

Hernias can also sabotage your GI tract. They occur when part of an internal organ, most often the intestines, protrudes into and obstructs your abdominal muscles, sometimes as a result of excessive straining while lifting.

"Before you lift, brace your stomach like you're about to be punched but are still able to breathe," says Pete McCall, M.S., C.S.C.S., an exercise physiologist with the American Council on Exercise. This supports and trains the muscles that line your abdominal wall. Plank exercises can also help strengthen your abs and could reduce the chances of a hernia. ■

Set a Good Habit in Stone

So you want to run every morning, choose oatmeal over Pop-Tarts, or remember to use sunscreen. Here's how to make healthy behaviors run on autopilot.

WATCH YOURSELF. People who keep track of their goals and record their progress are better able to make healthy behaviors a habit, notes a 2008 study in the *International Journal of Obesity*.

"It helps people keep in mind what they're trying to achieve and boosts their ability to make it happen," says study author Phillippa Lally, Ph.D. Write down a list of the habits you're trying to establish, and create boxes for every day of the week. Check off your successes each day.

MAKE STRESS WORK FOR YOU. If you're under stress, you're more likely to persist with behaviors that have unwanted outcomes, according to a 2009 study in the *Journal of Neuroscience*. This suggests that stress can promote bad habits. But the stress hormone cortisol, which appears to enhance habit-forming systems, might also impair systems associated with more flexible behavior, says study author Lars Schwabe, Ph.D. So going to the gym after tough workdays, for example, might help you stick to a fitness regimen.

REPEAT, REPEAT, REPEAT. Simply repeating good habits makes them more automatic. A 2007 study published in *Personality and Social Psychology Bulletin* found that after people chose an option associated with a goal (such as selecting fruit for dessert instead of ice cream) just three times, they were less tempted by the unhealthy alternative (the ice cream).

The Prosta Protection

te-
Plan

"I want my prostate back." The urologist diagnosed writer Laurence Roy Statins's prostate cancer. A high-tech robot removed the diseased organ. Then came two common after effects: sexual dysfunction, and nagging questions. Was it all a monstrous mistake?

It's June 20, the first day of summer in 2008. I'm knocked out on an operating table and a robot is removing my prostate gland. In April I learned I had stage II prostate cancer, and after questioning experts and survivors, I've decided surgery is the way to go. Let's git 'er done. My mom died of cancer, but not me. No way.

Now, almost 2 years later, I'm not going to say, "Thank God they caught it in time . . . I'm so blessed, each new morning is a miracle . . . Blah blah blah blah."

No, what I'm thinking is more along the lines of: I want my prostate back.

Your prostate gland labors in obscurity. The size of a golf ball, it's tucked away under your bladder, biding its time until you and your reproductive system decide to emit the sacred seed. Then the semen assembly line kicks in: The sperm swim up from your testicles to the seminal vesicles, and there they are mixed in a happy bath of fructose, vitamin C, and prostaglandins. This brew then proceeds to your prostate, which tops it off with enzymes, citric acid, and zinc before your man milk is propelled out of your body and into hers with rather pleasant smooth-muscle contractions. This long bomb triumphantly delivers your DNA into the end zone.

Ah, glory days.

But around the time in your life when you start to think more about your 401(k) than foreplay, your prostate starts to misfire. It swells in size, and the swelling clamps your urethra in a vise grip. If the cause of the swelling is benign, you're lucky. That's what those running-to-the-men's-room commercials for Flomax are all about. But some of the very same symptoms can also be caused by a prostate-cancer tumor.

Prostate cancer is the second most common cancer among men; only some skin cancers are more rampant. In 2009, it caused an estimated 27,360 deaths—long, slow, embattled deaths, as the cancer spread beyond men's prostates to nearby bones, notably their spines. Once the cancer advances past your prostate, you have only a 30 percent chance of surviving 5 years. But catch it early, before the cancer cells escape, and your chance of surviving 5 years is 100 percent.

Here's the good news about prostate cancer: Deaths are down because it is being diagnosed much earlier. In fact, 94 percent of all diagnoses these days peg the malignancy at stage I or stage II, before it metastasizes beyond the prostate. (Stage III cancers have begun to break out of the prostate; stage IV cancers have invaded nearby tissue and bone.) That has resulted in a steadily declining death rate of 4 percent a year since 1994. The declining mortality has generally been attributed to the widespread use—starting in the 1990s—of a simple test for the prostate-specific antigen, or PSA.

These days, the PSA test is so routine for middle-aged men that your doctor might order one for you without even asking. My internist did that for me in the summer of 2007, as part of a regular physical. Mostly he was worried about my cholesterol levels. The results showed mildly troubling cholesterol—but a very troubling PSA number. Standards in place at the time held that it should be less than 4; some evidence has suggested that it should be less than 2.5 if you're younger than 50. Mine was 12.6.

My doctor sent me to a urologist, who suspected that my high number was caused by a prostate infection. The only way to confirm those suspicions, unfortunately, was by collecting some prostatic fluid. He sat there grinning apologetically as he held up one gloved and well-lubricated index finger and asked me to bend over a chair. Then he stuck his finger up my ass and pushed on my prostate like it was a doorbell on Halloween night. About 10 minutes later, after I'd recovered, he gave me a scrip for an antibiotic and told me to come back at the end of the summer so he could retest my PSA.

I really didn't want to go back. So I didn't.

I put it off repeatedly until the night, months later, when I met the person I later called, only half-jokingly, the Angel on the Train. I was sitting in the dining car having chicken à la Amtrak with my wife and son when suddenly a disheveled old man tottered up the aisle carrying a little plastic bag full of pills. The steward swung him around and plopped him into the booth with us.

Nobody said a word for 15 minutes. Awkward! Then I started talking to him, and before I knew it we were comparing prostates. My wife ratted me out: "He had a high PSA reading," she said, waving her fork in my direction. "But he won't go back to the doctor."

The old guy turned to me. And, establishing eye contact for the first time, he said, "You really need to have that checked out."

When I returned home I had another PSA test. It was 9.2. That's better, right?

Well, as it turns out, nothing about the PSA test is accurate, starting with the name. The letters stand for a protein produced by the prostate. When PSA was first identified, the prostate appeared to be its only source, but it has even been detected, albeit in smaller amounts, in women. Clearly, there are non-prostate sources of PSA.

"I want my prostate back."

When your prostate is healthy, PSA is mostly contained within it, but if there is trouble in the tissue, more PSA can leak into the blood. By the time cancer has ransacked and spread beyond the gland, PSA levels can soar into the thousands. But the PSA test is so exquisitely fine-tuned that it picks up leaking PSA at the very lowest levels, measuring it in nanograms per milliliter of blood. That's right: nanogram, as in one-billionth of a gram.

As it turns out, the common threshold of 4 nanograms per milliliter is rather arbitrary. You can have cancer even if your PSA reading is below 4. That was definitively shown by a 2004 study of 2,950 men who were followed for 7 years as part of the Prostate Cancer Prevention Trial. These men never had a PSA level above 4, or an abnormal digital rectal exam, for the entire length of the study. They all underwent a prostate biopsy, and cancer was found in 449 of them, or 15.2 percent.

On the other hand, you can have a PSA reading above 4, and it could be caused by two common maladies: prostatitis, which is an inflammation usually caused by an infection, and benign prostatic hyperplasia (BPH), which is the fancy name for the benign swelling that plagues aging glands. Both can cause PSA leakage. In fact, the majority of high PSA readings are due to these noncancerous causes. Only one man in four with a PSA level between 4 and 10 will be found to have cancer after a subsequent biopsy.

The PSA test is no pregnancy test.

So what good is this PSA test, anyway? Even its defenders admit, sheepishly, that it's no pregnancy test. And its detractors say it's useless. In 2004, a team of Stanford urologists looked at pathology results of more than 1,300 surgically removed prostates and found that the PSA number predicted nothing more than the gland's size. The lead author, Thomas Stamey, M.D., now retired, declared at the time, "The PSA era is probably over." Which is noteworthy: Dr. Stamey is one of the inventors of the method used to prepare PSA for testing, and in 1987 he published the first study linking increased PSA levels to prostate cancer.

But nobody listened, and a lot of men continue to get biopsies they don't really need. If an estimated 192,280 men were diagnosed with prostate cancer in 2009, you can bet another 575,000 men endured biopsies that turned up nothing. If that statistic makes you shrug, you've never had a doctor come after you with a biopsy gun.

April 11, 2008. I'm lying on my left side on a gurney in my urologist's office. As instructed, I've lowered my pants to my knees. I'm here for a biopsy, but first comes the ultrasound. My doctor lubricates the ultrasound wand, which is about the size of my son's Spider-Man toothbrush, and slides it into my rectum. All is well until he starts to muscle it into various positions to improve the camera angles; then it feels less like a medical device and more like a broom handle.

Can a biopsy be any worse? Yes, it can. He inserts a syringe into my rectum to inject lidocaine into my prostate—six shots, in six separate locations, and all I can say is, never have a prostate biopsy without serious sedation. But by the time my doctor goes back up there to grab his 12 tissue samples, I don't feel a thing. I just hear the spring-loaded biopsy gun go off, bang, each time.

Then I go home to rest. And hope. Only a one in four chance they'll find something. I like those odds.

Five days later, the report comes back. Two of the 12 tissue cores are positive for cancer. I talk to people, even though the last thing I want to do is talk to people. Why are women so much better at this? They have "races for the cure" and that pink ribbon. A freakin' logo for their cancer! It must be a girl thing.

As for me, I just quietly call some strangers whose names have been passed along to me—by women, of course. One guy, John, had a biopsy that came back with only 1 percent cancer in one core. But his father had died of prostate cancer, so after 2 years of "watchful waiting," he finally went under the knife. I could opt for watchful waiting, but . . . waiting for what? For cancer to colonize my spine?

I have three treatment options: (1) surgery to remove my prostate, (2) external beams of radiation, or (3) brachytherapy, which involves implanting radioactive pellets in my prostate. Radiation treatments and their side effects can stretch out over months. I just want this to end. I'm in my 50s, so I'll recover from surgery, no problem. I choose surgery.

Besides, some 75,000 radical prostatectomies were performed robotically in the

TO TEST OR NOT TO TEST?

If you skip the PSA test, you'll never undergo an unnecessary biopsy, and you'll avoid treatment for a tumor that may not harm you (or even exist). But you'll also have no way of knowing if there's aggressive cancer in your prostate until it's too late. What's a guy to do?

"While many men risk being overdiagnosed and overtreated, PSA testing can undeniably save lives," says Judd W. Moul, M.D., FACS, director of the Duke Prostate Center and a *Men's Health* advisor. Here's how to make the best of a flawed test.

START AT AGE 40.

Your first test will provide a baseline PSA value, so when you're tested again (usually at age 45), your doctor can observe whether your levels have risen, and if so, how quickly a.k.a. your "PSA velocity." The greater the velocity, the more likely it is that you have not only prostate cancer, but aggressive prostate cancer at that.

RULE OUT IMPOSTERS.

Elevated PSA doesn't always mean you have prostate cancer. Case in point: Only one in four men with a PSA level of 4 to 10 actually has the disease. If your score falls in that range (and even if the velocity is high, too), talk to your doctor about eliminating other possible PSA-boosting culprits, such as benign prostate enlargement, infection, or trauma to the area.

CONSIDER RISK FACTORS.

Race, age, and family history of prostate cancer can all play a role in your risk. African Americans' prostate-cancer rates are nearly 60 percent higher than those of Caucasians; Asian Americans have among the lowest rates. Between ages 40 and 60, your odds of developing it are 1 in 40. If your father or brother has had a tumor down there, your risk doubles.

SCHEDULE THAT "OTHER" TEST.

Yes, a digital rectal exam (DRE) is unpleasant. And the results, considered alone, aren't any more accurate than those from a PSA test. But combine the diagnostic power of the two tests, and accuracy increases. Consider scheduling a DRE with an experienced urologist if your PSA velocity is high and you've ruled out non-cancer causes.

United States in 2008. The surgeon sits across the room at a console that looks like a video-game booth, manipulating a set of robotic arms over the patient. Unlike traditional surgery, there's no 8-inch incision and not as much blood loss; instead, the procedure is done through six dime-sized cuts in and below the navel. The best part, of course, is that the surgeon can be incredibly accurate, because he's seeing the tissues magnified 10 times and controlling the arms to make microsized movements. And if he sneezes, hey, no problem! As two doctors wrote in the British medical journal *The Lancet*, a nice feature here is the "elimination of a surgeon's physiological tremor."

Oh, yeah. I like that feature. When the whole point is to remove my prostate while sparing the surrounding nerves that create my erections, I totally love that feature.

It's June 18, 2008, two nights before surgery. I'm in bed with my wife, and I miss my prostate already. I tell her that if and when we have sex again, there will be no ejaculate, no man milk, no wet spot. Henceforth I shall be seedless. You can see where I was going with this, can't you, guys? I was hoping I'd receive a happy send-off.

My wife says, "You should talk to your doctor about that."

Gosh, honey. Thanks.

Here's what patients think their doctors say:
If you undergo the relatively new "nerve-sparing" prostate surgery, you will eventually return to the level of erectile function you enjoyed before you had the surgery. It may take weeks, months, or a couple of years, depending on age and prostate size, but that mojo will return. That's what

patients want to hear, too, so maybe they miss the doctors' qualifiers about "most men" and "in certain cases . . ."

Unfortunately, that's just not the truth, says John L. Gore, M.D., an assistant professor of urology at the University of Washington. "Even with a perfect surgery there's going to be some shutdown."

Dr. Gore is qualified to say this; he conducted one of the most recent studies of prostate-cancer patients and how surgery affects them. He and his UCLA colleague, Mark Litwin, M.D., followed 475 prostate-cancer patients for 4 years. These patients received more scrutiny than the typical so-how's-your-erection questions from their doctors. They filled out a 20-minute questionnaire in the privacy of their homes before surgery and at 1, 2, 4, 8, 12, 18, 24, 30, 36, 42, and 48 months afterward. And, no, things were not as they had been before.

"We're not saying sexual function is terrible after surgery," says Dr. Gore. "We're saying the likelihood of that function being exactly what it was before surgery is essentially zero." And, he adds, you'll recover what you're going to recover within 2 years. "Beyond that, it is what it is."

Okay, so . . . just how messed up are prostate patients? That question was answered by a nine-hospital study of 1,201 men, led by Martin Sanda, M.D., director of the prostate-cancer center at Beth Israel Deaconess Medical Center. After 2 years, radiation and brachytherapy patients complained most about urinary and bowel troubles; the 603 prostatectomy patients (93 percent of whom had nerve-sparing surgery) complained more about sexual function. To be blunt: Sixty-four percent of them said their erections were not firm enough for penetration (compared with 17 percent who had erection trouble before surgery), and just under half did not recover erections suitable for sex. This is, remember, 2 years after their surgery.

"One problem is that doctors often don't spend enough time with their patients to fully explain that sexual recovery typically takes years, not months, and often does not occur," Dr. Sanda says. "Men might assume that as long as they can have a nerve-sparing procedure, their sexuality will be fine. In reality, nerve sparing provides a reasonable chance for erection recovery, but it by no means guarantees it."

I'm not trying to pick a fight with urologic or cancer surgeons, but rather to help prostate-cancer patients have expectations that are more realistic. "Patients live a long time after treatment and many die with, rather than from, prostate cancer," notes Dr. Gore. "It's critical that they participate in shared decision making with their physicians so they don't come out of the process with regret."

I had no regrets. At first. I spent one night in the hospital, and 5 days later I taught a 3-hour class. Soon I'd quit inserting pink panty liners into my boxers. And urination became a reclaimed pleasure: I could piss like a racehorse, just like in my teens.

As for what's clinically called "restoration of sexual function," here's my official report: I dunno. My marriage was a mess, so you can imagine the amount of sexual healing that didn't happen. But plenty of guys' marriages are, you know, meh—just okay. So I wonder: Do a lot of wives think

this is a dandy time to close up shop? How many other wives make it a habit to come to bed long after he's asleep?

I also wonder how much of the sexual wreckage is more than just nerve damage. Without any ejaculate, I feel like a broken toy. Like a water pistol that squirts jelly. (Or nothing.) If love ever comes my way again, I'll sort of dread it. I'll be a spectator at my own sexual rehab, and we all know what that does for an erection.

> "Nerve sporing provides a reasonable chance for erection recovery, **but it by no means guarantees it.**"

While wondering whether I'd ever again throw the high hard one, I read everything I could about prostate cancer. Within weeks I was filled with remorse. In early August— less than 2 months post-op—the U.S. Preventive Services Task Force, the nation's leading independent panel of experts in prevention and primary care, said doctors should no longer screen for prostate cancer in men age 75 and older. At that age, the panel reasoned, the harms from treating the cancer outweigh the benefits.

This was a big deal: As recently as 2002, the panel was neutral on the topic. But the evidence of the last several years led the panel to conclude that the benefits of screening in the 75-and-older age group are "small to none," while the harms from treatment are "moderate to substantial."

As a recent cancer patient, I was totally

confused. Wait a minute, I'm thinking. This is cancer we're talking about. If you don't kill it, it kills you. Right?

Wrong.

As it turns out, prostate cancer is "heterogeneous," as the panel's report puts it. That is, one man's prostate cancer differs from another's. Some prostate cancer is aggressive, spreads rapidly, and will kill you. But screening tends to pick up the more slow-growing cancers. They can stop growing. You can live with them for years, symptom-free. Some may even regress on their own, says one theory, without nuclear bullets or robot intervention. I'm not 75, but I still had reason to wonder: Was my cancer the dangerous kind or the benign kind?

Here's the real problem with screening based on the PSA test: It can't tell the difference! So why operate on a 76-year-old man who is more likely to die of something else? By age 80, most men have some cancer in their prostate. And the question is even harder to answer for younger men.

PSA screening is too good. The panel concluded that in the 75-and-up crowd, screening finds cancer that "will never cause symptoms during the patient's lifetime." Here's a jarring thought: In 1980, a white man's lifetime risk of a prostate-cancer diagnosis was one in 11; today it's one in six. Yet his chance of dying of cancer is lower, not higher. So we're finding more cancer, with fewer fatalities. Just how much cancer is not worth finding? The panel wasn't sure, but noted this: "Incidence data suggest overdiagnosis rates ranging from 29 percent to 44 percent of all prostate-cancer cases detected by PSA screening."

Almost 8 months later, with my toy still

Your Gland-Protection Plan

Taking these six steps now can reduce your risk of prostate cancer.

1 **Drink more coffee.** Regular, decaf, half-caf, whatever—it's all good, say Harvard researchers. They found that men who drank six or more cups of regular or decaf coffee were 59 percent less likely to develop advanced prostate cancer than those who eschewed the brew. More research is needed to determine what's in java that might make it beneficial, says study author Kathryn Wilson, Ph.D.

2 **Give your gland a regular workout (i.e., have lots of sex).** A 2004 study in the *Journal of the American Medical Association* analyzed data on 29,342 men and found that guys who had 21 or more orgasms a month were about 30 percent less likely to develop prostate cancer than those who racked up only four to seven a month. A possible explanation is . . . wait, who cares? Tell your wife it's doctor's orders.

3 **See red, eat red.** For the 1,324th time, eat more cooked tomato products to reduce your risk of prostate cancer. This quirky link was first noticed in the 1990s by Harvard researcher Edward Giovannucci, M.D., Sc.D., and subsequent studies have confirmed the power of edible red. Credit lycopene, a pigment in tomatoes that's more potent after they're cooked. Aim for two-plus servings a week.

4 **Move it.** Exercise reduces the risk of fatal forms of prostate cancer by 41 percent. What's more, among survivors of prostate cancer, those who exercised vigorously (playing tennis, running, swimming, or biking) for 5 hours a week had a 56 percent lower risk of death from the disease.

"More activity is more protective," says lead researcher Stacey A. Kenfield, Sc.D., of the Harvard School of Public Health.

5 **Top off your oil.** Fish don't have prostates, but if they did, we're betting they wouldn't get prostate cancer. In studies on lab animals, the omega-3 fatty acids DHA and EPA in fish oil inhibited tumors. Plus, Harvard researchers found that men who ate fish three times a week reduced their risk of aggressive prostate cancer by 25 percent.

6 **Ditch the doughnuts.** Men with the highest blood levels of trans fats have more than twice the prostate-cancer risk of men with the lowest levels. Trans-fatty acids increase inflammation and insulin resistance, both of which may play a role in prostate cancer. Avoid commercially baked doughnuts and cookies, as well as packaged baked goods containing hydrogenated oil.

broken and my heart breaking, I read the results of two huge trials that assessed regular screening—similar to what I received. They were published in the *New England Journal of Medicine (NEJM)*, accompanied by an editorial by Michael J. Barry, M.D., a prostate disease outcomes researcher and the chief of general medicine at Massachusetts General Hospital. His conclusion: "Serial PSA screening has at best a modest effect on prostate-cancer mortality during the first decade of follow-up. This benefit comes at the cost of substantial overdiagnosis and overtreatment."

Overdetection. Overdiagnosis. Overtreatment. These are the new buzzwords of 21st-century cancer research—not just on prostate cancer but on breast cancer, too.

Here are the particulars. In one of the *NEJM* studies, nearly 77,000 men from 10 U.S. study centers were divided into two groups. Either they received an annual PSA test and a digital rectal exam, or they received "usual care," which may or may not have included screening. After 10 years, there was no reduction in the death rate for the screened group.

The other study followed 182,000 men in seven European countries. The 73,000 men who were screened an average of every 4 years for prostate cancer underwent 17,000 biopsies and had a 70 percent higher rate of disease. They also, not surprisingly, received much more treatment. According to estimates, 277 per 10,000 of those men underwent radical prostatectomy (versus 100 in the control group), and another 220 per 10,000 had radiation therapy (versus 123 per 10,000 in the control group). That's a lot of treatment—with few lives saved. The

study's conclusion: If you aggressively screened 1,410 men, and cut or irradiated 48 of them, you'd save exactly one man's life.

Were those my odds? I hate those odds.

Did I need surgery or not? Because if I didn't, I want my prostate back.

I'm in the hospital's pathology lab to visit my prostate, or what remains of it. After my surgery it was sent here, where it was sliced up like proscuitto. Then 24 tissue slices, each just 3 millimeters thick, were stained bubblegum pink and made into microscope-friendly slides. We look at slide F-4 because I want to see what cancer—my cancer, specifically—looks like. It doesn't look like anything. It looks like the Blob.

"It's actually not very interesting," the pathologist is telling me. It's just a ho-hum, garden-variety cancer. If I had left it in my body, she thinks it would have begun to bother me in another 4 or 5 years.

"Probably," she says. She thinks a moment, then tells me: "You made the right choice."

The surgical pathology report on my operation notes that a 57-year-old white male received a robotic prostatectomy. Several specimens were examined, including surrounding fat tissue, vas deferens, and seminal vesicles. All were cancer-free. Finally, the prostate itself arrived: 40 grams. With plenty of cancer to go around. There is tumor present on the left and right sides of the gland, in nine of the 24 sections, and most worrisome of all, it's present at the margin of the prostate on the lower left side.

It's given a Gleason score of 7 (on a 10-point scale), which means it's moderately abnormal. It's staged at T2c, the last stage before cancer begins to spread beyond the prostate gland.

I call someone who will know what it all means: Eric Klein, M.D., chairman of the Glickman Urological and Kidney Institute at the Cleveland Clinic. He thinks I might have gone another decade without symptoms. But based on the grade and volume of the tumor, "I would say, yes, you definitely needed to have that tumor removed."

In another decade, I'll still be in my 60s. My father is 92.

I wonder what my urologist thinks; he knows my prostate better than anyone. After all, he's the man who removed it. So I make my 1-year follow-up appointment. Maybe he's completely changed his position on prostate cancer. Maybe he's prescribing herbal teas these days. Who knows?

If you aggressively screened 1,410 men, and cut or irradiated 48 of them, you'd save exactly one man's life.

My urologist sits down with me and patiently looks over my pathology report. Yes, there was a lot of tumor volume. Furthermore, it was on both sides of the gland. Furthermore, it was at the margin of the gland in one spot. Then he notes a detail I'd neglected to tell Dr. Klein: The cancer was located at the bottom of the gland, a site where, according to a Vanderbilt University study, small margins of cancerous prostate cells commonly remain after surgery.

"By age 70, you would probably have had metastatic disease," he concludes. "Or earlier."

"When would I have begun to feel pain?" He's silent.

"What are you thinking?"

He's slow to answer. "I'm thinking, dying of prostate cancer is horrible," he finally says. The cancer, once it spreads, causes immense pain. It can obstruct the bladder and everything else down below, so the patient needs to have tubes inserted. Multiple tubes. Requiring multiple hospital stays. And there's the hormone therapy, which is so often in vain.

"If we could know whose cancer is going to progress and whose won't," he says, "that would be great."

Great for him, I have the feeling, as much as for his patients.

He tries to be helpful. We talk about the odds of recurrence, and PSA doubling time, and various treatments, and what works best. But again, there's nothing you can hang your hat on.

I tilt my head back and scream at his ceiling tiles: "There's nothing about prostate cancer you can hang your hat on!"

Except for this fact: Nobody wants to die of it. So I guess it was a good thing my prostate was taken out.

My friend John is not so sure. Here it is, 18 months later, and he still has erectile problems, leaky bladder problems. Does he regret it? "A lot of times, yes," he says.

As for you? I hope you or your father or one of your friends will not be among the unlucky many to receive a diagnosis of prostate cancer. And this year, there will be enough men to fill nearly three Superdomes. Picture it: row upon row of silent men with full agendas and empty stares. And no place to hang a hat.

Extra-Strength Pain Relief

Wincing and yelling take you only so far.
Here's how to stop the suffering.

Pain lets you know that health trouble has arrived. But sometimes pain won't go away after delivering the message.

Consider the case of Dave Brown of Lancaster, Pennsylvania, who develops GPS systems for fire departments. He's 27, but when he rolls out of bed he feels like he should be AARP-eligible next June.

"My pain is nearly constant," says Brown, who attributes his achy back and neck to 14 years of soccer. "I deal with it, but it makes me less productive." At night he usually winds up on the couch, too drained to move.

"When pain is no longer useful, it becomes detrimental to the body," says Carol A. Warfield, M.D., a professor of anesthesia at Harvard Medical School. "It can affect everything from mood to quality of life." But with the following tips from top medical experts, you can learn to control pain, not be a slave to it.

A SCORCHED MOUTH (PIZZA BURN)

Understand it: "The tissue in the roof of the mouth is very thin, so it's sensitive and prone to a painful burn when hot food meets your palate," says Michael W. Smith, M.D., chief medical editor for WebMD.

Stop it: Pop an ice cube for damage control; you're numbing the area and reducing swelling. Anbesol or another oral-use topical anesthetic can help, too.

Still hurts? After eating, rinse with a solution of ⅛ teaspoon of salt in 8 ounces of warm water. The salt will help disinfect your mouth. Just don't swallow.

Prevent it: Be careful with foods coming out of the microwave. "While the outside may feel just warm, the inside may be scorching hot," says Dr. Smith. Let any nuked meal rest for at least a few minutes before digging in.

PLANTAR FASCIITIS

Understand it: The band of tissue that runs along the arch of your foot is inflamed from hitting the treadmill or pavement.

Stop it: Ease up on the cardio until the stabbing pain's edge dulls. If it flares back up, take ibuprofen (e.g., Advil) and ice your heel for 15 to 20 minutes. Loosening up the area might also help. "Men with this problem often have tight calf muscles and Achilles tendons," says Matthew Matava, M.D., an associate professor of orthopedic surgery at Washington University. Try rolling each foot over a tennis ball for 10 to 15 minutes, several times a day.

Still hurts? Use a night splint to keep your foot, calf, and plantar fascia stretched overnight, reducing the pain, says Nicholas A. DiNubile, M.D., an orthopedic surgeon and the author of *FrameWork: Your 7-Step Program for Healthy Muscles, Bones, and Joints.*

Prevent it: Don't set the treadmill on an incline. "Running uphill strains the plantar fascia," says Dr. Matava, who recommends finding running shoes with strong arch supports that fit your foot's structure to relieve pressure. (We like the Asics Gel-Evolution 4.)

HEARTBURN

Understand it: Stomach acid spills into your esophagus, burning like a forest fire.

Stop it: Reach for an over-the-counter acid blocker such as Pepcid AC or Zantac 75, or chew sugarless gum. A study in the *Journal of Dental Research* found that chewing gum for 30 minutes after a high-fat meal lessens acid reflux by generating

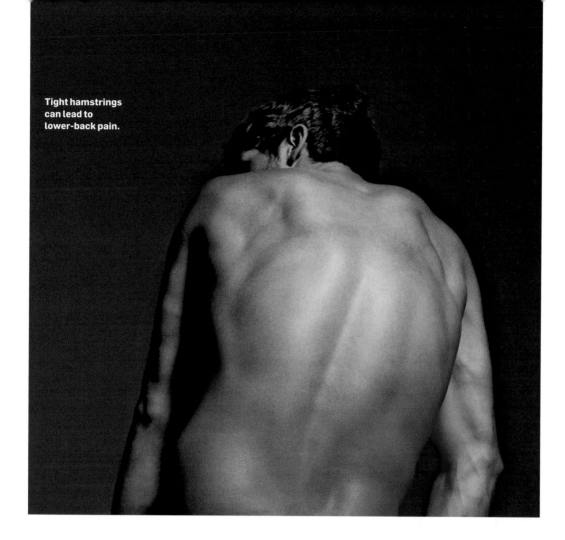

Tight hamstrings
can lead to
lower-back pain.

enough saliva to make you swallow more and push acid back down.

Still hurts? You might have gastroesophageal reflux disease, or GERD. See a doctor; GERD can lead to esophageal cancer.

Prevent it: Make stomach acid work against gravity at night by placing 2-inch blocks under the legs at the head of your bed, says Ted Epperly, M.D., president of the American Academy of Family Physicians.

Also, if you're a smoker, here's one more reason to quit. "Nicotine relaxes the LES valve, the muscle at the end of the esophagus, which usually opens only to allow food to pass into the stomach," says Dr. Smith. "Once it's loosened, acid can shoot back into the esophagus."

HEMORRHOIDS

Understand them: The veins in or around your anus are swollen and irritated.

Stop them: Apply a hemorrhoid-shrinking nonprescription ointment (such as Preparation H) in the morning, at night, and after each bowel movement. And soak the offending area in a tub filled with several inches of warm water for 15 to 20 minutes, three or four times a day. This can help decrease the painful swelling, Dr. Smith says.

Still hurts? If the pain persists after 2 weeks, you may require surgery.

Prevent them: Consume at least 25 grams of fiber and slug back no fewer than eight 8-ounce glasses of water a day.

CARPAL TUNNEL SYNDROME

Understand it: A nerve running from your forearm to your wrist is squeezed or inflamed within the narrow passageway of ligament and bones at the base of the hand.

Stop it: Hit the mat. A study in the *Journal of the American Medical Associa-* *tion* found that a twice-weekly yoga regimen practiced for 8 weeks eased symptoms and improved grip strength. You can also wear a wrist splint at night or while typing or driving.

"It keeps your wrist neutral, which prevents further compression and irritation of the nerve," says Tanya J. Lehky, M.D., director of the Clinical EMG Lab at the NIH's National Institute of Neurological Disorders and Stroke.

Still hurts? Ask your doctor for a referral to a hand surgeon, who can either inject corticosteroids into the carpal tunnel to reduce swelling and inflammation, or perform surgery to correct the problem.

Prevent it: "Set your keyboard at a height that allows your hand to work in a

The Pain Scale

Sure it hurts, but it's hard to convey your inner pain to medical professionals. Use this chart to let your doctor know how badly an ailment is bothering you.

NUISANCE	DISTRACTION	UNBEARABLE
Yes, it's a nuisance, basically. It's aggravating and noticeable, but most men can distract themselves from it. Nonmedical means should work, from applying ice or heat and stretching to preoccupying yourself with an activity.	The pain itself is distracting you, inhibiting you from participating in some of your daily activities. You might need medical intervention, including an OTC painkiller such as ibuprofen. You also might need a physical therapy or an exercise program.	You're experiencing a major reduction in function. This level of pain usually requires medical intervention that might include prescription drugs, injection therapies, and/or surgical procedures. Rehab might be required. Psychological therapies, like biofeedback, guided imagery, and other behavioral techniques to reduce pain perception, may help.

straight or neutral position," says Dr. Lehky. "Bending your wrist too far forward or backward pressures the nerve."

SUNBURN

Understand it: Ultraviolet rays inflame skin cells and irritate nerves. Reinforcements —bloodborne repair cells and nutrients— arrive on the scene. Skin temperature rises. Friends remind you of this crazy new invention called sunblock.

Pain delivers an important message, but sometimes it can overstay its welcome.

Stop it: To reduce inflammation, take a few ibuprofen and apply a cool, wet cloth. Next, slather yourself with skin cream. (We like Neutrogena Skin Aid; it contains glycerin, which is used in burn centers.)

"Nerves that are exposed to the air hurt," says Adnan Nasir, M.D., an adjunct clinical assistant professor of dermatology at UNC Chapel Hill. "Covering them with a moist ointment can reduce the pain on contact." For extra cooling, pop the lotion into the freezer for 10 minutes or so before application.

Still hurts? Take 900 micrograms of vitamin A and 15 milligrams of vitamin E every day for 2 weeks after a toasting.

"Sunburn creates cell-damaging molecules called free radicals," says Dr. Nasir. "Damaged cells increase inflammation, causing even more pain. These two vitamins help by scavenging free radicals."

Prevent it: Read the sun-exposure warnings on your Rx labels. "A whole range of medications, from antibiotics to blood-pressure medications, increases sensitivity to the sun," says Dr. Nasir.

MIGRAINE HEADACHE

Understand it: Changes in brain chemicals activate neuropeptides that invade the brain's covering, resulting in increased bloodflow and inflammation. The result is a throbbing, pulsing headache that can last for hours or days.

Stop it: Try Excedrin Migraine for a mild to moderate migraine. It has caffeine, which will help your body absorb the pain-relieving ingredients faster. You, on the other hand, should slow down.

"People with migraines have hyperexcitable brains, so they're more prone to headaches after experiencing stressors," says Steven M. Baskin, Ph.D., director of the New England Institute for Behavioral Medicine. Laying a pack of frozen peas across the back of your neck for 10 to 15 minutes can help, too.

Still hurts? If your condition is severe, talk to your doctor about migraine-specific drugs called triptans, which are very effective when taken in moderation, says Dr. Baskin.

Prevent it: Decipher your migraine triggers by downloading a headache diary at achenet.org/tools/diaries. Then add 600 milligrams of magnesium (gradually —too much at once can cause diarrhea) and 400 milligrams of riboflavin to your daily vitamin intake. Studies have linked low levels of magnesium to migraine attacks, and in one *Neurology* study, nearly

60 percent of people who took riboflavin daily for 3 months cut their migraine days by at least half.

TOOTHACHE

Understand it: Bacteria-filled plaque that settled on your teeth has been feasting away on sugars and other carbohydrates. The acidic by-products ate away at the tooth enamel; the resulting cavity allowed bacteria to invade the tissues and nerves inside, causing a painful infection.

Stop it: Take a few ibuprofen to help with the pain, and ask your dentist to call in an antibiotic before your appointment if you can't come in right away. "Although the antibiotic won't cure the toothache, it can reduce the infection in the gum and jaw around the tooth, easing pain," says Jerry Gordon, D.M.D., owner of the Dental Comfort Zone in Bensalem, Pennsylvania. He recommends rinsing with warm salt water four to six times throughout the day to ease any swelling associated with the infected tooth.

Still hurts? "Once a toothache occurs, the only solution is a root canal or having the tooth pulled," says Dr. Gordon. Too late for a mere filling, your cavity has now reached the pulp inside the tooth.

Prevent it: Limit your intake of high-carbohydrate foods like candy and sugar-frosted cereal. "Every exposure to these foods allows an acid attack on the teeth for about 20 minutes," says Dr. Gordon. If you must drink soda or sugar-filled drinks, he says, sip through a straw to bypass your teeth. To rid your mouth of cavity-causing plaque, brush three times a day, floss, and

consider using an oral irrigator, such as the Conair Interplak Dental Water Jet.

TENDINITIS

Understand it: The thick cord that attaches muscle to bone becomes worn, irritated, or inflamed, causing pain or range-of-motion limitations at your shoulder, elbow, Achilles tendon, or knee. Blame repetitive use, such as swinging a golf club or a tennis racket too often, or using incorrect technique, or both.

Stop it: Take a week off from the activity, during which time you can dull the pain with a nonsteroidal anti-inflammatory drug, such as naproxen (e.g., Aleve). Dr. Matava also recommends icing the tendon for 15 to 20 minutes, two or three times a day, until the pain subsides.

Still hurts? See a physical therapist or certified athletic trainer, says Dr. Matava.

Prevent it: "Cross-training helps relieve stress on the muscles and tendons involved," says Dr. Matava, who encourages incorporating swimming, cycling, and weight training into your workout regimen along with regular tendon-testers like running or tennis. Just be sure it doesn't involve the affected area.

LOWER-BACK PAIN

Understand it: "The most common problem is muscle strain," says Dr. Matava. "The muscles are stretched and microscopic tears occur in those fibers, which release chemicals that activate nerve endings throughout the area."

Stop it: Take ibuprofen and heat the area for 10 to 15 minutes a few times a day. But don't stop completely. "Bed rest leads to stiffness and decreased flexibility, both of which only increase pain," says Dr. Smith. Dial down activity a bit, and then dial it back up as the pain begins to ease.

Still hurts? If dialing down your activity level doesn't work, the next steps might include physical therapy, deep-tissue injection, or even surgery. So see your doctor.

Prevent it: Stretch your hamstrings once your body is already warmed up, not before. "When the hamstrings are tight, they can pull on the small postural muscles of the low back, causing pain," says Perry Fine, M.D., a professor of anesthesiology at University of Utah School of Medicine. ∎

Pin Down Your Pain

For weeks, Nathan Suver had a serious pain in the neck. It was a recurring problem, related to a back injury, and nothing made it go away. Until, that is, his doctor jabbed him with pins.

The National Institutes of Health reports that more than 3 million Americans tried acupuncture in 2007.

"He did it as part of a routine visit," recalls Suver, a 35-year-old software developer from Southington, Connecticut. "He has acupuncture training. He just said, 'This will help with the pain,' and stuck 10 little needles in me. He first put one in my neck, and then one in my wrist. It felt like lightning shooting through my body from my neck to my wrist. But it was actually only slightly uncomfortable."

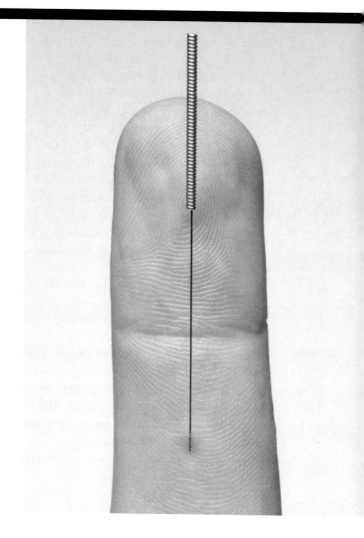

The treatment was worth that slight discomfort, because Suver's pain went away. A week later, he bragged about the success on Facebook. "What's even more amazing is that while I was convinced it wouldn't work, it did anyway," he wrote. "So much for the placebo effect."

Acupuncture, from an Eastern perspective, is all about energy and its flow through your body. If that flow is blocked, the thinking goes, pain or illness results. By gently tapping as many as 20 thin needles into your body at strategic points, acupuncturists try to reestablish the flow. That's a compelling but not necessarily convincing explanation. So Western medicine is working to understand the mechanisms of acupuncture.

"There are many details we still don't understand, but essentially, acupuncture seems to stimulate specific muscles and nerves, activating changes that reduce pain and symptoms and promote healing," says Kwokming James Cheng, M.D., whose June review in *Acupuncture in Medicine* aimed to identify the precise neurological significance of common "acupoints"—areas targeted in acupuncture.

How acupuncture works might be unclear, but the benefits stick out. Research shows that this ancient therapy can be an effective treatment for a wide variety of ailments, from back pain and sciatica to headaches, nausea, and asthma.

We consulted experts and recent studies to find out which conditions seem to benefit most from acupuncture. So if you're struggling with one of the following ailments, you might consider going under the needle.

Headaches

For most men, popping an aspirin can thwart the occasional skull attack. If headaches become intense or unremitting, though, OTC therapy might not keep them at bay—while the pins-and-needles approach might. Acupuncture taps directly into recent research theorizing that tension headaches—the most common kind—are not caused by muscles alone. Neurochemicals associated with mood and emotional well-being, such as nitric oxide and serotonin, may also play a role.

"The needles appear to send signals to the brain to adjust the levels of these neurochemicals," says Dr. Cheng.

SCIENCE SAYS: If your headaches tend to rebound or linger for days, some deft needling can help reduce the frequency of their intrusions into your life.

How acupuncture works might be unclear, but the benefits stick out.

"Acupuncture is a preventive treatment to reduce headache frequency and intensity," says Klaus Linde, M.D., a complementary-medicine researcher at Technical University Munich in Germany.

In a recent review of 11 studies on people with frequent tension headaches, Dr. Linde found that nearly half of patients who had acupuncture reported a 50 percent decrease in the number of days they had headaches, compared with a 16 percent drop in study participants who received painkillers and other routine care instead.

Gastrointestinal Problems

Saverio Mancina couldn't eat a thing. "I had severe cramping and diarrhea constantly," the Boston marketing exec says of his digestive troubles of 3 years ago. No prescription drugs helped, and tests for parasites and celiac disease came back negative. In addition to altering his diet and exercise regimen, he also turned to acupuncture. After three sessions, his symptoms nearly vanished.

When Mancina had acupuncture, his practitioner poked not just in his torso but also in his arms and legs. Acupuncturists insert needles into seemingly unrelated parts of your body because they believe there are local points—areas from where the pain radiates—and distal points, which correspond to remote areas of your body.

The Western explanation: "Your extremities have more nerve endings than your abdomen, so poking them can trigger a stronger response than a needle near your stomach can," says Dr. Cheng.

SCIENCE SAYS: Acupuncture's ability to combat basic stress might be a key part of its effectiveness with gastrointestinal disorders, says Tony Chon, M.D., chairman of the acupuncture practice at the Mayo Clinic in Rochester, Minnesota. "We know there's a strong link between stress and some GI symptoms, including indigestion," Dr. Chon says, "and acupuncture has been used for centuries for relief and treatment."

For upper-GI problems, acupuncture can beat antacids by a mile. In a 2007 University of Arizona study, people with chronic heartburn who didn't respond to prescription antacids underwent twice-weekly acupuncture. Their symptoms improved far more than those of people who took a double dose of the drug. Their chest pain decreased 82 percent, heartburn dropped 83 percent, and acid reflux fell 77 percent. Researchers speculate that the needle treatments prompt a decrease in stomach acid and speed up digestion, so less acid backs up into the esophagus. "It also seems to reduce pain perception in the esophagus," says study coauthor Ronnie Fass, M.D.

Sports Injuries

Many injured athletes use acupuncture. When he was playing in the NFL, former New York Giants running back Tiki Barber used it frequently for his muscle strains.

"It helps your body recover from injury faster," says Marianne Fuenmayor, M.S., L.Ac., chairwoman of the acupuncture department at the Pacific College of Oriental Medicine in New York City. One theory, according to Dr. Cheng, is that your body may respond to the needles by further increasing the flow of oxygenated blood to the injured area, which helps speed the healing process.

SCIENCE SAYS: You should see your doctor if you're injured, but if he or she says you don't need any treatment beyond rest, then ask if it's okay to go to an acupuncturist to help manage the pain or discomfort.

"I've used it very effectively to treat ankle sprains, muscle soreness, tennis elbow, and tendinitis," says John Cianca, M.D., a rehabilitation specialist at Baylor College of Medicine in Houston and the president of the American Road Race Medical Society.

This year, a Johns Hopkins study found that people with chronic tendinitis or arthritis who had 20-minute acupuncture sessions twice a week for 6 weeks had less pain and disability than people who only thought they were receiving acupuncture (the needles didn't penetrate the skin). Additionally, a 2008 study in the *Journal of Alternative and Complementary Medicine* found that participants who were jabbed

> ## When needles enter your earlobes, hands, or feet, Dr. Cheng says, your brain releases neurotransmitters and other chemicals that affect stress and mood.

for muscle soreness 24 and 48 hours after they exercised to exhaustion reported significantly less pain than people who didn't receive the treatment.

STICK A PIN IN
Anxiety and Depression

A little setback—say, your team falling behind in the playoffs—can trigger mild anxiety. A big bummer—losing your job,

for example—can cause serious depression. In either case, acupuncture can help.

"In the recent recession, I've been treating a lot of men who are under stress," says Nicholas Zimet, a licensed acupuncturist with Prime Meridian Acupuncture in Minneapolis. "After treatment, they feel more relaxed and able to deal with the pressures of life." Why the mental boost? When needles enter your earlobes, hands, or feet, Dr. Cheng says, your brain releases neurotransmitters and other chemicals that affect stress and mood.

SCIENCE SAYS: A recent study published in the *Journal of Alternative and Complementary Medicine* found that depressed patients with severe anxiety can benefit from acupuncture. The study, which paired acupuncture with the medication fluoxetine (a generic form of Prozac), also reported benefits for patients who couldn't tolerate the side effects commonly caused by the medication, including decreased sex drive, difficulty maintaining erections, and delayed ejaculation. Not a bad trade-off.

STICK A PIN IN
Back Pain

Treating back pain is by far the most common reason people turn to acupuncture.

"It simply works much better than any of the pills we prescribe," says Dr. Cheng. Just as with sports injuries, the needles seem to increase bloodflow to muscles and tissues. (Sometimes the practitioners will also run electric current through the needles. Physical therapists have been using electrical stimulation for years to promote healing, and Dr. Cheng says the needles help the current travel deeper into the muscles.)

SCIENCE SAYS: A University of Michigan study this year backed up Dr. Cheng's assessment. The researchers used brain imaging to see how needling the skin affects the brain's ability to control pain.

"Acupuncture seems to help pain receptors in the brain bind more easily to opioids such as endorphins, our body's natural painkiller," says Richard Harris, Ph.D., coauthor of the study. It also helps the receptors bind to painkilling drugs such as codeine or morphine. And the better those work, the less you hurt.

If you decide to give acupuncture a try, look for a licensed or a medical acupuncturist. States issue the licenses (which may require certification), and most use examination results from the National Certification Commission for Acupuncture and Oriental Medicine. (Search its database at nccaom. org.) A licensed, NCCAOM-certified acupuncturist has graduated from an accredited school and passed NCCAOM's exam, and has at least 1,800 hours of training. Medical acupuncturists (DABMA or FAAMA) are board-certified physicians who've had training approved by the American Board of Medical Acupuncture. Search for one at medicalacupuncture.org. ■

The Alzheimer's Virus

It's a memory-destroying disease that has baffled scientists for decades, but one researcher has a controversial theory: that we can catch it with a kiss.

Rich P. is only in his 20s, but these days he finds himself obsessing over something most guys his age never think twice about: Am I doomed to lose my mind?

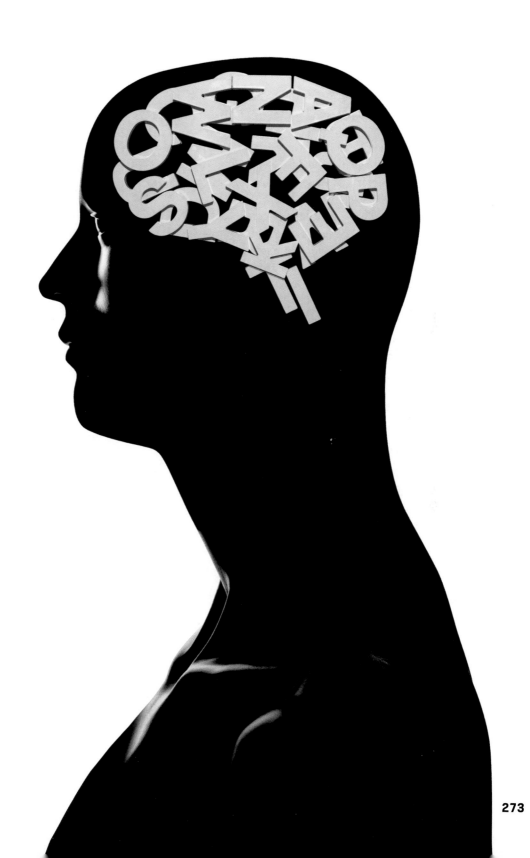

In some ways, Rich's anxiety is understandable. "My girlfriend is a social worker who works with the aged, specifically people with Alzheimer's," he says. "So I've seen close up what the disease does to you."

Indeed, Alzheimer's disease is characterized by memory loss and confusion and typically ends with complete disconnection from the world. People in its advanced stages can't care for themselves, recognize loved ones, or remember the lives they lived.

There's also another, even more personal connection for Rich: His girlfriend's father recently passed away from Alzheimer's. He was one of more than 70,000 Americans who die from the disease every year.

Still, what should worry Rich most isn't what he's witnessed in other people but what he sees in the mirror. Because there, literally right under his nose, is evidence that the monster that could be responsible for Alzheimer's is already skulking about inside his body, preparing itself—at some point, decades down the road—to attack and destroy his brain.

So here's the question: Is it in you, too?
For years, physicians and Alzheimer's experts have said that the earliest symptoms of the disease typically don't appear until you're in your 60s, 70s, or beyond. But now there's reason to believe that the first warning signs might actually crop up much earlier than that, and in a seemingly much more benign way: as cold sores, those embarrassing blisters that can erupt on the lips of people who are sick or run-down.

The sores are triggered by the herpes virus —most often, herpes simplex virus type 1

In the advanced stages of Alzheimer's disease, people can't care for themselves, recognize loved ones, or remember the lives they lived.

(not to be confused with HSV-2, which predominately causes genital herpes). In recent years, a growing body of research, much of it championed by a British scientist, has begun to suggest a startling fact: The same virus known for sabotaging people's social lives could be responsible for the majority of Alzheimer's cases.

"There's clearly a very strong connection," says the researcher, Ruth Itzhaki, Ph.D., speaking one afternoon in her office at the University of Manchester in northwestern England. A neurobiologist, Dr. Itzhaki has spent the better part of two decades studying the link between herpes and Alzheimer's.

"I estimate that about 60 percent of Alzheimer's cases could be caused by the virus." As viruses go, herpes is a particularly devilish bugger. The ancient Greeks were among the first to record the sores it causes (the virus's name is derived from a Greek word meaning "to creep"), and today the microbe is ubiquitous. As many as 85 percent of us have been infected by it, though experts say as few as 15 percent show symptoms. Worse, once you have it, you have it forever: After the initial infection, the virus lies dormant in your peripheral

nervous system, occasionally flaring up during periods of stress, illness, or fatigue. But it never completely disappears.

And it's that fact—herpes as the viral equivalent of The Thing That Wouldn't Leave—that lies at the heart of the herpes-Alzheimer's relationship. Research suggests that as we age, HSV-1 actually spreads to our brains, where in certain people, Dr. Itzhaki theorizes, it can cause the buildup of deposits—known as amyloid plaques and neurofibrillary tangles—that attack and destroy the cells responsible for memory, language, and physical functions. In short, those people develop Alzheimer's.

It's a provocative theory, one that would sound preposterous if it weren't for the steadily accumulating evidence. Last January, for instance, Dr. Itzhaki and her colleague, Matthew Wozniak, Ph.D., published a study in the *Journal of Pathology* in which they searched for the presence of the herpes virus in people's brains. They found that it resided in 90 percent of the amyloid plaques.

"The link between herpes and Alzheimer's has been there for a while, but more people are starting to pay attention," says Howard Federoff, M.D., Ph.D., an expert on neurodegenerative diseases and the executive dean of the school of medicine at Georgetown University. "It's no longer just a curiosity."

Unfortunately, while the theory might be on more researchers' radar, it's perhaps becoming a blip in the one area that matters most: the fight for funding. Sure, on the surface, the possible discovery of a

cause for Alzheimer's looks like Nobel-caliber news because it suggests a way forward in treating a disease that scientists have struggled—largely unsuccessfully—to understand.

What's more, if a new treatment does emerge, it could be just in the nick of time: Thanks to a combination of changing demographics and longer life spans, experts are predicting nothing less than an Alzheimer's epidemic in the decades ahead.

And yet all the promise held in the herpes connection may vanish as quickly and completely as the memories of an Alzheimer's patient. That's because despite Dr. Itzhaki's nearly 20-year struggle to get

Thanks to a combination of changing demographics and longer life spans, experts predict an Alzheimer's epidemic in the decades ahead.

her work noticed, an entrenched Alzheimer's research establishment remains skeptical. Worse, she now finds herself on the brink of having to shut down what might be the most promising avenue of investigation in ages.

"Our remaining funds are sufficient for only several more months," she says, "so unless we obtain a donation or grant, the work will then stop completely, because nobody else in the world is directly doing such research."

For young men like Rich P., who wonders what's in store for him in the decades ahead, this would appear to be an enormous scientific misstep—particularly since Rich believes he's seen firsthand the link between herpes and Alzheimer's.

His girlfriend's father, the one who passed away from Alzheimer's? He battled cold sores all his life.

Dr. Itzhaki says there are two reasons why herpes became a Virus of Interest in the hunt for an Alzheimer's cause. First was the observation, almost 3 decades ago, that a rare infection called herpes encephalitis affects the same regions of the brain that Alzheimer's does. Like people with Alzheimer's, encephalitis patients can be plagued by memory problems.

The other factor, she says, is the prevalence of the herpes virus itself. "Most people get it as children," Dr. Itzhaki says. "It's in your saliva, and it can easily be passed along with a kiss from a family member." She says it's not really that puzzling that most people who carry the virus never show symptoms—as she puts it, not everyone who's infected with a microbe is necessarily affected by it. "It depends on the person harboring the virus," she says. "It's probably based on genetic factors."

How might a germ you could have contracted from, say, a grandparent potentially destroy your brain when you become a grandparent?

In the early 1990s, researchers, including Dr. Itzhaki, found evidence suggesting that as we age, the herpes virus begins moving from its hideout near the bottom of the skull directly into the brain (possibly because our immune systems lose some bite). Indeed, one *Journal of Pathology* study found the virus in a high proportion of postmortem brain samples taken from people who'd died in their later decades, while it was absent in those from people who'd died in youth or middle age.

What effect does the virus have when it reaches your brain? The short answer: That depends. In certain people it seems to do much less damage than in others; just as some of us never develop cold sores, some of us can have the herpes virus inside our brains without any horribly ill effects. But Dr. Itzhaki believes that in other people—specifically those who carry APOE e4, a gene

As your age, herpes might spread to your brain and lead to its destruction.

form, or allele, strongly linked to Alzheimer's—the virus is not only reactivated by triggers like stress or a weakened immune system, but also actually begins to create the proteins that form the plaques and tangles presumed to be responsible for Alzheimer's.

If you're looking for evidence, Itzhaki can show you a stack of it. In two studies, for example, she and several colleagues took brain samples from 109 deceased people—61 of whom had had Alzheimer's, 48 of whom hadn't—to search for any correlation between herpes, APOE e4, and Alzheimer's. Their results: People who had both the APOE e4 gene and the herpes virus in their brains were 15 times more likely to have Alzheimer's than people who had neither. (The researchers also found, intriguingly, that people who suffered from recurrent cold sores were almost six times as likely to have the APOE e4 gene as those who didn't get cold sores.)

A decade later, Dr. Federoff, then working at the University of Rochester, administered the herpes virus to four different groups of mice, each of which had a different variation or absence of the APOE gene. He found that in mice with the specific APOE e4 variation, the virus was slower to become dormant than it was in mice with APOE e2, APOE e3, or no APOE gene, suggesting that the virus could be replicating faster in the e4 mice.

"The results definitely suggest there's something different about having APOE e4," says Dr. Federoff.

Still other research shows the direct impact of HSV-1 itself. In 2007, a study by Drs. Itzhaki and Wozniak found that infecting lab samples of brain cells with the virus caused a buildup of the protein (beta amyloid) that's the primary component of the plaque clogging the brains of Alzheimer's patients. The same study also found a similar result in the brains of mice that had been infected with HSV-1.

Then there was January's study in the *Journal of Pathology*. In it, Dr. Itzhaki and Wozniak looked at brain samples from 11 deceased people; six had had Alzheimer's and five hadn't. While both groups had plaques (not surprisingly, the Alzheimer's group had far more) and evidence of the herpes virus in their brains, there was

a crucial difference in the concentration of the virus: In the Alzheimer's patients, 72 percent of the virus's DNA was found in the plaques, compared with only 24 percent that was found in the plaques of the non-Alzheimer's brains. Not surprisingly, all but one of the Alzheimer's sufferers also carried the APOE e4 gene, compared with none of the samples from the non-Alzheimer's people.

Dr. Wozniak is confident that these last two studies point to the same conclusion: "The results strongly suggest that HSV-1 is a major cause of amyloid plaques—and probably of Alzheimer's disease."

For Drs. Wozniak and Itzhaki, the next step is to test whether antiviral drugs like Zovirax and Valtrex, both of which are used to shorten the duration of cold sores, might alleviate or slow the progression of Alzheimer's. The pair is seeking funding for two experiments with antiviral drugs— one testing them on mice, the other testing them on Alzheimer's patients.

"If the treatment is successful, it would stop progression of the disease, rather than just stopping the symptoms," Dr. Itzhaki says.

But that funding isn't likely to materialize if the rest of the research community continues to dismiss Itzhaki's theory—or ignore it altogether. When John Trojanowski, M.D., Ph.D., a respected Alzheimer's researcher at the University of Pennsylvania, was contacted to find out his take on the connection between Alzheimer's and herpes, he shot back a one-sentence reply: "Do not know of any connection."

When I pressed and asked him to take a look at two of Dr. Itzhaki's recent studies,

You vs. the Virus

Here's how to keep herpes from wreaking havoc on you.

STAY CALM UNDER FIRE.

Stress can allow herpes to emerge from its hiding place in your nervous system, say British researchers. It seems that chronic tension can impair the function of your T cells, white blood cells whose job it is to prevent the virus from reactivating. Feeling tense? A 15-minute stroll through a park can cut your level of the stress hormone cortisol in half, according to a Japanese study.

COVER YOUR MOUTH.

Think of herpes as a slumbering giant, one that can be roused by sunlight. That's because when UV rays hit your lips, they're thought to stimulate the nerves that run from the site of the original infection back to where the virus sleeps. So cover your kisser with a balm that blocks both UVA and UVB rays, such as Dermatone's SPF 23 Skin Protector ($5, dermatone.com).

BOOST T CELLS WITH TEA.

When your immune system is battling a cold or the flu, the herpes virus tries to sneak past your distracted defenses. Stop it by downing a few glasses of green tea every day you're sick. Pakistani researchers noted that EGCG, an antioxidant in green tea, may turbocharge your T cells. Try Honest Tea Organic Honey Green Tea; it has more EGCG than 13 other iced teas we had tested.

DISRUPT ITS DNA.

Antiviral drugs can't kill herpes, but they can stop it from making the DNA it needs to reproduce, says Robert Brodell, M.D., a professor of internal medicine at Northeastern Ohio Universities College of Medicine. Talk to your doctor about taking the antiviral Valtrex. If you pop 2 grams at the first hint of a cold sore, and then again 12 hours later, you may prevent an outbreak.

---

he was equally dismissive. "This is an old story," he said, "so I do not think there is much new news here."

Even those more familiar with the research remain skeptical.

"One of the things we see a lot in science is relationships—two things happening together," says Bill Thies, Ph.D., chief medical and scientific officer at the Alzheimer's Association. "But they often turn out to be independent events, or you can't tell which thing is causing which. It could be, for example, that there's something about amyloids that attracts HSV."

Dr. Wozniak says that the study he published with Dr. Itzhaki—in which the herpes virus caused amyloid accumulation in cells and mice—refutes that criticism. He also dismisses another critique—that

he and Dr. Itzhaki haven't established the mechanism by which HSV-1 brings about that accumulation. Again, he argues, this study indicates an increase in the enzymes that are responsible for forming amyloid from its precursor protein, called APP.

"Surely, the mechanism is clear: HSV-1 causes an increase in these enzymes, which in turn causes degradation of APP, leading to amyloid formation." He pauses, and then adds wryly, "It's interesting that people raise this criticism when, until our research, no other underlying causes of amyloid production linked to Alzheimer's disease were known."

Dr. Itzhaki is more sanguine about the skepticism. "We've seen this before when a virus or bacterium is suggested as the cause for a chronic illness," she says, noting the reticence people had when *H. pylori* was suggested as a cause of ulcers and when the human papilloma virus was suspected as a cause of cervical cancer. Both are now largely considered medical fact. "And the Alzheimer's establishment is very conservative."

Georgetown's Dr. Federoff agrees that in some ways the theory isn't conventional enough to be embraced by many mainstream Alzheimer's researchers. "Herpes is a common virus, but in this case we're talking about it behaving in an atypical way," he notes. That said, would he like to see further research on the connection between HSV and Alzheimer's? Absolutely.

There is one matter on which the opposing camps agree: With each passing day, the stakes for Alzheimer's research grow higher. Over the past century, the only thing that has prevented the disease from becoming even more widespread and devastating is that most people passed away from something else before they were old enough to develop it.

Drop dead of a heart attack when you're 52, and Alzheimer's is one malady you probably won't have to worry about. But the more progress we make against our most common killers—heart disease, stroke, and cancer—and the more we extend our life spans, the greater the number of Alzheimer's cases we're likely to see. Indeed, as the 33-million-plus-strong baby boom generation enters its golden years and sees its risk of Alzheimer's

increase, we are potentially looking at an epidemic. By 2010, the number of cases is expected to have increased 10 percent from its 2000 total, and from there the number is projected to more than double— to more than 950,000 new cases a year— by 2050.

"Alzheimer's has always been a big problem, but it's going to be even bigger," says Dr. Thies. "And the people who are now in their 20s, 30s, and 40s are the ones it's especially going to affect."

So what do you do if you're part of that group—especially if you tend to develop cold sores? One future option could be to have yourself tested for the APOE e4 gene—though Wozniak isn't a fan of that idea. "It would just cause a lot of worry for the person involved and his or her family."

Another possibility might be to take an oral antiviral drug preventively—essentially, to attempt to keep the herpes virus in check before it can do any damage to your brain. The hitch here, however, is that no clinical trials have ever evaluated the safety of taking a daily antiviral, such as Valtrex, for longer than a year. Plus, the average physician would consider the link to Alzheimer's too tenuous to let you play guinea pig.

In the end, the best option may simply be to wait and hope. When I ask Dr. Wozniak whether he and Dr. Itzhaki feel like they're running out of time, he says, "Of course. We are all getting older. Our parents are getting older. Soon we'll all be affected one way or another by Alzheimer's disease . . . if we haven't already." ■

Mike Genevie was the kind of guy who always came ready with a joke. But when his relationship with his girlfriend went sour, his sunny outlook on life turned overcast. "She stopped returning my calls," says the 27-year-old auditor from Levittown, Pennsylvania.

The Bad Mood Buster

Maybe you're not clinically depressed, but you are a little bummed out. Try these strategies before you start popping pills.

MILK DOES A BRAIN GOOD.
The tryptophan in 3 cups a day
can help you chill.

"I found out that she was with someone else." Suddenly, when a commercial for an antidepressant appeared on television, he found himself reaching for a pen and pad instead of the remote control.

Genevie has plenty of company. A 2005 study from the Centers for Disease Control and Prevention found that people take antidepressants even more often than they pop pills for high blood pressure, asthma, and high cholesterol. But men often don't need to be medicated; they're just feeling down at the moment.

"Antidepressants are prescribed too often," says Stuart Shipko, M.D., a psychiatrist and the author of *Surviving Panic Disorder*. Dr. Shipko cautions that taking a pill can lead to *real* problems: addiction, sexual impairment, or both. "Unless a person has a serious mental-health problem, the risk-benefit ratio doesn't favor these drugs," he says.

Fortunately, there are plenty of DIY ways to boost your body's own feel-good forces. Try a combination of the following blues-busting strategies, and your life view can brighten up in no time.

DO YOUR MIND GOOD WITH MILK

WHY IT WORKS: Milk is rich in tryptophan, which is an amino acid needed for the production of serotonin, a mood-boosting brain chemical. Not surprisingly, lower levels of tryptophan coincide with reduced serotonin levels. But your body can't make tryptophan on its own. So it has to come from dietary sources like milk, where the amino acid is plentiful. Otherwise, your mood could suffer from the shortfall.

DO THIS: Drink three 8-ounce servings of whole milk a day, which translates to 0.6 grams of tryptophan, enough to lift your spirits when combined with a protein-rich diet, according to Susan M. Kleiner, Ph.D., R.D., author of *The Good Mood Diet*. Yogurt, cheese, poultry, eggs, bananas, and peanuts are also good sources.

"A selection of these foods should be in your diet every day to raise serotonin levels and elevate mood," says Dr. Kleiner.

> "A selection of these foods should be in your diet every day to raise serotonin levels and elevate mood."

STACK THE DECK WITH SEAFOOD

WHY IT WORKS: Two types of omega-3 fatty acids are abundant in seafood—eicosapentaenoic acid (EPA) and docosahexaenoic acid (DHA). In humans, high DHA levels are linked to raised levels of dopamine and serotonin, the same brain chemicals that antidepressants boost. What's more, a shortfall of DHA in animals has been linked to symptoms and markers that mimic depression.

"You're at greater risk of being depressed, anxious, and irritable by avoiding fish," says Joseph R. Hibbeln, M.D., acting chief of nutritional neurochemistry at the NIH's National Institute of Alcohol Abuse and Alcoholism.

DO THIS: Eat cold-water fish (salmon or mackerel) at least twice a week. Otherwise, take a daily 1-gram dose of Jarrow Formulas EPA-DHA Balance (jarrow.com). The 2-to-1 ratio of EPA to DHA makes for good brain food, because EPA seems to hold more sway than DHA over mood and behavior, according to Parris Kidd, Ph.D., a nutrition educator and contributing editor for the *Alternative Medicine Review*. Be patient, Grasshopper. It takes 8 to 12 weeks for most men to feel a full response kicking in.

AX YOUR WAY THROUGH DOWN DAYS

WHY IT WORKS: If you're feeling down, the best way to change your tune might be to listen to or even play one. A 2006 *Journal of Advanced Nursing* study found that listening to music for an hour a day for a week could reduce symptoms of depression by up to 25 percent. Music may also

Listening to music can reduce depression by as much as 25 percent. (This doesn't apply to death metal, though.)

improve the outlook of a guy whose blues aren't yet clinical.

DO THIS: Even better for your mood than simply listening to music is creating some on your own.

"Just working out a few chords or melodies can be therapeutic," says Anna Maratos, a certified music therapist and the head of Arts Therapies at the Central and North West London Foundation NHS Trust. If you want to channel your inner guitar god but can't play a lick, try Guitar Hero with some friends.

If the way to a man's heart is through his stomach, the way to his mood-selector switch might be through his nostrils.

LIFT YOUR SPIRITS WITH GOOD SCENTS

WHY IT WORKS: If the way to a man's heart is through his stomach, the way to his mood-selector switch might be through his nostrils. A *Physiology & Behavior* study found that people sitting in a dentist's office were less anxious and in better moods when the waiting room smelled like orange or lavender. If those scents can distract you from the drone of a dentist's drill, imagine what they can do in less torturous settings.

DO THIS: You're probably not the kind of guy who drives around with an air freshener dangling from his rearview. Instead, spritz on Giorgio Armani's citrusy Acqua Di Gio or Calvin Klein Eternity for Men before work or a date.

BONUS: Nothing will boost your mood faster than the cute girl one cube over commenting on how swell you smell.

SET A GOAL—AND THEN NAIL IT

WHY IT WORKS: Setting higher expectations for yourself doesn't create stress; it actually provides a release valve for stress. A 2006 study found that people who set goals were less anxious, felt better about themselves, and found more meaning in their lives than did their free-floating counterparts.

"Setting goals boosts mood by increasing the likelihood of success, which results in better feelings about yourself and life in general," says Jennifer S. Cheavens, Ph.D., the study's lead author and an assistant professor at Ohio State.

DO THIS: Cheavens recommends setting reasonable, concrete goals and using multiple avenues to meet them. For example, commit to hitting the gym three times a week instead of vaguely declaring that you'll drop 10 pounds. If you miss a workout, vow to skip the starch at dinner.

"You want goals to have smaller accomplishment points along the way, so you enjoy the mood boost that comes with success," says Dr. Cheavens.

CHASE YOUR BLISS

WHY IT WORKS: A running trail is one path to happiness. Compared with sedentary subjects, men who ran regularly were

> ## "Setting goals boosts mood by increasing the likelihood of success, which results in **better feelings about yourself.**"

70 percent less likely to experience high stress and life dissatisfaction, according to a study of more than 12,000 people published in the *Scandinavian Journal of Medicine & Science in Sports*. Regular exercise increases adrenal activity, which facilitates stress adaptation and enhances the release of hormones like noradrenaline, serotonin, beta-endorphin, and dopamine. These hormones all improve mood, says Peter Schnohr, M.D., the study's lead author.

DO THIS: Dr. Schnohr suggests running, brisk walking, or any cardiovascular workout for half an hour, five times a week. Interval-style training is particularly effective, especially during a time crunch.

HIT THE SACK—FOR SEX

WHY IT WORKS: Oxytocin, a feel-good hormone that reduces fear and lowers your cortisol (a stress hormone) and blood-pressure levels, peaks in your body 1 to 2 minutes after climax. But whether you've had sex with a partner or simply flown solo, your body chemistry won't stay in the stratosphere for long.

"Levels return to normal within 10 minutes of orgasm," says Debby Herbenick,

The best way to heat up your life is to make *her* happy.

Joy to the Girl

If she's the one bummed, lifting her mood can do you both a world of good. Here's what to do to help her so that your brain waves will spike in happy unison.

WRITE IT DOWN. Clicking on an e-mail isn't the same as opening an envelope. You live with her? Mail a card anyway.

PLAN A LUNCH DATE FOR HER WITH A LONG-LOST FRIEND. In advance, arrange for the tab to disappear. Her friend will lift her spirits, and your effort will boost her brain chemicals, such as dopamine (pleasure) and oxytocin (trust).

BE THERE, BUT DON'T SMOTHER. If she's on the couch and doesn't want to talk, sit on the chair next to her and read.

"The thing for any guy to do is to let his girlfriend or wife know that he's there for her and that he loves her," says Patricia A. Farrell, Ph.D., the author of *How to Be Your Own Therapist*.

LET HER REST. Sleep can be the most valuable gift card of all, so unplug her alarm clock on a Saturday and cross off a few easy but time-consuming tasks (laundry, grocery shopping, gift wrapping) from her to-do list.

Ph.D., a sex researcher and educator at Indiana University.

DO THIS: Cuddle after coitus. "Oxytocin can be released not only during masturbation and intercourse but also during close touching," says Dr. Herbenick. The longer she keeps her arms wrapped around you, the more oxytocin is released and the better you'll feel.

LAY OFF THE SAUCE

WHY IT WORKS: There's a reason a regular advice column in *Men's Health* magazine is penned by a bartender: He gets more practice than Drs. Drew and Phil combined.

"Alcohol can reduce anxiety immediately after intake," says Clyde W. Hodge, Ph.D., a professor in the department of psychiatry at the University of North Carolina at Chapel Hill. "It also has antidepressant properties."

Problem is, this temporary lift is followed by a mood hangover. Hodge and his researchers found that mice consuming a moderate amount of alcohol every day for 28 days seemed bummed out after 2 weeks of abstinence. What happens, says Dr. Hodge, is a reduction of new neurons in the part of the brain that appears to regulate mood.

Men who run are 70 percent less likely than the sedentary to be dissatisfied with their lives.

DO THIS: Plan social activities that aren't centered on dining, which inevitably involves drinking. Plus, your gloom might just be cabin fever. Head outside.

ELEVATE YOUR TEST SCORES

WHY IT WORKS: Testosterone's effects can be felt above the belt, too. A 2008 *Archives of General Psychiatry* study found that older men with the lowest levels of free testosterone were at a higher risk for depression than men with the highest levels. Researchers haven't pinpointed the link, but other studies have shown that waning testosterone levels may lead to increased fat mass, irritability, and a lower sex drive. No wonder the guys are bummed out.

DO THIS: To help sustain testosterone levels, Dr. Kleiner recommends snagging 30 percent of your calories from healthy fats, such as the monounsaturated and polyunsaturated fats found in olives, fish, nuts, and avocado.

PICTURE HAPPINESS

WHY IT WORKS: Photos do more than freeze the past: They can unlock a current bad mood, assuming the shots bring to mind happier times. Researchers from the University of Southampton found that feeling nostalgic increases self-regard, social bonds, and positive feelings.

DO THIS: Trade that static wallpaper on your iPhone for a photo of the kids or your most recent vacation shots. Compile a downloadable gallery at me.com.

YOU SNOOZE, YOU WIN

WHY IT WORKS: Sleep is a much-needed sanctuary from stress. In fact, researchers from the Stanford Sleep Epidemiology Research Center found that people with sleep disorders such as sleep apnea are five times more likely to experience depression than those who sleep soundly.

Studies have shown that waning testosterone levels may lead to increased fat mass, irritability, and a lower sex drive.

"Individuals with sleep apnea generally have a sleep efficiency between 65 and 85 percent," says Maurice M. Ohayon, M.D., Ph.D., the center's director and the study's lead researcher. So those 7 hours of bedtime could become a fragmented, nonrestorative 5 hours of shut-eye.

DO THIS: If you have a flabby midsection, snore like a foghorn, or often wake up tired, find a specialist at sleepcenters.org.

LET THE SUN SHINE IN

WHY IT WORKS: Too little sunshine can lead to a vitamin D deficiency, and a 2008 study published in the *Archives of General Psychiatry* found that vitamin D levels were 14 percent lower in depressed people. The sun on your skin needs exposure time to bring about the change that produces vitamin D, according to Reinhold Vieth, Ph.D., a professor in the University of Toronto's department of nutritional sciences.

DO THIS: Dr. Vieth recommends popping 1,000 IU of vitamin D daily, because using food alone as a supply of vitamin D can be tough. Worried your levels are low? Ask your doc for a serum 25-hydroxyvitamin D test. ■

The Fountain of Youth

Writer Tom McGrath asks, "What if you didn't have to grow old?" Teams of scientists working at Harvard and MIT are tampering with the cellular power plants that determine how you live and when you'll die. Their goal for you: energy, health, and youth for a very long time.

There are many reasons a major leaguer can fall into a batting slump: losing his timing at the plate, bailing out on pitches, thinking too much about dinner after the game. But the funk that Tampa Bay Rays outfielder Rocco Baldelli fell into over the past two seasons was on a whole different level.

The dude's mitochondria were letting him down.

No bells ringing for you? Let me help you out: sophomore year in high school . . . specifically, biology class . . . the unit on cells . . . the discussion of the cell's power source . . .

Mitochondria! Yes!

Although Baldelli didn't realize it when his muscle soreness started or when his injuries began to pile up, his mitochondria were in serious trouble. And they weren't just causing a slump at the plate, they were causing a slump in his *life*. Early last year, he couldn't work out for more than a few minutes without becoming exhausted. He had cramping and other strange sensations in his limbs. By the start of the season last April, things were so bleak that the Rays had put him back on the disabled list.

Fortunately, this is a story with a pretty happy ending. Doctors eventually determined that Baldelli was suffering from mitochondrial myopathy—damage to those power plants. He began a course of treatment, and by early August the Rays were on the verge of making their first trip to the playoffs. He played well in the regular season, and in the postseason, as TV announcers struggled to pronounce "mitochondria," he stepped up his performance even more, hitting two postseason home runs and driving in one of the runs that sent the Rays to the World Series.

But don't let Baldelli's struggle spook you too much. His disease, however scary, is rare. And even though damaged mitochondria can do bad things to you, as Baldelli will attest, the opposite is also true: Strong, healthy mitochondria can make you strong and healthy now, and maybe for a very, very, very long time.

"Expanding lifetimes for another hundred, some say a thousand years, is . . . science fiction," says David Sinclair, Ph.D., his Australian drawl rising softly. "We can't even extend the life of a mouse that far. How could we do it for ourselves? I don't know of anything we're doing yet that would allow us to accomplish that."

Yet.

It's Friday afternoon, and I've come to Dr. Sinclair's lab at Harvard medical school to talk to him not only about the prospects for supercharging our mitochondria but also about the long-term effects of keeping these cellular power plants humming. Dr. Sinclair, a slight, intense man of 39, dismisses the idea of adding centuries to our lives, but he's more

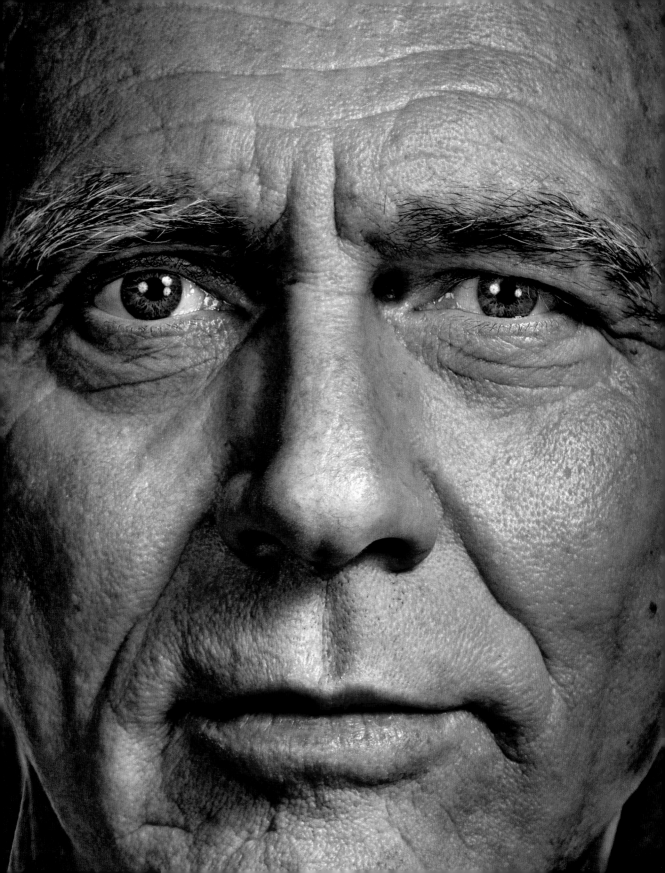

optimistic about the possibility of adding a few decades of, say, competitive softball.

"In the future, people will be thinking, 'When I'm 80, I'll still be playing tennis . . . and at 90 I'll still be around to see my great-grandkids graduate from college,'" he says.

Over the past couple of decades, researchers have gained an increasing understanding of just how crucial mitochondria are to, well, just about every aspect of human health and fitness. On the positive side, for example, research shows that properly functioning mitochondria pave the way for an array of benefits—from muscle growth and increased energy to greater endurance and a great head of hair. On the negative side, damaged mitochondria are associated with an equally wide array of diseases and conditions—from diabetes, heart disease, and obesity to the type of neuromuscular disorder that sucked the spirit out of Rocco Baldelli.

AS YOUR MITOCHONDRIA GO, SO GOES THE REST OF YOU

That's why Dr. Sinclair has been trying to pinpoint a genetic way to keep our mitochondria charged up. Currently, he and a group of researchers are focused on enzymes called sirtuins, which, when activated, have been shown to invigorate mitochondria.

Dr. Sinclair himself has made several of the most recent, high-profile breakthroughs involving sirtuins. In 2003, he discovered that the sirtuin known as SIR2 could be activated with resveratrol, which is a compound best known for its presence in red wine. In subsequent studies, he and other researchers found that giving lab mice large amounts of resveratrol not only made them healthier and more energetic but, in some cases, extended their lives by up to 30 percent. (Don't reach for the Beaujolais just yet, though—you'd have to drink at least 35 bottles a day for an equivalent dose). Then, last year, Sirtris Pharmaceuticals— the company Dr. Sinclair cofounded to develop antiaging drugs—announced that it had cooked up a chemical compound that's a thousand times more potent than resveratrol.

What does all this mean? In the short term, it means lots of enthusiasm for what Sinclair and his colleagues are doing. Pharmaceutical giant GlaxoSmithKline, for example, is so bullish on Sirtris that in June 2008 it bought the company for $720 million. Meanwhile, Dr. Sinclair himself believes that a sirtuin-activating, mitochondria-boosting drug could be on the market within a decade and possibly within 5 years.

If that happens, the impact on all of us is potentially profound. For starters, it would be a step toward a whole new type of treatment for some of the most common and debilitating human diseases, including heart disease, diabetes, and even cancer. Just as significant, though, is the fact that the drugs could allow us to remain healthy, active, and energetic years beyond what we're capable of now. So both Father Time and the Grim Reaper are in the crosshairs.

And for Dr. Sinclair, it seems, that is precisely the point.

"We have such a short time on the planet—on a geological scale, we're around for a second," he says. "And our loved ones are not going to be around forever. I'd like to do something about that. I think aging is the curse of mankind."

He leans forward in his chair. "It's really not fair for conscious beings to be aware of their own mortality."

Mitochondria are tiny, but their effects are large. You can easily see the difference between an animal whose mitochondria are working perfectly and one whose mitochondria are worn out.

Dr. Sinclair beckons me over to his computer.

Onto the screen pops a video of two mice running side by side on two tiny treadmills. The mouse on the left—which Dr. Sinclair explains was part of the control group in a recent study, one that was fed a diet of pellets—is struggling like an overweight chain smoker trying to run the New York City Marathon. The mouse on the right, whose mitochondria were fired up with megadoses of resveratrol, is sprinting forward gleefully.

So how exactly do mitochondria turn one mouse into a near-superhero while leaving another looking like a rodent version of Jack Black? The answer goes back to the role mitochondria play in cells. The main function of mitochondria is to transform nutrients that enter cells into supplies of the energy molecule ATP— something they accomplish through a complex process called aerobic respiration. ATP, in turn, provides the energy the cells need to function. (The number of mitochon-

dria in a cell varies, depending on how much energy the cell requires. Heart cells, for example, have thousands of mitochondria, while skin cells have only one mitochiondrion each.)

Now when your mitochondria are functioning properly, good things happen. Your body runs the way it's supposed to— your heart beats, your neurons fire, your muscles contract, your eyes see, and your liver, kidneys, and other organs operate as they should. You are, in essence, a perfectly tuned piece of physiology.

Unfortunately, at least two factors stand in the way of properly functioning mitochondria. The first is genetic mutation. Mutations may be inherited, or caused by

Strong, healthy mitochondria can make you strong and healthy now, and maybe for a very, very, very long time.

diet and lifestyle, or simply random. And they're associated with a vast array of conditions ranging from neuromuscular ailments to dementia, atherosclerosis, and diabetes. In such cases, the genetically damaged mitochondria fail to process all the nutrients in the cell, leading to an energy crisis within the cell. Without enough power to function, the cell falters . . . and presto, bad stuff happens.

The second force working against your mitochondria is, simply, time. The great

CAN MITOCHONDRIA REVERSE BALDING?

Writer Peter Moore conducted a hair-raising experiment:

On the Norwood-Hamilton scale of male-pattern baldness, I'm a III vertex; if my scalp were planet Earth, my ice cap would be melting. Which is why I was intrigued when the HairMax LaserComb was cleared by the FDA in 2007. Last summer, I was trained in laser-combing at a plastic surgeon's office in New York and started treating my (relatively minor) baldness in the prescribed way: For 10 to 15 minutes, 3 days a week, I dragged the comb over my scalp. Once, in the morning gloom, my wife encountered me doing so, and pronounced it (or maybe me) "creepy."

She had a point: The red laser light casts an eerie glow. But if you want to wake up the mitochondria (intracellular power plants) in sleepy hair follicles, you make sacrifices.

Beginning my therapy in 2008, I was roughly 40 years behind some shaven mice in a lab in Budapest, Hungary. Endre Mester, a Hungarian physician, had trained a laser (which had only just been invented) on shaven mouse skin and was shocked to

see accelerated hair growth under the lights. One theory about how it works: Laser light delivers photons to mitochondria, goosing them to increase production of ATP—the chemical energy source that powers cells. More ATP means that slacker hair follicles develop new mojo, which means less chrome on your dome.

At my first appointment, the dermatologist in New York warned me that it might take 3 months or longer for my mitochondria to take the hint. And according to those who look at my head every day, they probably have been so cued.

My experience is in line with an as-yet unpublished study submitted by HairMax to the FDA during the application process for marketing approval. A 6-month trial of 110 men, ages 30 to 60, found that the men who used the laser comb wound up with about 30 more scalp hairs per square centimeter than guys who used placebo combs. And, if it works the same for you, that'd be plenty for her to run her fingers through.

You'll note, of course, that it's an unpublished study, meaning it lacks the peer review that would tell us if the deep thinkers in laser therapy accept the results. And we'll note that FDA clearance simply means the comb is safe to use, not necessarily that it's effective.

Marc Avram, M.D., a New York hair-transplantation expert, conducted a small study of the comb and gives it a limited thumbs-up: "If a patient couldn't take Rogaine or Propecia, or needed an alternative, I would recommend the laser because it's safe and it may work. I just don't know how well it works." His reasoning: No large-scale studies have been published (especially not compared with the number of studies of such bona fide hair growers as Rogaine and Propecia).

Okay, so I've seen some success. So has the unpublished study, and so has Dr. Avram. The comb is pricey: $550. If you want to experiment on your own head, go for it. Just make sure you close the bathroom door first.

paradox of mitochondria is that even as they're providing energy to your body, they're essentially sowing the seeds of their own destruction. During aerobic respiration, by-products, such as free radicals, leak out. Over time, they harm both the mitochondria and other parts of the cell. The result: damage that looks a lot like aging.

THE MISSING LINK

The link between mitochondria and aging was most definitively established in a 2004 study published in the journal *Nature*. In the study, researchers at Stockholm's Karolinska Institute developed a strain of mice with damaged mitochondrial DNA. For the first 25 weeks (until young adulthood) the mice were normal. But then they suddenly began to show signs of premature aging. They displayed the sorts of symptoms you typically see at a 50th high school reunion: creaky joints, failing mojo, even baldness. Typically, wild mice live for about 2 years (100 weeks), while pet or lab mice live for 3 years or so (150 weeks). All of these mice were dead by 61 weeks.

Is there anything you can do to help your mitochondria withstand the ravages of time? The happy answer is yes. Exercise, for example, is known to have a major impact on mitochondrial function. In a 2003 study, Mayo Clinic researcher Kevin Short, Ph.D., put 65 healthy nonexercisers on a bicycle-training program 3 days a week. Not only did their aerobic capacity increase significantly, but their mitochondria were pumping out more ATP-boosting enzymes as well.

Alas, you can't exercise your way to immortality, which is why Dr. David Sinclair and others are trying to find a pharmacological way to keep those mitochondria revving. The mouse who's a stud on the treadmill and his resveratrol-stoked

Mitochondria pave the way for an array of benefits—from muscle growth to a great head of hair.

brethren, for example, had significantly less heart disease and diabetes and lived 30 percent longer than their resveratrol-deprived friends.

"They were healthier, fitter mice, all thanks to resveratrol in their food," says Dr. Sinclair.

David Sinclair may be on the brink of a mitochondria-boosting drug, but the quest actually began more than 70 years ago, long before he was born. In the 1930s, a group of researchers made a fascinating finding: Significantly reducing an organism's calorie intake lengthens its life. From an evolutionary standpoint, this makes sense. It suggests that organisms that could slow their own aging during food shortages were able to survive and reproduce, while organisms that couldn't saw their genetic lines die off. Still, while scientists have repeatedly shown that caloric restriction works in all sorts of organisms, they never really understood exactly how this magic took place.

Power Up Your Workout

Want to burn more fat? Focus on your mitochondria. These microscopic generators turn nutrients, including fat, into fuel for your muscle cells.

The more intensely you exercise, the more mitochondria you bring online, which means your muscles can work harder and longer, according to *Men's Health* advisor Alex Koch, Ph.D., an exercise scientist at Truman State University.

To boost your energy output, use this 3-day cardio workout from Koch. You can do it on a flat surface outside, a treadmill, or a stationary bike. Bonus: Interval plans like this one have been shown to torch more calories per minute to help you lose belly fat as you add mitochondria.

DIRECTIONS

Warm up with 5 minutes of easy jogging or cycling. For each workout, gauge your intensity by estimating your effort on a scale of 1 (sitting on the couch) to 10 (the hardest you can go). Then follow the directions for each day here.

THE PROGRAM	MONDAY	FRIDAY
Week 1	5 intervals	5 intervals
Week 2	6 intervals	5 intervals
Week 3	6 intervals	6 intervals
Week 4	7 intervals	6 intervals
Week 5	7 intervals	7 intervals
Week 6	8 intervals	7 intervals
Week 7	8 intervals	8 intervals

YOUR CHARGE

Monday and Friday: Sprint for 15 seconds at an intensity of 9; recover for 30 seconds at an intensity of 3 to 4. That's one interval. Repeat according to the chart.

Wednesday: For this workout, run or cycle continuously for 10 minutes at an intensity of 6. Each week, try to progress so you're eventually exercising for a total of 30 minutes.

In the early 1990s, an MIT researcher named Lenny Guarente, Ph.D., decided to take a crack at solving the caloric-restriction riddle. As career moves go, it was pretty risky, given that the study of aging had long been seen as a backwater of science.

"There were a lot of claims that turned out to be wrong," Dr. Guarente says as we chat in his MIT office, which is just across the Charles River from Dr. David Sinclair's lab. Now 56, Dr. Guarente is bald and has dark, deep-set eyes. "Aging was also seen as too complicated, too

chaotic" to solve, he continues. "And evolutionary theory holds that it should be that way. Aging occurs late in life, when natural selection has waned. The things that happen haven't been selected for and honed."

Dr. Guarente was undeterred by his colleagues' skepticism, though, and with the help of a couple of graduate students, he studied aging in yeast. (That's about as simple an organism as you can think of.) In 1996, he and his team discovered that a strain of yeast that lived longer than its counterparts had a mutation in a particular set of genes—namely, its sirtuin enzymes. Eventually, Dr. Guarente added an extra copy of one of those genes, SIR2, to a normal yeast cell, and found that—voilà— it extended the cell's life span by 50 percent.

It was around this time that Dr. Guarente was joined in the lab by Dr. Sinclair, then a 27-year-old Australian who'd just earned his doctorate in biology at the University of Sydney. The two had met by accident—they'd sat next to each other at a scientific forum in Sydney— but as soon as Dr. Sinclair heard what Dr. Guarente was working on, he wanted to join him.

"I basically told Lenny, 'I'm coming to your lab whether you like it or not,'" Dr. Sinclair remembers. "I didn't want to do anything else with my life."

Over the next few years, Dr. Guarente and his team made two more significant discoveries. In 1999, one of Dr. Guarente's lab assistants found that adding an extra copy of the SIR2 gene had a similar effect on roundworms. Dr. Guarente says this was a pivotal moment for him, because the finding suggested that the same process was at work in a variety of organisms.

The other breakthrough, equally crucial, was the discovery of a link between SIR2 and caloric restriction—the life-extending diet that had first been recognized back in the 1930s. While previous theories had speculated that caloric restriction worked by slowing an organism's metabolism, Dr. Guarente's research suggested the exact opposite was happening—slashing calories actually activated SIR2, which in turn revved up the cell's mitochondria and kept them young and vital.

In the nearly 10 years since then, Drs. Guarente and Sinclair, as well as a number of other Guarente protégés, have been researching sirtuin. Dr. Sinclair founded his own lab at Harvard in 1999, and he's made significant advances there, including the discovery that resveratrol can activate SIR2. He's also created a new chemical compound that's a thousand times more potent than resveratrol. In 2006, Dr. Sinclair and his team launched the first human studies of this new compound, and he's clearly excited by the results.

"The trials have shown that blood glucose levels are lowered in people with diabetes, as we saw in the mice," he says. "So far, we are seeing the same kind of improvements in glucose metabolism in humans that we saw in the mice. And we've seen no evidence of toxicity or side effects."

How much time does he think the drugs might potentially add to human life?

"It's feasible that we could help people live 5 or 10 years longer in a healthy state," he says. "Ultimately, they could have a far greater effect on healthy longevity based on what we know about caloric restriction in animals and its ability to keep animals healthy for an additional 30 percent longer."

Not everyone is convinced that Dr. Sinclair is onto the next big thing. Some scientists argue that studies of mice don't guarantee that resveratrol will work—or be safe—in humans. A handful of others are skeptical of any significant life-extension benefits, arguing that from an evolutionary perspective, humans might have already reached their maximum life span.

Dr. Sinclair acknowledges that plenty of obstacles are still ahead, but he has faith that he's on the right track.

"Caloric restriction works in every organism, and so far, these molecules have worked in every organism," he says. "I'm hoping humans are not the planet's only exception. People who think that are usually disproven when it comes to biology."

So what will these sirtuin-activating, mitochondrial-boosting drugs look like if they ever hit the market? The drugs that Sirtris is now working to develop will be targeted at specific diseases and not the aging process itself, largely for practical reasons. For a drug to be approved by the FDA, its manufacturer must show it has a measurable effect. To demonstrate an impact on aging would take at least 10 to 20 years, something no drug company has the time, resources, or interest in doing. Diabetes, in contrast, can be tested relatively quickly.

"It's probably never going to be sold as an antiaging drug," Dr. Sinclair says. "But if a drug comes to market and is capable of doing what we see in mice, then there will also be approved trials by doctors to treat other ailments. And the hope is that people will then start to see the other benefits."

Included in those other benefits are nearly all the things you see when mitochondria are working properly: abundant energy, improved memory, reduced chance of heart disease and cancer—the list goes on.

Dr. Sinclair says that sometimes people complain about what he's doing, but he

"People think we're extending the years of life. We're actually increasing the years of youth."

insists they simply don't understand it.

"I occasionally get letters from people saying, 'I'm 75, I can barely walk, I'm in pain. The last thing I want is a pill that extends my life.' " His voice falls to a near-whisper. "I think they miss the point. People think we're extending the final years of life, when what we're actually doing is increasing the years of youth. So it's keeping people out of nursing homes, not keeping them alive longer in nursing homes."

Given all of that, the more intriguing question might be this: What impact could these drugs have on society? Sinclair believes that reducing levels of age-related diseases would create a huge economic benefit to society. "If you make people live longer in a healthy way, it's far cheaper," he says. "I've read that if you reduce one disease—cancer, for example—by 10 percent, the savings to the United States would be about $5 trillion. Well, we're talking about drugs reducing disease maybe more than 10 percent—and many of them at once."

The more profound impact may be on each of us individually. On a practical level, you'd no longer be able to retire at 65. On the positive side, you'd have more years to enjoy the things you love, and probably watch your great-grandchildren grow up. And on a deeper level, perhaps the very arc of your life would be affected. In a world where 95 is the new 65, and 65 the new 40, would we stop going to school in our early 20s, or would we extend education another decade or so? Or go for repeated educations and careers? And how about marriage—would most of us still marry before we're 30? Would one spouse remain the ideal, or would we slap a 50-year expiration date on marriage and change partners later in life?

It's a lucky thing that mitochondria give us energy; we're going to need plenty.

For Dr. Sinclair, any complications pale in comparison to the benefits.

"When I was working for my Ph.D., my mom got lung cancer. The doctor said, basically, say good-bye to your mom, there's only a 5 percent chance she'll survive. It was pretty traumatic for her and us kids. And for a time I wasn't going to come to the United States because I figured I might never see her again. But I resolved that if I was going to leave her, I would devote myself to making practical use of discoveries.

"Fortunately, she's still alive. But that was a turning point in my life. People probably think I'm just spinning it, but I'm only doing this because I want to help people and prevent them from dying. Or delay it, at least."

Despite his heroics in baseball's postseason, Rocco Baldelli isn't cured, and he knows it. He's said that he sleeps twice as much as he used to, and he takes a daily cocktail of medications to combat his condition. His baseball future is unclear, as well: A few days after the Rays lost the World Series, Baldelli became a free agent.

"I don't anticipate that the state of my health will be changing," he told a sportswriter recently.

But that doesn't mean he's without hope. As any Tampa Bay Rays team member knows, miracles do happen sometimes. ■

PROVE IT.

CLICK— YOU'RE SICK

Never mind doorknobs and faucet handles—the real viral hot spot in your home is the TV remote control. A University of Virginia study discovered that **half of TV remotes belonging to people with colds were contaminated with the rhinovirus.** What's more, the bug, which causes 35 percent of colds, survived on the channel changers for 2 days.

"The microscopic secretions of mucus embedding the virus may help it survive so long," says study author Birgit Winther, M.D. **Debug your remote** with disinfecting wipes that contain ammonium chloride.

HARD TRUTH

2

Number of days the cold bug can survive on TV remotes

GET STUCK

If you don't usually get your flu shot, here's more incentive to roll up your sleeve: The influenza vaccine might help prevent potentially fatal blood clots. French researchers recently found that **people who'd been vaccinated were 48 percent less likely to develop the dangerous blood-clotting condition known as deep-vein thrombosis** than those who skipped the injection. Inflammation produced by the viral infection might cause your blood to thicken, increasing the odds of deadly clotting.

BE A WHIZ KID

Can you pass it? **A simple urine test can reveal if you're at risk for diabetes,** according to new research in the *Journal of Hypertension*. In the study by French scientists, men with even moderately high urine levels of albumin, a protein that regulates blood volume, had up to a 97 percent greater risk of developing diabetes than men with the lowest levels—even in the absence of common risk factors, such as obesity or cardiovascular disease.

While more research needs to be done to understand the connection, the study authors speculate that elevated levels of albumin could cause artery damage, which may in turn lead to insulin resistance. Ask your doctor for an albumin test: Urine levels above 9 milligrams per liter might signal a problem.

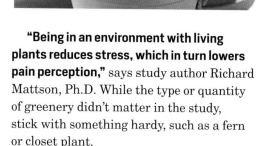

BEE WELL

Bees might someday take the sting out of sinus infections. In a test-tube study, Canadian researchers discovered that **honey is highly effective at killing the bacteria** that are sometimes at the root of chronic sinusitis.

In fact, honey was such a powerful bug zapper that it outperformed even the most commonly prescribed antibiotic. The next challenge is to identify the active compounds so they can be tested in a nasal spray.

Honey can also speed burn healing when spread over singed skin.

HAVE A GREENER HOSPITAL STAY

The next time you visit someone in the hospital, **skip the flowers and bring a potted plant** instead. Researchers at Kansas State University found that when people recovering from appendectomies had plants in their hospital rooms, they needed up to 36 percent less pain medication than those whose rooms were foliage-free.

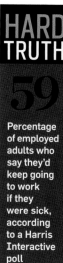

HARD TRUTH

59

Percentage of employed adults who say they'd keep going to work if they were sick, according to a Harris Interactive poll

"Being in an environment with living plants reduces stress, which in turn lowers pain perception," says study author Richard Mattson, Ph.D. While the type or quantity of greenery didn't matter in the study, stick with something hardy, such as a fern or closet plant.

Besides bringing a plant, crack open a window. Fresh air can reduce a patient's risk of catching TB by 72 percent.

SIP DOWN HYPERTENSION

Concerned about your heart health? Before you turn to meds, maybe you should try tea. **Drinking 3 cups of hibiscus tea a day can lower your blood pressure,** say Tufts University scientists. When prehypertensive and mildly hypertensive people drank the brew for 6 weeks, their average systolic blood pressure levels dropped by as much as 13 points.

"Flavonoids in hibiscus plants may work by dilating the blood vessels," says study author Diane McKay, Ph.D., which allows blood to flow through more easily. Celestial Seasonings Red Zinger contains the same amount of hibiscus that was used in the study, but talk to your doctor beforehand.

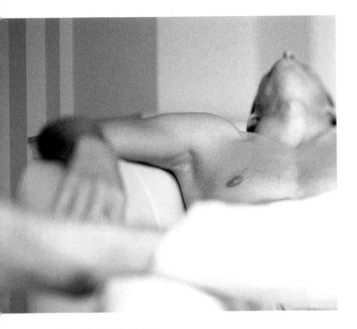

END APNEA

Apnea sufferers, take off the mask. The usual treatment for sleep apnea is a CPAP mask, which increases air pressure to keep your airway open. But Brazilian researchers found that simple throat exercises might also help treat sleep apnea. People who performed the exercises for half an hour a day reduced the severity of their condition by 39 percent in 3 months. The workout strengthens your upper airway, so it won't collapse during sleep.

If you have moderate sleep apnea, talk with your doctor about trying the exercises. Find sleep apnea exercises at MensHealth.com/apnea.

DEFUSE A BRAIN BOMB

Tough day at the office? Work stress can send your stroke risk skyrocketing. A new Japanese study found that men with demanding jobs in which they feel micromanaged have a 2½ times higher risk of stroke than men in less taxing positions. Chronic job stress keeps your sympathetic nervous system on high alert, which in turn might push your blood pressure into the red zone, says study author Akizumi Tsutsumi, M.D.

If the boss asks for one more thing, tell him that your brain will explode. Because it just might.

YOU ASKED.

I need to find a new primary-care doctor. What's the difference between an M.D. and a D.O.?

A: Other than one letter, not much. Doctors of medicine and doctors of osteopathy are educated in very similar ways, except D.O.s are trained in manipulative therapy, which involves moving and stretching a patient's joints and muscles to treat musculoskeletal complaints, such as pain in a person's neck or lower back. This reflects how D.O.s also used to differ from M.D.s in taking a more holistic approach to patient care, addressing the underlying causes as well as the symptoms of a person's medical problem.

These days, however, most M.D.s have adopted the D.O. philosophy, virtually eliminating the difference, says Steven Lamm, M.D., a clinical assistant professor of medicine at New York University's medical center.

If you're looking for a primary-care physician, Dr. Lamm says it's more important to find someone who is board certified in either internal medicine or family medicine. (Go to abms.org/wc/preregister.aspx to check.) Both specialties mean the doc is able to handle all the typical ailments you're likely to stumble in with.

Q: I know I should keep an eye on my sugar intake, but does that include fruits?

A: "No, fruits also provide vitamins, minerals, fiber, and compounds whose health benefits we're only beginning to understand," says Mary Ellen Camire, Ph.D., a professor of food science in the department of food science and human nutrition at the University of Maine. "But limit your juice intake to one or two of your daily fruit servings. Too much juice can spike blood sugar and lead to weight gain."

Q: Is there any way to make LDL cholesterol less deadly?

A: "LDL circulates as large, buoyant particles (form A), and as small, dense particles (form B)—the real heart killers," says John Elefteriades, M.D., chief of cardiac surgery at Yale University School of Medicine and a former president of the International College of Angiology. "It's not easy to convert a type-B pattern to a type A, but regular exercise and achieving your optimal weight can help."

Q: I slashed my carb intake, and my triglycerides fell from 289 to 98. Why?

A: "By going low carb, you're reducing the amount of sugar in your bloodstream. (Carbs are sugar.) This makes your body burn an alternative energy source, triglycerides, which are a kind of fat that circulates in your blood and which at high levels can increase your risk for heart disease," says Dr. Elefteriades.

Q: I am 30 and having trouble seeing when I drive at night. Do I need glasses?

A: "You should have an eye exam to determine if you need glasses and to assess your overall eye health," says Kimberly Cockerham, M.D., who has a private practice and teaches ophthalmology at Stanford University School of Medicine. "You could have a retinal problem; eat a diet rich in vegetables, fruits, fish, and whole grains to maintain good eye health.

"If you have a family history of macular degeneration, consider taking Ocuvite or OcuPlus. These supplements provide essential minerals and vitamins key to eye health."

Q: I just turned 30 and seem to be having fewer morning erections. Are my T-levels falling?

A: Don't be so quick to pin the blame on your age. Your lifestyle is the more likely culprit, says Steven Lamm, M.D., author of *The Hardness Factor: How to Achieve Your Best Health and Sexual Fitness at Any Age.*

"Anxiety, alcohol, and lack of exercise affect sleep quality, and poor sleep leads to fewer morning erections," Dr. Lamm says. Healthy men achieve three to five arousals a night, which are sparked by sexy dreams; these happen during rapid eye movement (REM) sleep. Morning wood results from waking during the final REM cycle. Your erections should resume with healthy lifestyle changes that lead to better sleep—such as exercising at least three times a week and limiting alcohol to two drinks or less a night. If nothing pops up over the course of a month, or if you have trouble achieving or maintaining an erection during sex, see your doctor.

"The absence of erections could signify an underlying cardiovascular issue, diabetes, cancer, or a hormonal problem," Dr. Lamm says.

Q: Is 40 too early for a PSA test?

A: "No. The latest guidelines from the American Urological Association and the National Comprehensive Cancer Network say that all men should have a baseline PSA blood test at 40, both to help estimate their risk for prostate cancer and determine how often they should have future tests," says Judd W. Moul, M.D., FACS, chief of the division of urologic surgery at the Duke University medical center in Durham, North Carolina, and director of the Duke Prostate Center.

Q: Can upgrading my pillow improve my sleep?

A: Yes, especially if what's currently cradling your cranium doesn't pass this test: "Your pillow should spring back after it's been folded in half," says Michael Breus, Ph.D., a sleep specialist in Scottsdale, Arizona. "And it should also align your head and neck in a straight line."

To find the right level of support, rest your noggin on a pillow (or pillows, if you use two) against the wall in the same position you sleep in. If your head tilts toward the wall, you need a firmer model. If it tilts away, go softer. Did it fail? Use the cheat sheet below to choose a new one.

1. DOWN

A luxurious landing spot for your head costs some dough, but down pillows can outlast most synthetic types. One caveat: Down is fertile ground for allergens. So sleep specialist Michael Breus recommends Ogallala's Hypo-down. The 700 is stuffed with 80 percent goose down and 20 percent milkweed syriaca, which prevents the buildup of dust mites. $165, ogallalacomfort company.com

2. THERMOREGULATING

No one has invented a self-flipping pillow, but the IsoCool Foam Side Sleeper could be the next best thing. It has microcapsules that absorb excess heat, preventing that hot-side, cold-side problem. The same stuff is also used in apparel, to make base layers for use in sports where overheating can inhibit performance. $80, sleepbetter.org

3. ANTISNORING

Specially designed for side sleeping, the Sona Pillow has a unique shape that positions your jaw to keep your airway open. In fact, company research published in *Sleep and Breathing* showed that people using the Sona snored less. The pillow also has two tunnellike sections that allow you to slide your arm under your head without it falling asleep. $80, brookstone.com

4. MEMORY FOAM

Your body heat causes memory foam to conform to your head and neck, making this kind of pillow worth considering if you sometimes crawl out of bed with a crick, says Breus. His pick is the Tempur-Pedic NeckPillow because of its shape and high-quality foam. $100, tempurpedic.com

5. HYPOALLERGENIC

For people who sneeze themselves to sleep, these pillows contain fills, such as wool, cotton, and polyester, to name a few, which repel dust mites and mold. Side sleeper? We like the extra neck support provided by the 2-inch gusseted side panels on the PrimaLoft Comfort Pillow. $45, garnethill.com

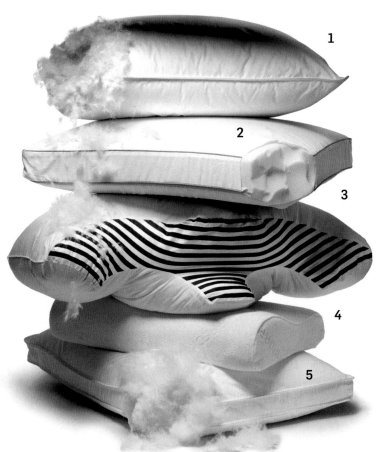

Improve Your Game

Your Best Shot

Grip it and rip it: five high-tech sticks that'll drive down your score.

Golf might as well be a game of tee shots with a bunch of other stuff in between— because, really, what's more satisfying than blasting a golf ball 240 yards? Recently, manufacturers released many new drivers to make the most of that first shot. We tested them for strengths and weaknesses and analyzed the different ways they can boost your own shortcomings on the course. Here are our winners, and how to save par every time.

NIKE SQ DYMO STR8-FIT
$540, nikegolf.com

TAYLORMADE R7 LIMITED
$360, taylormadegolf.com

MH
TOP PICK

**CLEVELAND GOLF
HIBORE MONSTER XLS**
$300, clevelandgolf.com

ADAMS GOLF SPEEDLINE
$300, adamsgolf.com

PING RAPTURE V2
$500, pinggolf.com

Ping Rapture V2

EXCELS AT: Power

It outslugged every driver we tested by an average of 12 yards, thanks to its plasma-welded titanium face, but the blast exaggerated off-center hits. This club's safe only for the most accurate players.

Center distance: **243 yards**
Center dispersion: **5.7 feet**
Off-center distance: **237.5 yards**
Off-center dispersion: **43 feet**

Cleveland Golf Hibore Monster XLS

EXCELS AT: Forgiveness

The horizontally stretched head can better correct off-center hits, and its scooped crown puts air under the ball. Best for guys who need all-around help.

Center distance: **234.7 yards**
Center dispersion: **16 feet**
Off-center distance: **227.1 yards**
Off-center dispersion: **21.8 feet**

Nike Sq Dymo Str8-fit

EXCELS AT: Adaptability

The clubhead fits the shaft in eight positions to help with draws and fades and negate hooks and slices. Perfect for a guy who plays many courses. But don't adjust it during play—that's against the rules.

Center distance: **231.2 yards**
Center dispersion: **10.6 feet**
Off-center distance: **228.5 yards**
Off-center dispersion: **36.8 feet**

Taylormade R7 Limited

EXCELS AT: Balance

The varied thickness of the clubface creates a wide sweet spot for more distance and accuracy on off-center hits. Best for a sprayer whose balls never land where he's looking.

Center distance: **232 yards**
Center dispersion: **14.8 feet**
Off-center distance: **227.2 yards**
Off-center dispersion: **25 feet**

Adams Golf Speedline

EXCELS AT: Speed

A raised crown, along with scoops in the toe and heel to improve aerodynamics, allows the club to cut through the air with ease. Best for a straight shooter who could use a few extra yards.

Center distance: **235.7 yards**
Center dispersion: **11.5 feet**
Off-center distance: **230.8 yards**
Off-center dispersion: **38.8 feet**

Professional golfer
Adam Scott

The New Rules of Golf

"You should be enjoying the game. Otherwise, why go out there?" says pro golfer Adam Scott. Here's how to keep your round fun—and fair.

SIMPLIFY YOUR STYLE

"Everything has relaxed in the past few years," says Scott. But he nods to tradition, wearing classic patterns like plaid or argyle with modern, slim-fitting pants and a thin belt.

COUNT THEM ALL

There's no ref on the course; players govern their own games. If your ball falls out of bounds, call a penalty immediately. You'll lose a stroke but set the precedent for fair play.

CELEBRATE AT THE END

Golf requires stillness and precision, so Scott embodies it—even after an amazing hole. "If I get too pumped," he says, "it's hard to calm down for the next shot."

Save Par Every Time

"The game's all about recognizing what makes a tough shot and adjusting your swing," says PGA Tour pro Marc Turnesa. Diagnose difficult lies and salvage strokes by following top golfers' advice.

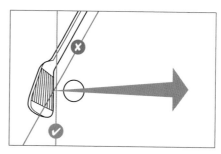

Short Chip from a Tight Lie

Bump-and-runs can sputter. High lobs can overshoot. So don't choke the club and scoop the ball. "Use soft hands and hit the ball with a square face," says Turnesa. This keeps the ball low—the safest bet. The faster you land it, the less work you'll need on the green.

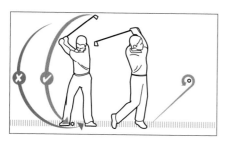

Long Iron from Deep Rough

You want loft to escape the grass without sacrificing distance. Set the ball back in your stance, take the club back steeply, and strike down on the ball, not deep underneath. "You'll create spin, which helps take your ball out of the rough," says PGA Tour pro Nicholas Thompson.

Drive into the Wind

Don't hit the ball hard; that'll create spin, allowing the wind to catch it. Instead, tee the ball lower than usual and back in your stance. You'll produce a low, straight shot that bores through the wind.

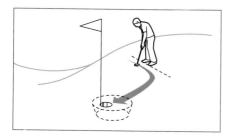

Sidehill Downhill Putt

Put more weight on your leading foot and resist the urge to direct the ball with your clubface. Just pick a line and commit to it. "Every putt is a straight putt," Turnesa says. Place your feet in the direction of your line, not toward the hole, and follow through.

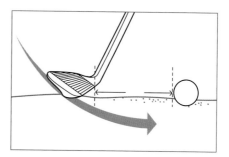

Green-Side Bunker Shot

You can't be afraid to thump the sand. Swing hard and use the acceleration of the club to propel the ball toward the hole. Hit about 6 inches behind the ball to create a tsunami of sand.

HARD
TRUTH

58

Percentage of
game injuries
caused by
player-to-
player
contact

Want to stay in the game and off the injury list? That's a no-brainer for sure. And that's why the protective sports gear industry is so huge, and growing. Here, says Cynthia Bir, Ph.D., lead scientist for FSN's Sport Science, separates the claims from the reality—and helps you keep some of your hard-earned cash in your pockets along the way.

Your Body Guards

Not all protective sports gear lives up to its promise. Navigate hype and conflicting claims with this primer.

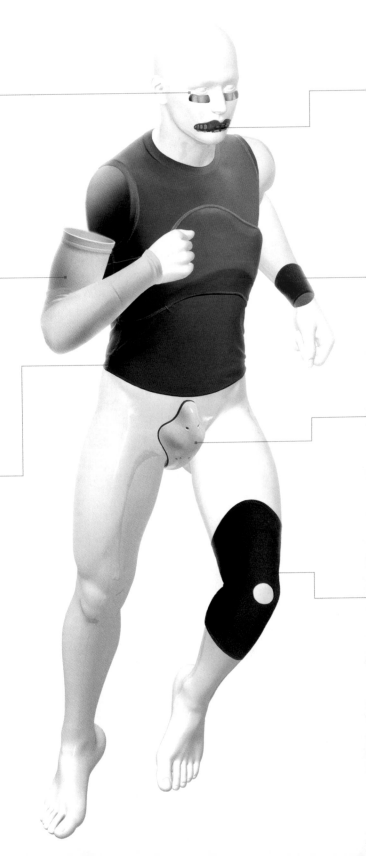

EYE BLACK

Claim: When used under eyes, it improves ability to see contrast.
Reality: Yale researchers found that the grease increases the eyes' sensitivity to contrast. A similar product, adhesive "antiglare" stickers, did not. Still, there's no official word on whether the improvement significantly affects performance.

SHOOTER SLEEVES

Claim: They improve muscle efficiency. Some manufacturers claim that the wraps help conserve power, boost endurance, or promote bloodflow.
Reality: "Shooter sleeves are great for keeping your arms warm, and that's it," says Douglas B. McKeag, M.D., M.S., director of the Indiana University Center for Sports Medicine. "This is the modern-day version of snake oil."

CHEST PROTECTOR

Claim: The exterior disperses impact by radiating it outward instead of simply cushioning a hit.
Reality: It's true, and you don't need a fancy one. "Any chest protector or shin pad with a hard outer shell and foam padding underneath will distribute force and reduce initial impact," says Dr. Bir.

MOUTH GUARD

Claim: It protects your teeth. Some mouth guards have shock absorbers and additional impact protection.
Reality: Custom-fit top and bottom guards outperform boil-and-bites by 50 percent, says Dr. Bir. The more snug the guard fits against your teeth, the better, she says. Visit your dentist for a custom grille.

BICEPS BANDS

Claim: They keep your arms dry and make them look better.
Reality: They won't hinder you, but expect nothing else from them. "Unless you have a serious sweat problem, biceps bands are purely cosmetic," says Dr. McKeag.

ATHLETIC CUP

Claim: It's supposed to transfer impact to your pubic bone so you can sustain a blow to your boys.
Reality: Dr. Bir's lab pitted the NuttyBuddy against an air cannon and measured the distribution of force. The cup's shape spread the blow better than some grade-school cups. $20, nuttybuddy.com

NEOPRENE KNEE SLEEVES

Claim: Wrapped around an injury-prone joint, neoprene aids stability while remaining flexible.
Reality: Dr. Bir hasn't found much purpose for these, but Belgian researchers have: A neoprene sleeve applies pressure and reminds your brain to "sense" your joint's position-ing, which could prevent injury as your muscles fatigue.

Halt the Hurt

Looks bad. Don't make it worse. Before you see a doctor for an injury, here are a few simple, immediate steps you can take to help minimize damage.

Cramp

"Stretch, but not to the point of pain. A 30-second stretch elongates muscles and increases the flow of fluid," says Philadelphia Flyers athletic trainer Jim McCrossin, A.T.C.

Sprain

Get off the leg as soon as possible, and then follow the RICE rule: rest, ice (for 15 minutes), compress, and elevate. Don't use the injured leg, says McCrossin.

Broken nose

Apply ice for 10 to 15 minutes and breathe through your mouth. If there's blood, pack your nostrils with gauze. Don't wipe; side motions may increase damage.

Black eye

Ice it to control swelling, but only for 10 to 15 minutes—no longer, says McCrossin. After about 20 minutes, the ice can make the injury look worse.

"When you accomplish something so great, you want to do it again."

The Champion Within

Paul Pierce overcame every obstacle in his way.
Each one made him work harder.

In Manhattan Beach, just outside Los Angeles, there is a city park with a 100-foot sand dune. Back when Paul Pierce was a nobody, just some poor kid who thought maybe he'd become a garbage man someday, he'd visit the park regularly. And with the other kids there, he'd charge up that dune.

It's a hell of a workout. It'll make you wheeze. Run that thing from bottom to top, and a basketball court might as well be a waterslide.

Flash-forward to summer 2008: Pierce, then captain of the Boston Celtics, had won an NBA championship by defeating the Lakers. His legacy was secure. He could rest, finally, after a career of struggles and doubts, after boos from the fans, after he was stabbed in a Boston bar. He deserved to celebrate until he forgot what stress felt like.

You've had the temptation, too. You land the job, you score the girl, and you feel secure. You feel in—as if you can finally rest. But you can't. Muscles atrophy if you don't work them; life can go slack, as well, if you don't make an effort.

Pierce has a tattoo, "My gift is my curse." He means basketball, but the phrase could apply to anything: When you succeed, you only raise the bar. It's a good thing, but it means you have to refocus and find new motivation. You must be ready with new goals. If you're not looking up, you're looking down.

Which is why the kids running the dune in Manhattan Beach were joined by a familiar face last summer. It was Pierce. He was out there scaling it six times a day—first walking, then jogging, then running. Running hard.

"Usually when you win the championship, you party all summer and don't work out," he says. "But when I won, I mean, I had my good times, but I used it as motivation to do it again. When you realize you can accomplish something so great, you want to do it again."

When Pierce took the championship, he thought he was at his peak form. Nobody would have disputed it. But there's always room for improvement. Start with food: Pierce was winning games, but he was also eating at all times of the night, scarfing pasta and popcorn. When you look good and feel good, it's hard to think about this stuff being bad for you. But after he took home an NBA trophy and washed the champagne off his head, he changed his diet. He ate regularly. He dropped junk food and excess carbs, and switched to fish, chicken, and salads.

And when he arrived at Celtics training camp in 2009, he was 9 pounds lighter and perhaps more prepared than he'd ever been. For the first time in his career, Paul Pierce was, in every way, starting on top.

"Mentally prepare yourself. I think about what I need to do to become better.

THE KEY TO MOTIVATION

"Michael Olowokandi!"

Swish.

"Robert Traylor!"

Swish.

Know those guys? Maybe not; they're no longer in the NBA. But Pierce knew them well. They were drafted before him, in 1998, the year Pierce was expected to be taken second but instead went tenth. He was disappointed, but then he was motivated: There were nine guys the league thought were better than he was, and that meant there were nine guys he had to show up. So as a rookie, when he practiced his free throws, he'd call out their names.

"Jason Williams!"

Swish.

A key to motivation is finding strength in a weakness—in his case, a perceived weakness. People won't always recognize your abilities. The better man is turned down for promotions all the time, but did that man make his abilities evident? Maybe not. It's your job to display your worth, not your boss's job to figure it out.

"You have to show them that they made a mistake, and that you're better than the guys who were chosen before you," Pierce says. "That was something I needed to do, and it drove me."

It also turned out to be a type of motivation Pierce would turn to again, and he'd really need it. The Celtics might be steeped in glory ("It's almost a religion around here," Pierce says), but Pierce's time with the Celtics was often difficult. He was the best man on a bad team, an all-star who rarely saw the playoffs. He was tense with reporters and not always loved by fans,

and he was even stabbed at a nightclub before the 2000–2001 season. He didn't miss a single game that season, but the failures shook his confidence. In the thick of it, during long losing streaks, Pierce described himself as Dr. Jekyll and Mr. Hyde. The good days were fine, but the bad days were really bad.

You can't bottle that up. Keep negativity inside and you'll start to believe the worst—that you're untalented, unaccomplished, everything you fear about yourself. So Pierce, a proud man who likes to rely on himself, started turning to others. He'd speak regularly with his mom and brothers and Celtics coaching legend Red Auerbach. They're optimistic people whose opinions mattered to him. Not everyone around him was positive, so he learned who to turn to. That's important: Even when you need advice, you still have control. You can pick the people who'll prop you up. That means you may already know what they'll tell you, but it's helpful to hear it anyway. It's important not to endure your troubles alone.

"Red always said to me, 'Your name is Paul Pierce, and just remember who you are,'" Pierce says. "Understanding who you are is saying, 'You're great, you have tons of confidence, and don't ever forget that.' And that helped me, man. Because when things weren't going right, I thought, *You've got to remember who you are. Don't stray from that. Don't let these things get you down.*"

These days, Pierce wakes up every day at 7:30. The Celtics have 11 a.m. practice, so he's often in the gym by 9:15. He's done this for years. It's sending a message not only to his teammates, who have seen him sweaty and ready by the time they're strolling in, but also to himself. He's reminding himself that work still needs to be done.

Try it. Show up at the office before your boss does, and see what happens. He'll take notice immediately. In the dead quiet, you'll see the office like you haven't before—not as a place of constant demands but as a space for strategizing and setting things in motion, for going on offense instead of defense.

"For that little moment while you're there alone, you can work on things without someone telling you what to do. You men-tally prepare yourself," Pierce says. "I think about what I need to do to become better."

But these days, that quiet is harder to find. Pierce has set an example. The team's younger guys are showing up at the gym when he does. They're watching him, learning from him. Blaze a path and you'll be followed. They'll give you credit; they'll take you seriously. It's why Pierce is the team's leader. It's why the city of Boston loves him. It's why he runs that sand dune, and why he'll keep running it, year after year, no matter what happens. ■

BREAK THROUGH THE HARD TIMES

The Celtics had some rough years, and Paul Pierce always looked for help. Here are ways he found it.

STUDY YOUR PREDECESSORS.

Pierce is an NBA historian, and not just because he's nostalgic for Bill Russell. He finds comfort in learning about the struggles of great players, because they remind him that success isn't bestowed; it's chased, and the hungriest catch it.

"That's what separates the top players today from the rest," he says. "Understanding history means knowing what motivates you."

GIVE YOURSELF A PRIZE.

Rewards, like money and fame, are universal. But they're ultimately empty if there's nothing truly personal at the center of your quest. That's what Pierce had when Red Auerbach gave him a few of his cigars. Pierce keeps three of them in his locker, and he'll light one up only if he wins a championship. Last year he took his first taste.

"It was stale," he says. "But I smoked it anyway."

BECOME YOUR OWN COACH.

Pierce works well with his coaches, but he also values his time away from them. "They tell you what to do," he says. "But you have to think about how you can help yourself, before the coach comes in." The most successful men know this balance. It's not only a matter of learning from others; it's about building on what you've learned in order to achieve something unique to you.

Raising the Stakes

Miami Heat guard Dwyane Wade is an NBA champ and an Olympic gold medalist. This year, the pressure reaches new heights.

The Miami Heat's star guard is goofing around on a basketball court, and someone asks if he has a signature move. "I don't," Dwyane Wade says. "I make it up as I go." In fact, that unpredictability pretty much is his signature. His best moments typically involve dodging a gauntlet of opponents, slamming into one of them, and then contorting, spinning, and collapsing to the floor just as his tossed-up shot tumbles through the hoop.

327

Wade's career has been similarly bruising. After joining the NBA in 2003 with little hype, he led the Heat to its first championship 3 years later and took home a Finals MVP trophy. He became a regular All-Star and signed high-profile sponsorships. But then the Heat grew sluggish and Wade sustained knee and shoulder injuries. He mostly watched from the bench in 2007–08 as the team posted the worst record in the league.

"One of the hardest things to do, once you win, is come out and do it again," Wade says. "But it's all about growth. As you grow older, the responsibilities turn to you." And they truly have: He's healthy again, and he has convinced superstars LeBron James and Chris Bosh to join the Heat. Wade's role is different now, but he has prepared for it. Here are his tips on recovering from even the toughest setbacks.

REMAIN RELEVANT

"I never wanted to be a vocal kind of leader," Wade says. "I've always said I would lead by example."

But exhorting teammates from the bench when he was injured led to a change. He became an observer and a motivator. "Some guys you can talk to a certain way and some guys you can't. As a leader you have to know the difference," he says.

Fill a need. Wade's style of play may be aggressive, but he refuses to play it safe. He has a specific purpose—to penetrate and set up plays.

"I wouldn't be any good to my teammates if I went out there and became what everybody else has become—just a jump shooter," he says. "That's an easy game to play. I don't like to play easy." It's important to know what others look to you for. That doesn't mean you box yourself in, but by cultivating a strength, you'll make sure you're always someone's go-to guy.

EMBRACE CHALLENGES

Wade, once king of the NBA, is now joined by King James, and expectations are high again. But that's not such a bad place to be, at least for now.

"As champion," he says, "you're everybody's biggest game. Somebody's going to come and try to take you down every night." But when the spotlight and pressure are on someone else, you're free to rebuild and grow stronger. When it's time to make a run at the top, you'll be ready.

PUSH YOURSELF

For the first 5 years of his career, Wade occasionally worked with renowned trainer Tim Grover, the same trainer Michael Jordan has used. But Wade couldn't commit to a regular schedule: He had commercials to shoot and an NBA life to enjoy. The injuries refocused his priorities. He spent one summer with Grover and came out stronger than ever.

"I'll tell you: Every year after this, I'm going to him continuously," Wade says. In fitness, coasting is costly.

SEEK INSPIRATION

During the off-season, Wade wanted to prove that he was healthy and agile. But he didn't want to start the Heat's year with that personal quest, because he knew his teammates would be looking to him for selfless leadership. Follow Wade's lead: Build yourself up beforehand, so you can start at your strongest. ■

Recover the Right Way

Dwyane Wade's doctor and personal trainer helped him regain strength and avoid reinjury. Do the same as you rebuild by following these basic tips from Bill Hartman, P.T., C.S.C.S.

RESTORE

An injury often limits your range of motion, and that can lead to trouble in other areas, such as a loss of hip-joint motion that causes lower-back or knee pain, says Hartman. Restore flexibility by applying gentle manual pressure at the point where your movement becomes limited. Hold the pressure for 30 seconds while you try to move your injured joint in the direction of the limitation. Do 3 reps, 4 times a day.

BUILD

Regain power by challenging the muscles near your injury before you add full-body exercises that incorporate the hurt area, Hartman says. So if your knee is the problem, sit with your legs extended, tighten your thigh muscles, and then relax. This builds your quadriceps and allows you to progress to more challenging exercises, such as stepups or squats. As the pain decreases, increase the resistance, speed, and range of motion of your exercises.

RESIST

Just because you're feeling better doesn't mean you're ready for the starting lineup. If basketball is your sport, build your skills—shooting, cutting, and running—before you play a game, to limit risk of reinjury.

As you increase your minutes, keep a close eye out for any recurring signs of pain, swelling, redness, weakness, or instability, Hartman says.

PREVENT

Once the pain is gone, head to the gym. To stay injury-free, you must train your body frequently, including the weak areas. Work out at least 2 or 3 times a week and focus on strength, power, and flexibility. Include full-body exercises like squats and deadlifts. Be patient. The long layoff will have set you back—strength gains are lost in less than a month, endurance declines after 2 weeks off, and your speed loses its zip in only 5 days, Hartman says.

The Persistence Factor

Professional beach volleyball player Phil Dalhausser and his partner have dominated the U.S. tour.

Phil Dalhausser began his drive for Olympic gold at 4 a.m., on the beach in Ocean City, Maryland. He was inflating an air mattress; it was his only hope for a good night's sleep.

He and a friend had spent their last few bucks flying cross-country and then taking a cab to this beach. The next morning, they'd compete in yet another volleyball tournament. They'd played many that summer, in 2003. They killed at some, were slaughtered at others. But they needed this one. A win was paid in cash—and without that, they might have to quit traveling and give up on their dreams of making it big.

Rare is the man who knows—just damn knows, early on—what he wants out of life. The rest of us find our passion later. It snaps into focus only after we've paid dues elsewhere. Dalhausser was like that: In 2003, he was a 23-year-old middle-school substitute teacher who couldn't discipline his kids. Boys with pubescent mustaches were picking on him. And all the while, Dalhausser dreamed of volleyball. He played a lot of it in college. He was pretty good. What if there was more to it?

"You have to give your passion a shot," Dalhausser says. "Otherwise, you'll always wonder."

And if you do it responsibly, without sacrificing what you already have, one of two things will happen: You'll make a big change, or you'll flush the what-ifs from your system and embrace your first path. Either way, you can't lose.

That's why Dalhausser didn't quit teaching. He tried volleyball during the summer, when it wouldn't interfere with his job. He gave himself 2 years: Succeed, or give it up.

Changing paths is equal parts exhilaration and fear. You're at the back of a new line. But just because those guys ahead of you decided on a path before you did doesn't mean they're better than you. They're just better trained. Put in more effort than they have, and you can pass them.

But you'll need patience.

When Dalhausser woke up on that air mattress, players were standing around

When people don't know what to expect from you, ==surprise them== with your strength.

laughing at him. But he and his friend just packed up their stuff, signed in for the tournament, and used the embarrassment to their advantage. When people don't know what to expect from you, surprise them with your strength. That's just as true on the court as it is with a new job: Opponents are defeated, bosses are impressed. Victory is in the blitz.

"And we got the last laugh," Dalhausser says, "because we won the tournament."

Five years later, Dalhausser received a gold medal in Beijing for beach volleyball. He was the summer star in the volleyball league AVP. And although his success may have begun in places like Ocean City, it went worldwide because Dalhausser knew he had much to work on.

Roam aimlessly, choose an exercise, go at it for a while, repeat. It's a familiar but ineffective gym routine, and it's how Dalhausser worked out for years. That's why, as he met with a professional trainer for the first time in 2006, he couldn't perform a deadlift. The trainer had to raise the barbell a few feet so Dalhausser didn't throw out his back.

"He could have laughed at me," Dalhausser says. "I was pathetic."

This was the problem: You can build muscles at random, but you'll plateau without a program to tie it all together.

Nail the Jump Serve

Here, Phil Dalhausser teaches volleyball's opening salvo.

TIME YOUR JUMP "You need to hit it at a high angle so the other team has less time to react," he says. Practice jumping so you connect with the ball at the highest point possible, with your arm fully extended.

TOSS IN FRONT If you toss the ball directly above or behind you, you'll look up and see nothing but ball. But if you aim it a few inches in front of you, you can watch the ball and keep your opponents—and more important, an open space on their side of the court—in your field of vision.

PLACE YOUR FINGERS Don't whap the ball with your palm the way most novices do. You'll have no control. Instead, connect with your fingers and the top of your palm. Your fingers will give the ball topspin and help guide it across the net.

That's because your muscles respond best to specific kinds of work. Dalhausser didn't have the core strength to perform deadlifts because his workouts hadn't built his abs, glutes, or hamstrings, among other muscles.

Plus, he'd been using weight machines, which are attractive because they're easy. But they're also limiting. Think of the difference between a leg-press machine and a squat. The first builds your legs, while the second builds your body—including all those small, unglamorous

> ## "You have to give your passion a shot. Otherwise, you always wonder whether it would have worked out."

back muscles you tend to ignore. But try to lift a weight from the ground, and you'll find out how much they matter.

You need motivation to become serious about training, and Dalhausser's came in the form of Todd Rogers. In 2006, Rogers, a veteran nicknamed "the Professor," asked Dalhausser to join him in a unique pairing: The two would be teammates, but Rogers would also be Dalhausser's coach. Dalhausser would have to learn when to lead and when to follow.

Who wants to work closely with the boss? You're never sure when to trust your instincts, and you're always being told what to do. You do it at work all the time, and it's nerve-racking. But Dalhausser saw it differently.

"We're a team, so I had to be good," he says. "He helps himself by making me the best player I can be. We have to have a successful partnership."

Look at your work that way, and those moments won't seem so complicated after all. Your boss might call the shots, but he's as dependent on you as you are on him. Your score is his score. He wants to move forward. So if you innovate and strive, you'll be rewarded as he is.

Dalhausser listened and learned and changed his game. As he improved, the team improved. And soon enough, the new guy could even perform those deadlifts.

Any passion is subject to being spoiled. It's like an overplayed song: The more it tosses around in your head, the more it becomes a chore. Same goes for last night's date or a meeting at work: There's healthy reflection, and then there's obsession. And that's why Dalhausser bought himself a 125-gallon salt water fish tank. It's his big, beautiful distraction.

"You can sit and stress, or you can occupy your mind with something you enjoy," Dalhausser says. So when he's at home, an hour outside Los Angeles, Dalhausser plays video games, admires the clown fish in his tank, and gives his mind a break from volleyball.

He does think about what'll happen when he retires from the game, though. It's inevitable; most players quit by their mid-30s. And now that he has pursued his passion, he's feeling free. The what-ifs that dogged him as a substitute teacher are gone. ■

PROVE IT.

GET THE ULTRAVIOLET EDGE

Go outside: Sunshine can increase athletic performance by as much as 10 percent, according to the journal *Medicine and Science in Sports and Exercise*. **Ultraviolet rays boost your vitamin D levels,** and a study review has determined that D improves reaction time, speed, and muscle strength.

Sun-activated vitamin D works as a steroid hormone that regulates genes associated with athletic performance, says study author John Cannell, M.D. Three out of four people have too-low levels of the vitamin.

Net gain: If you're low on vitamin D, 10 minutes of sun on your legs and arms 3 times a week can boost your D to healthy levels.

DRINK IT IN

Maybe we've been brainwashed. **Just looking at a sports drink increases exercise endurance,** according to research reported in the journal *Psychology of Sport and Exercise*. People who were shown a bottle of Gatorade were able to raise one leg for 149 percent longer than those who viewed a bottle of springwater. The boost probably occurs because of the inherent association between Gatorade and exercise, which cues our brains that it's time to work hard, says study coauthor Ron Friedman, Ph.D. Advertising has reinforced the link, he says, noting that it would probably work for other beverages that are strongly associated with endurance and hard work.

REFUEL RAPIDLY

Have a cup of joe with your post-workout meal; it could help you with tomorrow's run. **Drinking caffeine along with carbohydrates refuels your muscles faster.**

Australian researchers found that when cyclists combined their carbs with caffeine, their supply of muscle glycogen refilled 34 percent faster than it did in people who ate only carbs. "Adding caffeine triggers a greater increase in blood glucose and insulin levels," says study author John Hawley, Ph.D., making it easier for muscles to store glucose as glycogen. Each cyclist ingested the equivalent of 6 cups of coffee, however. More research is needed to see what smaller amounts might do.

GET THE WINNING EDGE

Logging lazy "junk" miles won't improve your race times. The more often you replicate high-intensity race-day conditions during practice, the faster you'll finish in actual competition, a new University of Wisconsin at LaCrosse study finds.

Rowers and **cyclists who performed six practice trials at a competitive pace improved their race times by 10 percent.** The reason: Athletes tend to hold back in practice and underestimate the effort needed to perform optimally in a race, says study author Carl Foster, Ph.D.

TAPER PERFECTLY

The taper is that glorious prerace period for marathoners (and half-marathoners) when training is scaled back. A review of tapering studies reveals that **reducing mileage while maintaining your pace and frequency is best.** Do your final long run—16 to 20 miles—21 days before the race. Then follow this plan.

3 Weeks Before

Training: Scale back your total mileage for the week to about 75 percent of what you've been doing.
Diet: Aim for 60 to 70 percent carbs, 15 percent protein, and the rest healthy fats. This maintains glycogen, your main energy source.

2 Weeks Before

Training: Halve your usual mileage. Your longest run should not exceed 10 miles. Stretch to help recovery.
Diet: Keep the same ratios, focusing on quality carbs. Try your prerace breakfast before a run to see how your body reacts.

1 Week Before

Training: Reduce your training to 25 percent of usual, at most. Keep your runs short, but stay on pace.
Diet: The last few days, your calorie intake should stay the same, but up to 90 percent of it should come from carbs. And no new foods!

Race Day

Training: You're done training, man. Save your energy for the gun.
Diet: Eat 300 to 500 calories (a bagel, some fruit, and an egg) 2 to 3 hours before the race. Drink 40 to 48 ounces of water over 2 hours.

HARD TRUTH

41

Optimum temperature (Fahrenheit) for the best marathon times, according to the U.S. Army Research Institute of Environmental Medicine

KNOW WHEN TO STAND UP

It's an eternal question among road cyclists: On your way up a hill, when is it most efficient to rise from the saddle and stand on the pedals? A new Norwegian study has found that magic point: **If you're climbing a 10 percent grade, stand when you're working at 94 percent capacity—or nearly as hard as you can.**

Anything less and you're likely to be more efficient in the seated position, says researcher Ernst Hansen, Ph.D. At less vigorous levels of uphill effort, standing might have biomechanical disadvantages.

MAKE A DRINKING PLAN

Cyclists and runners hit the road intending to stay hydrated, but rarely do. A new British study in the *Journal of Sports Sciences* found that explicit planning can ensure proper hydration. **Cyclists who wrote down a drinking strategy before an hourlong ride drank 55 percent more of a sports drink than cyclists who didn't map out their strategy.**

Study author Martin Hagger, Ph.D., of the University of Nottingham, suggests writing down, for example, "Three mouthfuls at the 15-, 25-, and 35-minute marks." Then do it. If you feel thirsty, you're probably already dehydrated.

WALK THIS WAY

Trekking poles are intended to make hiking easier. But surprisingly, hikers using poles work out harder without feeling any extra effort. Hikers with poles used 10 percent more oxygen and had heart rates 6 percent higher than hikers walking at the same speed sans poles—yet they reported no perceived increase in exertion, says a new study from James Madison University.

"They burned more calories without feeling the extra effort," says Mike Saunders, Ph.D., possibly because "the workload is spread over the entire body, not just the legs."

DETECT INJURIES SOONER

Knowing how badly an athlete is hurt is crucial for treatment. **A late diagnosis can exacerbate an injury, delaying a comeback.** But Spanish researchers have discovered that measuring blood levels of the protein alpha-actin helps identify muscle damage faster than current methods do. This could lead to quicker treatment, before an injury worsens and becomes chronic.

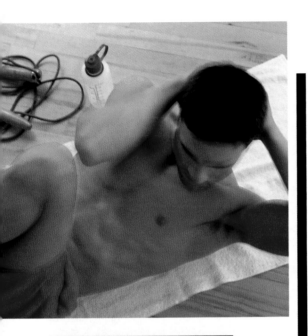

STRENGTHEN YOUR CORE FOR FASTER TIMES

It's not all about your legs. **Runners on a 6-week core-strengthening program shaved 47 seconds off their 5-K times,** a new study reports. A control group didn't do the core work and improved by only 17 seconds.

A strong core helps you maintain good posture, which leads to consistent stride length and frequency. This may reduce fatigue, says author Kimi Sato, Ph.D.(c).

These exercises, performed 4 days a week for 6 weeks, led to faster 5-K times: Crunches, back extensions, hip raises, Russian twists, supine opposite single-arm/single-leg raises, and all but the last exercise were done on a Swiss ball.

LIFT YOUR ENDURANCE

Turns out, muscular legs won't slow you down. In fact, say University of Connecticut scientists, **pumping iron improves running performance.** Among the many benefits of resistance training, the enhanced communication between your mind and muscles is key.

That's because it allows you to activate more muscle fibers, which can help you climb hills or sprint to the finish, explain the researchers. Just be sure to push yourself. Improvements were seen in study participants who used heavy weights.

YOU ASKED.

Does it matter what time of day I strength-train?

A: "No. Just be consistent in order to maximize your muscle growth. Your testosterone levels fluctuate during the day and will adjust to your workouts. Therefore, exercising at the same time every day ensures that you will have higher levels of testosterone during your workout, which can lead to bigger strength gains," David Pearson, Ph.D., C.S.C.S., a professor of exercise physiology at Ball State University and a senior editor for the *Strength and Conditioning Journal* of the National Strength and Conditioning Association.

Q: I'm trying to build bigger leg muscles, but I feel like my running is suffering. What are my options?

A: You need an efficient workout that provides a three-way payoff: more leg strength, additional explosive power, and better muscle elasticity, says Craig Friedman, M.S., C.S.C.S., a trainer at Athletes' Performance in Phoenix. Do three rounds of the following circuit twice a week while continuing your running. Soon you'll be as fast as you look.

Reverse lunge: Holding a pair of dumbbells at your sides, step back with your left leg and lower your body until your front leg is bent 90 degrees and your back knee nearly touches the floor. Keeping your torso upright, push yourself back up to the starting position; repeat with your other leg. That's 1 repetition. Use dumbbells heavy enough that you find it difficult to do 5 repetitions.

Reactive stepup: Place your right foot on a sturdy 6- to 10-inch step with your arms back. Jump vertically, driving off your right leg by extending your hip, knee, and ankle. Land in the same position and repeat. Finish 6 reps on one leg and then repeat with the other.

Quad/hip flexor stretch: Stand in front of a bench in a staggered stance. Kneel so that your front leg is bent 90 degrees, your back knee is on the floor, and the top of your back foot rests on the bench. Keeping your core tight and your back straight, lean forward and tighten the glute muscle on your back leg. Hold for 2 seconds. Complete 6 reps on each leg.

Q: I can't run more than a 5-K without having to stop and take a leak. What can I do?

A: You're probably too paranoid about dehydration. Relax and dial back the timing and quantity of your liquid intake.

"On race day, try limiting your extra fluid intake to 4 to 12 ounces a few hours—not minutes—before the race," says Liz Applegate, Ph.D., the director of sports nutrition at the University of California at Davis.

She recommends 4 to 8 ounces if you weigh 150 to 200 pounds, and up to 12 ounces if you're over 200 pounds. This should leave you sufficiently hydrated and ensure that any excess fluid will end up in the urinal before the race starts. That said, you may need to fine-tune your fill-ups on your training runs: Act like it's race day, record how much you drink, note how you feel, and then calibrate accordingly.

Q: How can I make my eyes less bloodshot after swim workouts?

A: "Before you put on your goggles, apply moisturizing gel drops. (Refresh Celluvisc is a good option.) Then, after your swim, soothe your eyes with tear drops, such as preservative-free Blink Tears," says Kimberly Cockerham, M.D., who teaches ophthalmology at Stanford University school of medicine and currently has a grant to investigate nanotechnology implants. "Skip the Visine; it relieves redness by constricting the blood vessels in your eyes, but using it regularly can condition those vessels to dilate when you stop using it."

Q: Basketball high-tops hurt my achilles tendons. Are low-rise sneakers okay?

A: "High-tops can rub the Achilles tendons and cause irritation, so changing to low-tops could help," says Nicholas A. DiNubile, M.D., an orthopedic surgeon, a clinical assistant professor of orthopedic surgery at the Hospital of the University of Pennsylvania, and the author of *FrameWork*. "So will warming up and stretching your calves. Stand on a step with your heels over the edge, and drop them down for 15 seconds. Do 3 reps. Also do this three times throughout the day on rest days."

Q: How can I continue to build strength without bulking up?

A: To a great extent, muscle size and muscle strength are interdependent: As you become stronger your muscles grow, and as your muscles grow you become stronger. That said, it is possible to fine-tune your regimen to emphasize strength over size, says Alex Koch, Ph.D., an exercise scientist at Truman State University in Missouri.

"To build strength, you have to train your nervous system to recruit and activate more muscle cells." The best way to achieve this is to lift heavier weights (around 85 percent of your 1-rep max) and do fewer reps (3 to 5). Placing your muscles under great tension for a short period not only forces them to fire in a more coordinated way but also signals them to increase the number of myofibrils, the bundles of filaments in your muscle fiber that power contraction. The result: You can generate more force.

Fizik Aliante Carbon Fiber Twin Flex: Designed to prevent the penile numbness that afflicts 61 percent of male cyclists, the Aliante has rails that support your pelvis and shift weight off your package, and a shell that dampens vibration. $200, fizik.it

Bontrager Race Lite Hardcase: A smooth tire handles better than one with tread, but it's also more vulnerable to flats. This slick has a Kevlar belt to guard against punctures. $80/set, bontrager.com

Topeak Two Timer: CO_2 pumps provide fast fixes, but they're useless if the cartridge runs out midrepair. As a backup, the Two Timer integrates a manual pump, too. $35, topeak.com

Specialized BG grips: These grips have a flat surface to help prevent the hand pain caused by clutching curved grips. $30, specialized.com

Polar CS600X: Coasting makes it easy to slack off, but a cycling computer, which tracks your cadence, heart rate, distance, and speed, serves as an on-board trainer. $420, polarusa.com

Q: What kind of bike will get me in shape fast?

A: Mountain bikes are overengineered for anything short of trails, and road bikes are really designed for speed. For everyday exercise, go for a fitness bike, like the **Cannondale Bad Boy Ultra** ($1,440, cannondale.com). This type combines the stability of a mountain bike— suspension fork and wider tires—with the lightweight frame of a road bike, says Kathleen Krumme of the Serotta International Cycling Institute. Have a shop fit the bike to ensure optimal comfort and control, and consider the upgrades above to max out your ride.

Credits

Index

Boldface page references indicate illustrations.
Underscored references indicate boxed text.

A

Abdominal muscles
  exercises for, 160–61, **160–61**
  function of, 158
  myths concerning, 158–59
  workout, 156–61
Accessories, for jeans, 193
Acetylcholine, 210
Achilles tendon, 342
Acne
  increase from dairy products,
    217
  red-light therapy for, 217
  scars, 219
Acupuncture, 267–71
Adams Golf Speedline, **313**,
    314, **314**
Additives. *See* Food additives
Aerobic exercise, benefits of, 26
Agave, 141
Age erasers, 207–13
  award winners 30s
    Derek Jeter, 209
    Mark Wahlberg, 209
    Tom Brady, 209
  award winners 40s
    Barack Obama, 211
    Daniel Craig, 211
    Will Smith, 211
  award winners 50s
    Bruce Springsteen, 213
    Denzel Washington, 213
    Matt Lauer, 213
  feeling younger, 210–12
    brain training exercises, 212
    erection improvement, 212
    laughter, 211–12
    reducing cognitive decline,
      210–11
  looking younger, 209–10
    hairstyle, 210
    shaving, 209
    skin care, 209, 210
    sleep, 210

  staying younger, 212–13
    breakfast, 212–13
    heart health, 213
    muscle maintenance, 213
Aging, mitochondria linked to,
    292–303
Albumin, in urine, 304
Alcohol, 244, 288
Aldo Clvtorigi, 205
Alfredo sauce, 70
Allergies, pesticides linked to, 132
Allura red (Red #40), 89
Almond butter, 140
Almonds, 68
Alpha-actin, 339
Alternating shuffle pushup,
    155, **155**
Alzheimer's disease
  increase risk with TV
    viewing, 236
  as viral disease, 272–81
American Heart Association
    certified food, 92–93
Ammonium chloride, 304
Amy's, 135
Anbesol, 262
Angiography, cardiac CT, 226–27
Antacids, 247, 269
Anthelios, 209
Anthocyanins, 138, 142
Antibiotics, in meat, 132
Antidepressants, 284
Anxiety, acupuncture for, 270
APOE e4 gene, 278–79
Apples, 4, 138, 140, 246
Arnold Grains & More Double
    Oat Hearty Oatmeal
    Bread, 143
Arsenic, 132
Arthritis, acupuncture for, 270
Artificial sweetener
  aspartame, 88, 141
  choosing, 141, **141**

  saccharin, 89, 141
  sucralose, 89, 141
Art of Strength Ropes Gone
    Wild, 177, **177**
Asics Gel-Evolution 4 running
    shoe, 262
Aspartame, 88, 141
Athletic cup, 319
ATP, 296
Attracting women, 214

B

Back health, bag choice for,
    220
Back pain, 266–67, 270–71
Bacon
  best for men, 65
  fat content, 102, 105
  pancetta, 111, 111–12
  preparation, 111, 111–12
Bad habits, breaking
  caffeine, 235–36
  loud music, 236–37
  smoking, 234
  talking and texting while
    driving, 237
  television, 236
Bag, 220
Bagel, 62
Baldness, 297
Banana Republic, 204
Barbell bus driver rotation, 33,
    33
Barbell drop squat and row, 34,
    34
Barbell overhead lunge, 32,
    32
Barbell press, 183
Barbell squat and one-arm
    press, 33, **33**

Basketball
    Dwyane Wade, 326–30, **327**,
        329, **331**
    Paul Pierce, **320**, 321–25,
        323, 325
    shoes, 342
BBQ sauce, 70
Beans
    canned, 66
    health benefits from, 138
    refried, 66
Beef
    cooking, 51
    frozen entrée, 65
    grass-fed, 5, 9
    hormones in, 8–9
    In-N-Out Burger, 57
    New American Burger, 5
Beef jerky, 68
Beer
    best for men, 69
    light, 69
    organic, 135
    Oskar Blues, 61
Bench jump, 21
Bench press, 37, **37**, 154, 181
Benign prostatic hyperplasia,
    252
Berries, blood pressure
    lowering by, 139
Beverages, calories consumed
    in, 86
BHA (butylated
    hydroxyanisole), 88
BHT (butylated
    hydroxytoluene), 88
Biceps bands, 319
Biceps curl, 184
Binge eating, 43
Bird dog, 164, **164**
Bisphenol A (BPA), 5, 6–8
Black eye, 319
Blink Tears, 342
Blood pressure
    decrease from
        berries, 139
        hibiscus tea, 305–6

increase from
    lifting weights, 182
    stress, 306
    testing, 228
Blue #1 (brilliant blue), 88
Blue #2 (indigotine), 88
Blueberries, 138
Blushing, 218
Body fat, measuring, 42
Body fat percentage, 183
Bone density scan, 227, 229
Bontrager Race Lite Hardcase
    tire, 343
BPA, 5, 6–8
BPH, 252
Brain, harm by pesticides, 131–32
Brain training exercises, 212
Bread
    best for men, 62
    burger bun, 63
    choosing most nutritious, 143
    organic, 134
Breakfast
    benefits of egg consumption, 138
    organic food choices, 134
    weight-loss, 212–13
Breakfast bar, 62
Breakfast sandwich, frozen, 66
Brilliant blue (Blue #1), 88
Broccoli, 41
Burger
    In-N-Out Burger, 57
    New American Burger, 5
Burns, healing with honey, 305
Burrito, frozen, 65
Butter, 125, 125
Butylated hydroxyanisole
    (BHA), 88
Butylated hydroxytoluene
    (BHT), 88

C

Cable face pull, 150, **150**
Cable pull-through, 165, **165**

Cafestol, 136
Caffeine
    breaking habit, 235–36
    carbohydrates combined
        with, 337
    for migraine headache, 265
Calories
    burned by
        aerobic exercise, 27
        muscle, 42
        weight training, 28
    consumed in beverages, 86
    inaccurate counting by food
        companies, 95
    restricting for life-extension,
        298–302
Calvin Klein Eternity for Men,
    286
Cancer
    chemicals in animal feed
        linked to, 132
    decreasing risk with
        coffee, 136
        green tea, 136
    prostate, 136, 250–59
Canned foods, 8
Cannondale Bad Boy Ultra,
    343, **343**
Canola oil, 125, 125, 135
Carbamates, 6
Carbon footprint, 133
Cardiac CT angiography, 226–27
Cardio activity
    after weight training, 183
    jumping rope, 183
    mitochondria boosting
        workout, 299
Carotenoids, 142
Carpal tunnel syndrome, 264–65
Carrageenan, 88
Cascadian Farms, 135
Casein, 121
Catalase, 216
Cataracts, 178
Catechins, in green tea, 92
CCK, 81
Celery, 80, 140

Celestial Seasonings Red
    Zinger, 306
Cereal
    best for men
        health cereal, 62
        sweet cereal, 62
    organic, 134
Cereal bar, 87
Certain Dri, 220
Cetaphil Gentle Skin Cleanser,
    215
Chandon Brut Classic, 49
Cheat meal, 42
Cheese
    all-purpose, 63
    cottage cheese, 64
    cream cheese, 64
    organic, 134
    Parmesan, 48, 49
    shredded, 64
    sliced, 63
    snacking, 64
Chemicals, in food, 129–30, 131–33
Chest exercises
    bench press, 154
    pushups, 154–55, **155**
Chest protector, 318
Chewing gum
    for heartburn relief, 262
    whitening, 219
Chex Mix Cheddar, 95
Chicken
    calories from fat, 10, 86
    frozen entrée, 65
    thighs, 52
Chili, 66
Chinup, 22, **22**
Chocolate
    antioxidants in, 137
    best bar for men, 68
Chocolate milk, 63
Chocolate sauce, 72
Cholecystokinin (CCK), 81
Cholesterol
    HDL, 125, 137
    LDL, 9, 125, 137, 307
    trans fat effect on, 85

Chukka boots, 205
CLA. *See* Conjugated linoleic acid
Claiborne, 201
Clamshell, 164, **164**
Cleveland Golf Hibore Monster
    XLS, **313**, 314, **314**
Clothing
    accessories, **193**, 193
    celebrity style tips
        Common, 199
        Jeremy Renner, 196–98
    denim jacket, 194–95, **194–95**
    jeans, 191–93, **192**
    labels
        Banana Republic, 204
        Claiborne, 201
        J.Crew, 202
        Pendleton, 203
        Woolrich, 203
    presidential, 189, **189**
    suit, 189, **189**
Coffee
    artisan, 54–55
    best for men, 69
    canned, 69
    decrease cancer risk with,
        136, 257
    iced, 54
    organic, 134
    post-workout, 337
Cognitive function
    improving, 212
    reducing decline, 210–11
Cola, 140
Cold cuts, 64
Cold sores, 274, 280, 281
Collagen, 210
Colonoscopy, 228
    virtual, 230
Common (rapper/actor), 199,
    199
Conair Interplak Dental Water
    Jet, 266
Condiments
    alfredo sauce, 70
    all-purpose condiment, 71
    BBQ sauce, 70

    best for men, 70–72
    chocolate sauce, 72
    cooking broth, 72
    cooking oil, 71
    cooking salt, 72
    dip, 71
    flavor enhancer, 72
    guacamole, 71
    hot sauce, 71
    hummus, 71
    jelly/fruit, 71
    ketchup, 70
    marinade, 70
    mayonnaise, 70
    mustard, 70, 134
    organic, 134
    pasta sauce, 70
    peanut butter, 71
    protein powder, 72
    salad dressing, 71
    salsa, 70
    sandwich spread, 71
    secret sauce, 72
    soy sauce, 72
    steak sauce, 70
    syrup, 72
    vinaigrette, 71
    vinegar, 72
Conditioner, 220–21
Conjugated linoleic acid (CLA)
    in butter, 125
    in grass-fed beef, 9
    in organic dairy foods, 130
Cookbook, 54
Cookie, 68
Cooking
    beef, 51
    chicken thighs, 52
    corn, 52
    molecular gastronomy, 107
    skillet, cast iron, 51–52
    Web sites, 49, 51
Cooking broth, 72
Cooking oil
    calories per tablespoon, 124
    canola oil, 125, 125, 135
    choosing, 125

Cooking oil *(cont.)*
Formula 47, 123
hydrogenated, <u>89</u>, 123–24,
137, <u>257</u>
olestra, <u>89</u>
olive oil, 124–25, <u>125</u>
organic, <u>135</u>
peanut oil, <u>125</u>
sesame oil, <u>125</u>
trans fats in, 124
using variety of, 124
Core-strengthening program,
for runners, 340
Corn
cooking, 52
genetically modified, 132–33
Summer Corn, <u>52</u>
Cornflakes, 92
Corticosteroids, for carpal
tunnel syndrome, 264
Cortisol, 178, 211, <u>247</u>, <u>280</u>, 287
Cosmetic surgery, <u>217</u>
Cotechino, 109
Cottage cheese, 64
CPAP mask, 306
Cracker, 67
Cramp, 319
Cream cheese, 64
Creatine, 179
Crossover box pushup, 155, **155**
Cycling
fitness bike, 343, **343**
hydration, 339
improvement with caffeine, 337
practicing at competitive
pace, 338
standing while climbing hills,
339

D

Daidzein, 9
Dairy products
acne promoted by, 217
best for men, 63–65

butter, 64
cheese
all-purpose, 63
shredded, 64
sliced, 63
snacking, 64
chocolate milk, 63
cottage cheese, 64
cream cheese, 64
eggs, 64
kefir, 64
milk, 63
mood improvement with,
283, 284
sour cream, 64
yogurt, 64
Dallhauser, Phil (athlete),
332–33, 333–36, **334**
Dark chocolate, 137
DDE, 5–6
Dean's Guacamole Flavored
Dip, 87
Deep-vein thrombosis, 304
Deli items
bacon, 65
best for men, 63–65
cheese
all-purpose, 63
shredded, 64
sliced, 63
snacking, 64
cold cuts, 64
hot dog, 65
salami, 65
sausage, 65
Dementia, linked to obesity,
41
Denim jacket, 194–95, **194–95**
Deodorant, 220
Depression, acupuncture for,
270
Dermatone's SPF 23 Skin
Protector, <u>280</u>
Dessert, binge eating, 43
DEXA scan, 227, 229
DHA. *See* Docosahexaenoic
acid; Omega-3 fats

Diabetes
albumin test, 304
cornflakes and, 92
description, 14
Diamond Organics, <u>135</u>
Diamond pushup, 155, **155**
Diet
cheat meal, 42
failure of traditional, 4
leanness laws, 5–50
sugar, 13–17
Diet cola, 140
Digital rectal exam (DRE), <u>254</u>
Dinner, organic food choices for,
<u>135</u>
Dip, 22, 71
Diphenyl, 131
Disappointment, expressing,
214
Docosahexaenoic acid (DHA)
in fish-oil supplement, 136, 140
for mood improvement, 284–85
for prostate cancer risk
reduction, <u>257</u>
Doctor
appointments
follow-up contact, 241
with physician's assistant,
241, <u>241</u>
scoring the appointment,
239–40
talking to the doctor, 240–41
M.D.s and D.O.s, 307
Doctors Without Borders, 58
Donald Pliner Firm, 205
Dopamine, 132, 287
Down, <u>309</u>
DRE, <u>254</u>
Drinks
alcohol content, 244
beer
best for men, 69
light, 69
organic, <u>135</u>
Oskar Blues, 61
best for men, 68–70
calories consumed in, 86

coffee
  artisan, 54–55
  best for men, 69
  canned, 69
  decrease cancer risk with,
    136, _257_
  iced, _54_
  organic, _134_
  post-workout, 337
flavored water, 68
fruit juice, 69
hot chocolate, 69
orange juice, 69
organic, _135_
recovery, _135_
sports drink, 69
tea
  best for men, 69
  bottled tea, 69
  caffeinated bag tea, 69
  catechins in, 92
  decaf bag tea, 69
  decrease cancer
    progression with, 136
  immune system boost from,
    _280_
vegetable juice, 69
wine
  choosing, 49
  organic, _135_
  red, 70
  sparkling, 70
  white, 70
Driving, talking and texting
  while, 237
Dual energy X-ray
  absorptiometry (DEXA)
  scan, 227, 229
Dumbbell, Powerblock U-90,
  176
Dumbbell bench press, 183
Dumbbell curl with static hold,
  35, **35**
Dumbbell row, **28**
Dyes (food colorings)
  Blue #1 (brilliant blue), _88_
  Blue #2 (indigotine), _88_

hyperactivity in children
  linked to, 93–94
Red #3 (erythrosine), _89_
Red #40 (allura red), _89_, 93–94
Yellow #5 (tartrazine), _89_,
  93–94
Yellow #6 (sunset yellow), _89_,
  93–94

E

Eating
  after workouts, 184
  binge, 43
  nighttime, 43
  before workouts, 182
EDCs, 3–5, 9
Eden Foods, 8
Edox, 212
EGCG, _280_
Eggs
  benefits of eating for
    breakfast, 138
  New American Omelet, _7_
  organic, _134_
Eicosapentaenoic acid (EPA)
  in fish-oil supplement, 136, 140
  for mood improvement,
    284–85
  for prostate cancer risk
    reduction, _257_
Encephalitis, herpes, 278
Endocrine-disrupting
  chemicals (EDCs), 3–5, 9
Endocrine system, effect of
  obesogens on, 3–4
Endorphins, 40, 271, 287
English muffin, 62
EPA. _See_ Eicosapentaenoic
  acid; Omega-3 fats
Epinephrine, 211
Erectile dysfunction
  after prostate surgery,
    255–56
  from bisphenol A exposure, 7

Erections
  improving, 212
  morning, 308
Erythrosine (Red #3), _89_
Estrogen, 3, 5, 8, 43
Excedrin Migraine, 265
Executive health exam, 226
Exercise(s)
  alternating shuffle pushup,
    155, **155**
  barbell bus driver rotation,
    33, **33**
  barbell drop squat and row,
    34, **34**
  barbell overhead lunge, 32, **32**
  barbell press, 183
  barbell squat and one-arm
    press, 33, **33**
  bench jump, 21
  bench press, 37, **37**, 154, 181
  biceps curl, 184
  bird dog, 164, **164**
  cable face pull, 150, **150**
  cable pull-through, 165, **165**
  chinup, 22, **22**
  clamshell, 164, **164**
  crossover box pushup, 155, **155**
  diamond pushup, 155, **155**
  dip, 22
  dumbbell bench press, 183
  dumbbell curl with static
    hold, 35, **35**
  dumbbell row, **28**
  extended plank, 161, **161**
  floor press, 150, **150**
  front plank, 158
  hammer curl, 184
  hands-on-box diamond
    pushup, 155, **155**
  hip raise, 164, **164**
  hip raise with feet on bench,
    165, **165**
  hip raise with feet on Swiss
    ball, 165, **165**
  hyperextension with
    dumbbell scarecrow and
    twist, 33, **33**

Exercise(s) *(cont.)*
  incline pushup, 168, **170**
  inverted row, 34, **34**
  jump rope, 21
  jump squat, 23, **23**
  kneeling cable pulldown, **173**
  lateral walk, 165, **165**
  lean-away lat pulldown, 150, **150**
  leg press, 185
  lunge, 39, **39**
  medicine ball crunch, 22
  medicine ball pike, 22, **22**
  medicine ball Russian twist, 22
  medium-grip barbell row, 151, **151**
  for mitochondrial function improvement, 298, <u>299</u>
  mountain climber, **29**
  mountain climber with hands on bench, 160, **160**
  mountain climber with hands on Swiss ball, 160, **160**
  one-arm pushup, 155, **155**
  plank on elbows, 160, **160**
  plank slideout, **176**
  plank with feet elevated, 160, **160**
  plate pushes, 32
  power clean, **174**
  for prostate cancer risk reduction, <u>257</u>
  pullup, 39, **39**
  pushup, 22, 35, **35**, 37, **37**, 154–55, **155**
  pushup and row combination, 34, **34**
  quad/hip flexor stretch, 341
  reactive stepup, 341
  reverse lunge, 341
  rotational, 159
  row, 39, **39**
  scaption, 151, **151**
  scissor bench jump, 21
  shadowboxing, 21
  shrugs, 184
  side-lying external rotation, 151, **151**
  side plank, 158, 160, **160**
  side plank with feet elevated, 160, **160**
  single-leg balance touch, 35, **35**
  single-leg side plank, 161, **161**
  single-leg squat-to-bench, 165, **165**
  squat, 38, **38**, 185
  squat thrust, 23
  stepup, 21, **21**, 165, **165**
  straight-leg deadlift, 38, **38**
  suitcase carry, 159
  swing, **28**
  Swiss-ball jackknife, 161, **161**
  T-pushup, **27**
  treadmill run, 21, **21**
  walking lunge, 23
  wide pushup, 155, **155**
  windshield wipers, 168
Extended plank, 161, **161**
Eye black, 318
Eyes
  affect on appearance, 214
  after swimming care of, 342
  black eye, 319
  Lasik surgery, 218
  vision loss prevention with exercise, 178

F

Farro, 58
Fat
  interesterified, <u>88</u>
  monounsaturated, 137
  omega-6, 124, <u>125</u>
  polyunsaturated, 124
  saturated, 102, 123, 124–25
  trans, 85, 123–25, 137, <u>257</u>
Fat burner workout, 31–35
Feeding America, 58
Fenbutatin, 66
Fiber, sources of, 138–39, <u>142</u>

Finca Santuario, 55
Fish
  frozen entrée, 65
  Grilled Fish Tacos with Chipotle Crema, <u>61</u>
  mackerel, 55
  for mood improvement, 284–85
  for prostate cancer risk reduction, <u>257</u>
  salmon, 67
  tacos, 61, <u>61</u>
  tuna, 67
Fish oil, 136, 140
Fitness Anywhere TRX Suspension Trainer Force Kit, 175, **175**
Fitness bike, 343, **343**
Fitness gear, 172–77
  Art of Strength Ropes Gone Wild, 177, **177**
  Fitness Anywhere TRX Suspension Trainer Force Kit, 175, **175**
  FreeMotion EXT Dual Cable Cross, 173, **173**
  Iron Woody Woody Bag, 174, **174**
  JC Predator Band, 174, **174**
  Nike Free 5.0, 176
  Polar FT80, 176
  Powerblock U-90, 176
  Valslides, 176, **176**
5-second muscle test, 146–47
Fizik Aliante Carbon Fiber Twin Flex saddle, 343
Flavonoids, 306
Flavor enhancer, 72
Floor press, 150, **150**
Flour, 63
Flu shot, 304
Folate, <u>142</u>
Food
  American Heart Association certified, 92–93
  best foods for men, 62–72
    breads and grains, 62–63
    condiments, 70–72

dairy and deli, 63–65
drinks, 68–70
frozen foods, 65–66
packaged foods and snacks,
    66–68
canned, 8
carbon footprint of, 133
feeding the hungry, 58
food industry secrets, 90–95
leftovers, 140
nutritiondata.com Web site, 229
organic, 126–35
packaging and bisphenol A,
    6–8
pesticides in, 4, 5, 5–6, 129–30,
    131–33
stealth health, 79–81
supermarket survival guide,
    82–89
umami flavor, 48–49
Web sites
    behindtheburner.com, 51
    imcooked.com, 51
    tastespotting.com, 49, 51
Food additives
    aspartame, 88
    BHA (butylated
        hydroxyanisole), 88
    BHT (butylated
        hydroxytoluene), 88
    Blue #1 (brilliant blue), 88
    Blue #2 (indigotine), 88
    carrageenan, 88
    guar gum, 88
    high fructose corn syrup
        (HFCS), 88
    hyperactivity in children
        linked to, 93–94
    interesterified fats, 88
    inulin, 143
    mannitol, 89
    olestra, 89
    partially hydrogenated
        vegetable oil, 89
    polydextrose, 143
    Red #3 (erythrosine), 89
    Red #40 (allura red), 89

saccharin, 89
sucralose, 89
Yellow #5 (tartrazine), 89
Yellow #6 (sunset yellow), 89
Food colorings, 88–89
Food For Life Wheat & Gluten
    Free Brown Rice Bread,
    143
Food labels, 86, 87, 133, 139
Food log, 40
Form, tips for perfecting, 36–39
Formula 47 cooking oil, 123
Fragrance, 198, 199, 204
FreeMotion EXT Dual Cable
    Cross, 173, 173
Free radicals
    created by sunburn, 265
    mitochondria harmed by, 298
Free Rice, 58
Frontal plane of motion, 180
Front plank, 158
Frozen foods
    beef entrée, 65
    best for men, 65–66
    breakfast sandwich, 66
    burrito, 65
    chicken entrée, 65
    family-sized pizza, 65
    fish entrée, 65
    fruit, 66
    ice cream, 66
    organic, 135
    pasta entrée, 65
    single-serving pizza, 65
    snack, 66
    treat, 66
    turkey entrée, 65
    vegetables, 66
    waffle, 66
Fructose, 16
Fruit juice, 69
Fruits
    canned, 67
    decline of nutrients in, 85–86
    dried, 68
    frozen, 66
    hybrids, 142

pesticides in, 131
sugar in, 307
Fuet, 112
Fungi, mycorrhizal, 134

G

Gastroesophageal reflux
    disease (GERD), 263
Gastrointestinal tract
    acupuncture for problems
        with, 268
    service plan for, 246–47
Gatorade, 337
Genesis 1:29 Sprouted Grain
    and Seed Bread, 143
Genetically modified organism,
    132–33
Genistein, 9
GERD, 263
Gillette Clinical Strength, 220
Giorgio Armani's Acqua Di Gio,
    286
Glasses, 308
Glucomannan, 96
Glucose, 14
Glutamate, 48
Glute workout, 162–65
Glycemic index, 15
Glycogen, 16, 337
Goals, for mood improvement,
    286
Golf
    drivers, 312–14, 313, 314
    new rules, 314
    tough shots
        drive into the wind, 315, 315
        green-side bunker shot,
            315, 315
        long iron from deep rough,
            315, 315
        short chip from a tight lie,
            315, 315
        sidehill downhill putt, 315,
            315

Green tea
  catechins in, 92
  decrease cancer progression
    with, 136
  immune system boost from, 280
Griswold skillet, 51
Groats, 139
Growth hormones, 8, 132
Guacamole, 71
Guar gum, 88
Guinness, 57
Gum
  for heartburn relief, 262
  whitening, 219

H

Habits, breaking bad
  caffeine, 235–36
  loud music, 236–37
  smoking, 234
  talking and texting while
    driving, 237
  television, 236
Hair
  gray, 216
  removal of chest, 216
  robotic replacement system,
    216
  shampoo-plus-conditioner,
    220–21
HairMax LaserComb, 297
Hairstyle, 210
Half-and-half, 94
Hammer curl, 184
Hamstrings, stretching for
    lower-back pain
    prevention, 266
Hands-on-box diamond
    pushup, 155, **155**
HDL cholesterol, 125, 137
Headache
  acupuncture for, 268
  migraine, 265–66
  tension, 268

Headcheese, 115
Health issues
  acupuncture, 267–71
  Alzheimer's disease, 272–81
  bad habits to break, 232–37
  doctor appointment, 238–41
  good habits, 247
  health tests, 225–31
  life extension, 290–303
  mood improvement, 282–89
  pain relief, 260–71
  prostate, 248–59
  questions and answers, 307–9
  service plan for your organs,
    243–47
    gastrointestinal tract,
      246–47
    kidneys, 244–46
    liver, 244
    lungs, 246
Health tests
  blood pressure, 228
  bone density scan, 227, 229
  cardiac CT angiography,
    226–27
  colonoscopy, 228
  digital rectal exam, 254
  lipid profile, 228
  nutritional evaluation, 230
  online self-tests, 229
  physical exam, 231
  PSA test, 228, 251–52, 254,
    257–58, 308
  treadmill stress test, 228
  urine albumin, 304
  virtual colonoscopy, 230
  VO_2 max test, 229–30
Hearing damage, from loud
    music, 236–37
Heart, pig, 112–13, 113
Heartburn, 246–47, 262–63, 269
Heart health
  cardiac CT angiography,
    226–27
  disease risk increase from
    saturated fat, 102
  trans fat, 85, 137

improving
  with chocolate, 137
  with strength training, 182
  as you age, 213
Heart-rate monitor, 176
Heifer International, 58
Hemorrhoids, 263–64
Hemp seeds, 80
Hernia, 247
Herpes simplex virus type 1
    (HSV-1), 274–81
Hibiscus tea, 305–6
High-fructose corn syrup
  dangers of, 139
  description, 5, 88
  in drinks, 86
  as food additive, 5, 88
  role in obesity, 9, 10, 15, 88
Hiking, with trekking poles, 339
Hip raise, 164, **164**
Hip raise with feet on bench,
    165, **165**
Hip raise with feet on Swiss
    ball, 165, **165**
Hogan, 205
Honest Tea Organic Honey
    Green Tea, 92, 280
Honey, 141, 305
Hormones, in meat, 8–9
Hot chocolate, 69
Hot dog, 65
Hot sauce, 71
HSV-1, 274–81
Hummus, 71
Hurricane training system,
    19–23
Hydration
  race-day, 342
  while cycling, 339
Hydrogenated oil, 89, 123–24,
    137, 257
Hydrogen peroxide, 216, 219
Hyperactivity in children,
    linked to food additives,
    93–94
Hyperextension with dumbbell
    scarecrow and twist, 33, **33**

Hyperglycemia, 16–17
Hypertension, lessening with
    hibiscus tea, 305–6
Hypoglycemia, 17

I

Ibuprofen
    for lower-back pain, 266
    for plantar fasciitis, 262
    for sunburn pain, 265
    for toothache, 266
Ice, applying to injuries, 262, 319
Ice cream, 66
Iced coffee, 54
Ice pack, 181
Immune system
    boosting with tea, 280
    weakening from pesticides, 132
Incline pushup, 168, **170**
Indigotine (Blue #2), 88
Inflammation
    in carpal tunnel syndrome, 264
    decrease with
        cruciferous vegetables, 139
        ibuprofen, 262, 265
    increase from omega-6 fats,
        124
    in migraine headache, 265
    in plantar fasciitis, 262, 265
    in sunburn, 265
    in tendinitis, 266
Influenza vaccine, 304
Injuries
    acupuncture for sports, 269–70
    black eye, 319
    broken nose, 319
    cramp, 319
    early detection, 339
    recovering from
        exercises that incorporate
            hurt area, 330
        limiting risk of reinjury, 330
        restoring range of motion,
            330

setbacks from, 330
    sprain, 319
In-N-Out Burger, 57
Instant oatmeal, 62, 139
Insulin resistance, 14, 138,
    210–11, 304
Insulin sensitivity, decrease
    with caffeine
    consumption, 235
Intelligentsia Coffee & Tea, 55
Interesterified fats, 88
Intervals, 299
Inulin, 143
Inverted row, 34, **34**
Iodine
    deficiency, 77
    role in body, 77
    sources, 77
Iron Woody Woody Bag, 174, **174**
Ito En Tea's Tea Lemongrass
    Green, 92

J

Jacket
    denim, 194–95, **194–95**
    fit, 189
Jamones, 111
JC Predator Band, 174, **174**
J.Crew, 202
Jeans
    accessorizing, 193
    fit, 192
    shoes to pair with, 193
    wearing to work, **192**, 192–93
Jelly, 71
Jennie-O Turkey Breast
    Tenderloin Roast Turkey,
    94
Johnson & Johnson Stim-U-Dent
    Plaque Removers, 220
Johnston and Murphy
    Matheson, 205
Jumping rope, 21, 183
Jump squat, 23, **23**

K

Kahweol, 136
Kenneth Cole Reaction Flow
    Theory, 205
Ketchup, 70
Kidneys, service plan for, 244–46
Kiwi, 130
Kneeling cable pulldown, **173**
Kokoretsi, 113
Konjac yam, 96

L

L-arginine aspartate, 212
Lasik, 218
Lateral walk, 165, **165**
Laughter, 211–12
LDL cholesterol
    increase from fat in dairy
        products, 125
    lowering with
        nuts, 137
        soy protein, 9
    type A and type B particles, 307
Lean-away lat pulldown, 150, **150**
Leftovers, 140
Leg press, 185
Lentils, 66, 81
Leptin, 10, 136
Leucine, 121
Limequat, 142
Lipid profile, 228
Liver, service plan for, 244
Loafers, 205
Locavore, 128
L'Oreal Paris Men's Expert
    Vita Lift Anti-Wrinkle &
    Firming Moisturizer, 210
Loud music, 236–37
Lower-back pain, 266–67
Lunch, organic food choices for,
    134–35
Lunge, 39, **39**

Lungs, service plan for, 246
Lycopene, <u>257</u>

M

Mackerel, 55
Macular degeneration, 178, 308
Maggots, in food, 92
Magnesium
  deficiency, 75–76
  for migraine headache
     prevention, 265
  role in body, 75
  supplementing, 76
Maneb, 131
Mannitol, <u>89</u>
Marathon
  optimum temperature for
     best times, <u>338</u>
  tapering prerace training, 338
Margarine, 125, <u>125</u>
Marinade, 70
Martin's 100% Whole Wheat
    Potato Bread, 143
Mayonnaise, 70
McDonald's, 123, 124
Meat. *See also* Beef; Chicken;
    Pork
  antibiotics in, 132
  bacon, 65, 102, 105, <u>111</u>, 111–12
  cold cuts, 64
  dark, 81
  hot dog, 65
  lunch, <u>134</u>
  organ, 112–15, <u>113</u>
  organic, <u>135</u>
  salami, 65
  sausage, 65, 112, <u>113</u>, 114
  sodium in, 94
Medicine ball crunch, 22
Medicine ball pike, 22, **22**
Medicine ball Russian twist, 22
Medium-grip barbell row, 151,
    151
Metabolic circuits, 29

Metabolic syndrome, 14
Metabolism, boost from
  protein, 41
  weight training, 42
Mexoryl, 209
Migraine headache, 265–66
Milk
  chocolate, 63
  mood improvement with,
    283, 284
  organic, <u>134</u>
Minneola tangelo, <u>142</u>
Mionetto Prosecco Brut, 49
Mitochondria, 292–303
Molecular gastronomy, 107
Monounsaturated fats, 137
Mood improvement
  methods
    goal attainment, 286
    milk, **283**, 284
    music, **285**, 285–86
    photos, 288
    refraining from drinking, 288
    running, 286–87
    scents, 286
    seafood, 284–85
    sex, 287–88
    sleep, <u>287</u>, 289
    sunlight exposure, 289
    testosterone elevation, 288
  for women, <u>287</u>
Motor overflow, 181
Mountain climber, **29**
Mountain climber with hands
    on bench, 160, **160**
Mountain climber with hands
    on Swiss ball, 160, **160**
Mouth, burnt, 262
Mouthguard, 319
Mouthwash, 215
MSG, 49
Muscle
  building/maintenance
    with creatine, 213
    with protein, 42
    as you age, 213
  calories burned by, 42

Muscle strain, as lower-back
    pain cause, 266
Music, for mood improvement,
    285, 285–86
Mustard, <u>57</u>, 57–58, 70, <u>134</u>
Mycorrhizal fungi, 134

N

Nabisco Honey Teddy
    Grahams, 94–95
Naproxen, for tendinitis, 266
Neoprene knee sleeves, 319
Neutrogena Oil-Free Acne
    Wash, 215
Neutrogena Skin Aid, 265
Newman's Own Organics, <u>135</u>
Nicotine, 263
Nike Free 5.0, 176
Nike Sq Dymo Str8-fit, **313**,
    314, **314**
Nitric oxide, 212, 268
Noodles, shirataki, 96–99
Noradrenaline, 287
Nose, broken, 319
Nutri-Grain Strawberry Cereal
    Bars, 87
Nutritional evaluation, 230
Nuts
  alternative to, 68
  best for men, 68
  improving cholesterol with, 137
  mixed, 68

O

Oatmeal, 62, 92
Oats, steel-cut, 62, 139
Obama, Barack (President),
    188–89, 189, <u>211</u>
Obesity
  dementia linked to, <u>41</u>
  denial of severity, 40

Obesogens, 3–5, 8–10
Obliques, exercises for, 159
OcuPlus, 308
Ocuvite, 308
OGTT, 16
Oil
  calories per tablespoon, 124
  canola oil, 125, <u>125</u>, <u>135</u>
  choosing, <u>125</u>
  Formula 47, 123
  hydrogenated, <u>89</u>, 123–24,
    137, <u>257</u>
  olestra, <u>89</u>
  olive oil, 124–25, <u>125</u>
  organic, <u>135</u>
  peanut oil, <u>125</u>
  sesame oil, <u>125</u>
  trans fats in, 124
  using variety in cooking, 124
Olestra, <u>89</u>
Olive oil, 124–25, <u>125</u>
Omega-3 fats
  balancing omega-6 fats, 124,
    <u>125</u>
  feeling fuller from eating, 136
  in grass-fed beef, 9
  in hemp seeds, 80
  in milk, 9
  for mood improvement, 284–
    85
  for prostate cancer risk
    reduction, <u>257</u>
  sources of, 136, **136**
  supplement, 136, 140
Omega-6 fats, 124, <u>125</u>
One-arm pushup, 155, **155**
Online weight loss program, 42
Oral glucose tolerance test
    (OGTT), 16
Oral irrigator, 266
Orange juice, 69
Organic food
  beef, 9
  benefits of
    environmental, 130,
      133–34
    list of, 129

  nutritional, 130
  pesticide avoidance,
    129–30, 131–33
best brands, <u>135</u>
best for men
  after workout, <u>135</u>
  breakfast, <u>134</u>
  dinner, <u>135</u>
  lunch, <u>134–35</u>
  snacking, <u>135</u>
cost, 128
labels
  "made with organic
    ingredients," 133
  "natural," 133
  USDA Organic, 133
pesticide-free, <u>5</u>, 6
research on, 128–29
Organ meat, 112–15, <u>113</u>
Organochlorine pesticides, 6
Organophosphates, 6
Organs, service plan for, 243–47
  gastrointestinal tract, 246–47
  kidneys, 244–46
  liver, 244
  lungs, 246
Oskar Blues beers, 61
Oxfords, 205
Oxytocin, 287–88
Ozone, 246

P

Packaged foods and snacks,
    best for men, 66–68
  almonds, 68
  beef jerky, 68
  canned beans, 66
  canned fruit, 67
  canned tomatoes, 67
  chili, 66
  chocolate bar, 68
  cookie, 68
  cracker, 67
  dried fruit, 68

  jarred vegetable, 67
  lentils, 66
  mixed nuts, 68
  nut alternative, 68
  nuts, 68
  pickle, 67
  popcorn, 68
  potato chips, 67
  pretzel, 67
  refried beans, 66
  salad topping, 67
  salmon, 67
  sandwich topping, 67
  snack bar, 68
  soup, 66
  tortilla chips, 67
  trail mix, 68
  tuna, 67
Pain
  acupuncture for, 267–71
    anxiety and depression,
      270
    back pain, 270–71
    gastrointestinal problems,
      269
    headaches, 268
    sports injuries, 269–70
  detrimental nature of, 262
  scale, <u>264</u>
  sources of pain
    carpal tunnel syndrome,
      264–65
    heartburn, 262–63
    hemorrhoids, 263–64
    lower-back pain, 266–67
    migraine headache, 265–66
    plantar fasciitis, 262
    scorched mouth, 262
    sunburn, 265
    tendinitis, 266
    toothache, 266
Pancetta, <u>111</u>, 111–12
Paraquat, 131
Parmesan cheese, 48, 49
Partially hydrogenated
    vegetable oil, <u>89</u>
Partial reps, 181

Pasta, 63, 65
Pasta sauce, 70
Peanut butter, 71, 140
Peanut oil, <u>125</u>
Pendleton, 203
Pepcid AC, 262
Pesticides
    accumulation in the body, <u>245</u>
    in food, 4, <u>5</u>, 5–6, 129–30,
        <u>131</u>, 131–33
    health dangers of, 129–33
Pesto
    Shirataki Noodles Al Pesto,
        99
PHisoderm Deep Cleaning
    Cream Cleanser, 215
Phosphoric acid, 140
Photos, for mood improvement,
    288
Phthalates, <u>5</u>, 6–8
Phthalides, in celery, 80
Physical exam, 231
Physician's assistant, <u>241</u>
Phytochemicals, in celery, 80
Pickle, 67
Pierce, Paul (athlete), **320**,
    321–25, **323**, <u>325</u>
Pillows, 308–9, <u>309</u>
Pimples, 218–19
Ping Rapture V2, **313**, 314, **314**
Piriformis muscle, 168
Pistachios, 137
Pita, 63
Pizza
    crust, 63
    frozen family-sized, 65
    frozen single-serving, 65
Planes of motion, 180, **180**
Plank on elbows, 160, **160**
Plank slideout, **176**
Plank with feet elevated, 160,
    160
Plantar fasciitis, 262
Plants, stress reduction from,
    305
Plastic, chemicals from, 6–8
Plate pushes, 32

Plumcot, <u>142</u>
Plumpynut, 58
Polar CS600X cycling
    computer, 343
Polar FT80, 176
Polycarbonate bottle, 7
Polydextrose, 143
Polyunsaturated fat, 124
Popcorn, 68
Pork
    butchering a pig, 100, 102,
        106
    buying in bulk, <u>117</u>
    cotechino, 109
    cuts
        belly, <u>111</u>, 111–12
        chops, <u>116</u>
        head, <u>115</u>, 115–16
        loin, <u>107</u>, 107–8
        organs, 112–15, <u>113</u>
        shoulder, <u>116</u>
        trotter and shanks, <u>109</u>,
            109–11
    fat content, 102, 105
    hog breeds
        Berkshire, <u>117</u>
        heritage, 105, <u>117</u>
        Magalitsa, <u>117</u>
        Ossabaw, <u>117</u>
        Red Wattle, <u>117</u>
    pancetta, <u>111</u>, 111–12
    pig anatomy, **101**
    roasting, <u>105</u>
    Soy Pork Shirataki Stir-Fry, 98
    versatility of, 102
Potassium
    deficiency, 76
    role in body, 76
    sources, 76, 80
Potato chips, 67
Powerblock U-90, 176
Power clean, **174**
Prediabetes, 16, 17
Preparation H, 263
Pretzel, 67
The Professional Chef
    (cookbook), 54

Progesterone, 8
Propecia, <u>297</u>
Prostate biopsy, 252
Prostate cancer, 136, 250–59
Prostate surgery, 254–56, 258
Prostatitis, 252
Protective sports gear, 317–19,
    318
    athletic cup, 319
    biceps bands, 319
    chest protector, 318
    eye black, 318
    mouthguard, 319
    neoprene knee sleeves, 319
    shooter sleeves, 318
Protein
    at breakfast, 212–13
    complete, 120
    metabolism boost from, 41
    for muscle building, 42
    recommended daily intake,
        120
    satiety from, 138
    sources of, 43, 120
    supplementing, 121
    timing consumption of, 120–21
    for weight loss, 42, 138
Protein powder, 72
PSA test, <u>228</u>, 251–52, <u>254</u>,
    257–58, 308
Psoas muscle, 168–69
Pullup, 39, **39**
Purpose Gentle Cleansing Bar,
    215
Pushup, 22, 35, **35**, 37, **37**,
    154–55, **155**
    alternating shuffle, 155, **155**
    crossover box, 155, **155**
    diamond, 155, **155**
    hands-on-box diamond, 155,
        155
    incline, 168, **170**
    one-arm, 155, **155**
    for serratus anterior muscle,
        167–68
    T-pushup, **27**
    wide, 155, **155**

Pushup and row combination, 34, **34**
Pycnogenol, 212

Q

Quad/hip flexor stretch, 341
Quaker Instant Oatmeal Maple & Brown Sugar, 92

R

Range of motion, restoring after injury, <u>330</u>
Reactive stepup, 341
Recipes
  Caprese Pasta Salad, 99
  for curing bacon, <u>113</u>
  Grilled Fish Tacos with Chipotle Crema, <u>61</u>
  Harbour Guinness Mustard, <u>57</u>
  iced coffee, <u>54</u>
  New American Burger, <u>5</u>
  New American Omelet, <u>7</u>
  Perfect Grilled Mackerel, <u>55</u>
  Shirataki Noodle Cake with Shrimp and Chorizo, 98
  Shirataki Noodles Al Pesto, 99
  Soy Pork Shirataki Stir-Fry, 98
  Summer Corn, <u>52</u>
  Web sites, 49, 51
Recovery drink, organic, <u>135</u>
Red #3 (erythrosine), <u>89</u>
Red #40 (allura red), <u>89</u>, 93–94
Red-light therapy for acne, 217
Reduced-fat foods, 92
Reflex test, 231
Refresh Celluvisc, 342
Remington Body and Back Groomer, 216
REM (rapid eye movement) sleep, 210, 308

Renner, Jeremy (actor), **196**, 197–98
Republic of Tea Pomegranate Green Tea, 92
Resistance bands, 174, **174**
Resistance training. *See* Weight training
Resveratrol, 212, 294, 296, 298, 301–2
Retin-A, 210
Retinoid X receptors, 6
Retinol, 210
Reverse lunge, 341
Rhinovirus, 304
Riboflavin, for migraine headache prevention, 265–66
Rice, quick-cooking, 63
RICE (rest, ice, compress, elevate) rule, 319
Rodale, J. I. (publisher), 128–29
Rogaine, <u>297</u>
Rotational, 159
Rotator cuff, exercises for, 171
Row, 39, **39**
Running
  core-strengthening, 340
  exercises, 341
  hydration, 339, 342
  mapmyrun.com Web site, <u>229</u>
  for mood improvement, 286–87
  practicing at competitive pace, 338
  resistance training, 340
  sprints, 29
  tapering prerace training, 338
  for vision loss prevention, 178

S

Saccharin, <u>89</u>, <u>141</u>
Sagittal plane of motion, **180**
Salad
  Caprese Pasta Salad, 99
  topping, 67

Salad dressing, 71
Salami, 65
Salmon, 67
Salsa, 70
Salt, cooking, 72
Sandwich spread, 71
Sandwich topping, 67
Sara Lee 45 Calories & Delightful 100% Whole Wheat with Honey, 143
Saturated fat, 102, 123, 124–25
Sausage, 65, 112, <u>113</u>, 114
Scallops, 81
Scaption, 151, **151**
Scarf, <u>193</u>, 194
Scents, for mood improvement, 286
Scissor bench jump, 21
Seafood. *See also* Fish
  for mood improvement, 284–85
  Shirataki Noodle Cake with Shrimp and Chorizo, 98
Seaweed, 80
Segura Viudas Brut Reserva, 49
Serotonin, 134, 268, 284, 287
Serratus anterior muscle, 167–68
Sesame oil, <u>125</u>
Sex, for prostate health, <u>257</u>
Sexual function, after prostate surgery, 255–56
Shadowboxing, 21
Shady Brook Farms Fresh Boneless Turkey Tenderloin, 94
Shampoo, 220–21
Shaving, 209
Shirataki, 96–99
Shirt, sleeve length of, 189
Shoes
  basketball, 342
  Nike Free 5.0, 176
  pairing with jeans, 193
  for plantar fasciitis prevention, 262
  styles, 205
Shooter sleeves, 318
Shoulders, exercises for, 149–51

Shrimp
  Shirataki Noodle Cake with
    Shrimp and Chorizo, 98
Shrugs, 184
Side-lying external rotation,
  151, **151**
Side plank, 158, 160, **160**
Side plank with feet elevated,
  160, **160**
Silver ions, in deodorant, 220
Single-leg balance touch, 35, **35**
Single-leg side plank, 161, **161**
Single-leg squat-to-bench, 165,
  165
Sinusitis, 305
SIR2 gene, 294, 301–2
Sirtuin, 294, 301–2
Skillet, 51–52
Skin
  acne, 217, 219
  matching cleanser to skin
    type, 215
  pimples, 218–19
  wrinkles, 209, 210
Skip pyramids, 183
Sleep
  affect on eye appearance, 214
  for mood improvement, 287,
    289
  pillows, 308–9, 309
  REM (rapid eye movement),
    210, 308
Sleep apnea, 289, 306
Smoking, breaking habit, 234
Snack bar, 68
Snacks
  best for men, 66–68
  frozen, 66
  100-calorie packs, 95
  nighttime, 43
  organic, 135
    crunchy, 135
    fiery, 135
    fruit, 135
    sweet, 135
  pre-dinner, 140
Snoring, 309

Soda, 15, 16
Sodium, in meat, 94
Sodium benzoate, 93–94
Soup, 66
Soy
  estrogen level increases from,
    43
  role in obesity, 9–10
Soy sauce, 72
Specialized BG grips, 343
Sperm count, lowering by
  pesticides, 132
Spice, organic, 135
Spinach, for muscle
  maintenance, 213
Sports drink, 69, 337
Sports gear, protective, 317–19,
  318
  athletic cup, 319
  biceps bands, 319
  chest protector, 318
  eye black, 318
  mouthguard, 319
  neoprene knee sleeves, 319
  shooter sleeves, 318
Sports injuries, acupuncture
  for, 269–70
Sprain, 319
Sprints, 29
Squat, 38, **38**, 185
Squat thrust, 23
Steak sauce, 70
Steel-cut oats, 62, 139
Stem cells, 3
Stepup, 21, **21**, 165, **165**
Stevia, 141, 141
Stinco arrosto, 110
Straight-leg deadlift, 38, **38**
Strength, building without
  bulking up, 342
Strength training. *See* Weight
  training
Stress
  bad habits promoted by, 247
  blood pressure increase from,
    306
  job, 306

relief
  with acupuncture, 269
  for herpes virus prevention,
    280
  with laughter, 211–12
  with plants, 305
  with weight training, 178
  weight gain from, 40
Stress test, treadmill, 228
Stretching
  quad/hip flexor stretch, 341
  tensor fasciae latae, 170–71
Styrofoam, 5, 8
Stumptown Coffee Roasters,
  55
Style. *See* Clothing
Subscapularis, 171
Sucralose, 89, 141
Sugar, 13–17, 307
Sugar alcohol, 89
Sugar substitutes, 141, **141**
Suitcase carry, 159
Suits, 189, **189**
Sunblock, 209
Sunburn, 265
Sunglasses
  aviator, 190, **190**
  keys to great, 190
Sunlight
  mood improvement from, 289
  vitamin D boost from, 289,
    337
Sunset yellow (Yellow #6), 89
Supermarket
  checkout lines, 93
  survival guide, 82–89
Supplements
  casein, 121
  eye health, 308
  fish-oil, 136, 140
  magnesium, 76
  omega-3 fats, 136, 140
  protein, 121
  vitamin B_{12}, 76
  vitamin D, 75, 289
Supraspinatus, 171
Sweetbreads, 112

Sweeteners, 15, 88–89
Swing, **28**
Swiss-ball jackknife, 161, **161**
Syrup, 72

T

Tartrazine (Yellow #5), 89
Taylormade R7 Limited, **313**, 314, **314**
Tea
  best for men
    bottled tea, 69
    caffeinated bag tea, 69
    decaf bag tea, 69
  green tea
    catechins in, 92
    decrease cancer
      progression with, 136
    immune system boost from,
      280
Teeth
  brightening, 219
  brushing, 220
  clenching during workout,
    181
  porcelain veneers, 219
  whitening chewing gum, 219
Television, breaking viewing
    habit, 236
Tendinitis, 266, 270
Tensor fasciae latae, 170–71
Testosterone
  in beef, 8
  depression from low, 288
  weight gain from low, 8
  weight related to level, 212
  during workouts, 341
TFL, 170–71
Thyroid function, impaired
    with pesticide exposure,
    6
Tie
  color, 189
  knot size, 189

Tomato
  canned, 67
  prostate cancer risk
    reduction with, 257
  umami flavor, 48, 49
Toothache, 266
Topeak Two Timer pump,
    343
Tortilla, 63
Tortilla chips, 67
Toxins, accumulation in the
    body, 245
T-pushup, **27**
Trail mix, 68
Trans fat, 85, 123–25, 137,
    257
Transverse plane of motion,
    180
Treadmill
  pace for conditioning, 32
  stress test, 228
Treadmill run, 21, **21**
Treats, frozen, 66
Trebolone acetate, 9
Trekking poles, 339
Tretinoin, 210
Tributyltin, 6
Trichinosis, 108
Triclosan, 220
Triglycerides, 16, 308
Triptans, for migraine
    headache, 265
Tryptophan, in milk, 284
Tuna, 67
Turkey entrée, frozen, 65
Tuscan melon, 142
TV remote control, viruses on,
    304, 304

U

Ultraviolet light
  herpes virus activation by,
    280
  vitamin D boost from, 337

Umami flavor, 48–49
Uniq fruit, 142
USDA Organic, 133

V

Valslides, 176, **176**
Valtrex, 280, 281
Vegetable juice, 69
Vegetable oil, 89, 125
Vegetables
  cruciferous, 139
  decline of nutrients in,
    85–86
  fat-fighting, 41
  frozen, 66
  jarred, 67
  pesticides in, 131
Vegetarians, protein sources
    for, 43
Vinaigrette, 71
Vinegar, 72
Virtual colonoscopy, 230
Virus
  as Alzheimer's disease cause,
    272–81
  influenza vaccine, 304
  rhinovirus, 304
Visine, 343
Vision, 178, 308
Vitamin A
  sources of, 142
  for sunburn, 265
Vitamin B_{12}
  deficiency, 76
  role in body, 76
  sources of, 76
Vitamin C, sources of, 142
Vitamin D
  boost from light, 74, 289, 337
  deficiency, 74–75
  role in body, 74
  supplementing, 75, 289
Vitamin E, for sunburn, 265
VO_2 max test, 229–30